PSYCHOANALYSIS
AND HISTORY

psychoanalysis
and history

Edited and with an Introduction by
by bruce mazlish

The Universal Library
GROSSET & DUNLAP
A NATIONAL GENERAL COMPANY

New York

Published simultaneously in Canada
REVISED UNIVERSAL LIBRARY EDITION
FIRST PRINTING, APRIL, 1971

LIBRARY OF CONGRESS CATALOG CARD NO.: 76-145736
ISBN: 0-448-00250-7

Printed in the United States of America

Table of Contents

Part II
THE APPLICATION OF
PSYCHOANALYSIS TO HISTORY

Introduction

It was an acute observer of men and matters who once remarked: "If you want to hide something, put it in the most obvious place." For centuries, mankind seems to have followed this advice: in an effort to avoid self-knowledge men ignored not only their dreams but the behavior of their children, until Sigmund Freud detected the hidden psyche under the disguises of commonplace and everyday life. Like Sherlock Holmes, Freud was a master logician and detective, and for him, too, his conclusions when once reached were "elementary."

Unfortunately, for most of us there is little that is elementary about psychoanalysis except its observed materials. The theories and the techniques are sophisticated, complicated, and often tenuous, which poses major difficulties to our acceptance of them. First, they touch us in our most sensitive area; ourselves the product of repressions, resistances, and sublimations, we are now asked to break through these to a new self-awareness. Second, as I have tried to suggest above, they appeal to a whole mass of clinical evidence which is so familiar to us that familiarity has bred, not overt contempt, but a more subtle version: dismissal. Everyday slips of the tongue, our dreams and fantasies, the desires and actions of our children, the all-too-frequent newspaper-reported "perversions" of our adult neighbors—to these we turn the averted eye of overfamiliarity. And when to all these are added psychoanalysis' pretension to be a science, of the most subtle kind, and its attempt to build theoretical constructions on the tensions of our dubious and ambivalent selves, we feel justified in throwing up our hands in protest. A science! Nonsense, psychoanalysis is only a strange collection of occult phrases and materials. Small wonder, then, that historians share the general attitude. Accustomed as they are to deal primarily with particular facts, and to eye theory and abstraction with a jaundiced look, they are perhaps additionally wary of this strange beast in the scientific jungle.

And yet one wonders. Why should history, the one discipline that deals especially with man's past and seeks explanation of that past largely in terms of men's motives, ignore so staunchly the one science (or, at least, attempt at a science) which centers itself on research into exactly these areas. Historians study man's collective past; psychoanalysts study his individual past. Surely, one would have thought that a mental bridge could be built to connect the two investigations.

That it has not been built is abundantly clear. There are economic historians and social historians who feel it requisite to know something about economic theory or sociological theory, and to apply these findings to historical research. There are only a few hardy pioneers in psychoanalytic history. When William Langer, the eminent diplomatic historian, in his Presidential address to the American Historical Association in December 1957, unexpectedly posed as the historian's "Next Assignment" the application of psychology to the study of human motivation and mass movements, he threw his voice, in part, into a void. How much of a void is seen in the fact that a book by Erik Erikson, perhaps the most important recent study in psychoanalysis and history, as well as on Luther, which appeared in 1958, was not even reviewed in either the *American Historical Review,* the official publication of the Historical Association, or in the *Journal of Modern History,* which, on chronological grounds, would be the other natural outlet for such a review.

The neglect—nay, the deliberate ignoring—of such works as Erikson's would seem to be on a par with the refusal to deal with the original documents and evidence themselves. This, as Donald Meyer points out in one of the articles we reprint, is the "sin of sins" for an historian: to overlook or ignore the documentary evidence; to explain it away on trivial grounds. Clearly, Luther used "dirty" language, shocking in its bluntness. Henry VIII married an unusual six times, and was seemingly compulsive in his treatment of his various wives. Are we simply to ignore the psychoanalytic tools and techniques that may help us to understand these "facts," which, if of private significance when they concern private individuals, take on public significance in the case of a German reformer and of an English King who "accidentally" became a reformer?

Leopold von Ranke, the great nineteenth-century German historian, posted a sort of Hippocratic oath for historians. Against those who ignored or distorted "the actual past" (*wie es eigentlich gewesen*), he announced that "We, in our place, have a different notion of history: naked truth without embellishments, thorough investigation of every single fact. . . . By no means fiction, not even in the smallest details; by no means fabrication." "Thorough investigation of every fact"—Freud could have taken this as his motto, too.

Here we have the clue to the major purpose of this present anthology: it is to suggest the aid psychoanalysis can offer in the task of investigating facts and reaching the "naked truth" of history. This anthology, then, is envisioned as a contribution to the vexing problem of historical explanation. Without becoming involved ourselves in the intricacies of this large topic, we need only point out that much of historical explanation takes place in terms of an appeal to generally accepted ideas regarding human nature and human behavior. To use a more impressive word, historians employ the method of *Verstehen,* or "understanding." This involves the claim that we understand human behavior by being able to share "states of mind." Presumably, to take a simplified example, we understand an explanation which tells us that crop failures produced a declining marriage rate in rural areas because we "understand," usually though not always from self-knowledge, that crop failure may produce a feeling of insecurity and that the feeling of insecurity may lead to a fear of taking on certain responsibilities; in short, we intuit or empathize.

There are two weaknesses in this method of psychological intuition, or empathy, as the grounds for explanation in history; and this, after all, is the method almost all historians use covertly if not overtly. One is that we may consider as natural or understandable only that which is so to our particular time and culture. Thus, Voltaire is reputed to have denied the "fact" of Greek exposures of defective new-born children on the grounds that it was against human nature. The second weakness is simply that the acceptance of "surface" psychology in history perpetuates the very same deception we practice on ourselves in everyday life. Never going beneath appearances, we settle for the unexamined clichés about human nature and behavior, and turn our backs on the insights and theories of a deeper and more refined psychology.

What, however, if we were to accept the aid of psychoanalytic techniques and theories? I should like to suggest that Freud's work has application to two areas of interest to historians. On the one hand, he has elaborated a fundamental historical explanation, that of the origin of human society. I have called this Freud's philosophy of history, and it forms the first part of this anthology. On the other hand, he has developed psychoanalytic approaches which can be applied to more limited problems of historical explanation, dealing with the more traditional questions as to the causes of specific events. As Freud himself remarked in his *General Introduction to Psychoanalysis,* "As a science, psychoanalysis is characterized by the methods with which it works, not by the subject matter with which it deals." I have labeled this section, "The Application of Psychoanalysis to History."

In both cases—the philosophy of history and the application of psychoanalytic methods to history—I have sought to reprint articles, some favorable and some unfavorable to Freud's ideas, which would illustrate the kind of work that has been and might be done. One purpose of this anthology, therefore, is to suggest future lines of investigation by showing past efforts. As already hinted at, psychoanalytic history, except for the work of a few hardy pioneers, can hardly be said as yet to exist. It is, in large part, to help bring forth this new branch of the ancient tree of historical knowledge that this collection has been undertaken.

2

Whereas Darwin's theories provided man with an explanation of his origin and evolution as a physical animal, Freud, in what I have called his philosophy of history, sought to give man an explanation of his origin and evolution as a cultural animal: a new "genesis." Freud, however, left no doubt that the author of the *Origin of Species* was his starting point. In one passage, he compared the effect of his own psychological blow to man's "narcissism"—the belief in man's unique and central creation— with the "biological blow delivered by the theory of descent." These two blows, together with Copernicus' cosmological discovery, "naturalized" man, i.e., turned him into a natural object for scientific study.

Darwin not only gave Freud the cue to study man as a natural being, subject to cultural as well as physical evolution, but he also gave him the initial idea of the particular way in which the development took place: the idea of the primal horde. As Freud put it, "In 1912 I took up a conjecture of Darwin's to the effect that the primal form of human society was that of a horde ruled over despotically by a powerful male." In his work of 1913, *Totem and Taboo,* Freud first set forth the powerful story—his philosophy of history—of how man arose from a physical to a cultural animal. It is a crime story. Without going into the details (see pp. 51-52, in Baron's review), we need only note here that it is from the murder of the powerful male, the father, by the sons leagued together, that human society takes its origin. After the murder, the sons, filled with guilt and fear, seek to prevent the dominance of another "powerful male" by hedging in man's instincts with the ghostly bonds of totem and taboo.

In a number of later works—*Group Psychology and the Analysis of the Ego, The Future of an Illusion, Civilization and its Discontents, Moses and Monotheism*—Freud developed his philosophy of history; and basic to them all is the "hypothesis," as he put it, of the primal horde and the resultant totem and taboo. What are we to say of this hypothesis, which Freud claimed should be judged on the grounds of whether "it proves able to bring coherence and understanding into more and more new regions"?[1]

---

[1] *Group Psychology and the Analysis of the Ego,* trans. James Strachey (New York: Liveright Publishing Corp., 1960), p. 69.

The first question we must answer is whether or not Freud intended his hypothesis to refer to a literal event. As an historical fact, did the murder of the powerful male occur in the way Freud outlined it? Or, to come to Freud's last development of his position, in the *Moses and Monotheism* of 1939, did a group of the Jewish people murder Moses, suffer the memory of this crime to lapse during a period of latency, and then "remember" this great misdeed of primeval times in the revived form of Jewish monotheism, later, indeed, developing into Christianity? We have reprinted two items—the Kroeber and the Baron reviews—which throw grave doubt on the literalness of Freudian "facts."

And yet, does this effectively discredit Freud's work? Or is he really getting at something else, a psychic instead of "historical" reality? As Kroeber suggests, paradoxically, the psychic reality may itself, therefore, be historical. Freud himself hints at this in *Civilization and its Discontents,* when he writes, "It is not really a decisive matter whether one has killed one's father or abstained from the deed; one must feel guilty in either case, for guilt is the expression of the conflict of ambivalence, the eternal struggle between Eros and the destructive or death instinct." [2] In this awareness, Freud is merely recapitulating his experience with individual patients, but now in terms of the entire human race. At the beginning of his psychoanalytic practice, Freud was struck by his patients' recitals of sexual attacks undergone in childhood, at the hands of their parents. He believed in the reality of these seduction scenes, for, as he commented, "Why should patients assure me so emphatically of their unbelief [in their own stories], if from any motive they had invented the very things that they wish to discredit?" [3] The shock of discovering that the supposed traumas had never really occurred tried Freud's character to the utmost. As his biographer, Ernest Jones, comments, it marked "a turning point in his scientific career, and it tested his integrity, courage, and psychological insight to the full." With reality seemingly lost, Freud came slowly to realize that "If hysterics trace back their symptoms to fictitious traumas, this new fact signifies that they create such scenes in phantasy, and psychical reality requires to be taken into account alongside actual reality." [4]

Here, then, is the clue. The murder of the primal father is "psychical reality." It is a myth; and as Freud wrote to a fellow scientist, Albert Einstein, "It may perhaps seem to you as though our theories are a kind of mythology. . . . But does not every science come in the end to a kind of mythology?" And, as Philip Rieff has pointed out in his brilliant book, *Freud: The Mind of the Moralist,* "Scientific myths in contrast to reli-

[2] *Civilization and Its Discontents,* trans. Joan Riviere (London, 1949), p. 121.

[3] Ernest Jones, *The Life and Work of Sigmund Freud,* Vol. I (New York: Basic Books, Inc., 1953) p. 264.

[4] *Ibid.,* pp. 265 and 267. [This latter quotation is originally from Freud's *On the History of the Psychoanalytic Movement* (1914.)] For an interesting comment on the importance of this discovery, see Norman N. Holland, "Freud and the Poet's Eye," *Literature and Psychology* (Spring, 1961), p. 44.

gious myths, are designed to free individuals from their psychological thralldom to primal forms." [5] May we not also substitute here for the word "myth," Freud's own usage of "hypothesis"?[6]

Basically, what Freud has done is to assume that man's cultural evolution—his history—is the story, as Rieff puts it, of "psychic states that work themselves out as events." Darwin had started from unexplained variations, and offered a theory of natural selection to serve as the mechanism whereby evolution took place. Freud starts from man's unexplained, "given" psyche—his ambivalence—and offers a theory of psychological conflict as the mechanism by which history unfolds.[7] A key element in this explanation is Freud's assumption that man, under the psychic necessity of repressing his instincts, "sublimates" himself in work, and thus creates civilization. Increasingly, as civilization grows and develops, the burden of guilt, the need for repression, becomes ever greater. As we shall see in a moment, history has become neurosis.

Before we turn to this theme, however, a word about Freud's psychological explanation of history. Rieff, for one, sees Freud mistakenly turning history into psychology. However, this may be seen to have its good as well as its bad aspects. Whereas in Hegel and Marx, for example, private psychological make-ups are secondary to world spirits and economic conditions of production, which merely use individual psyches for their own cunning purposes, in Freud it is the private psychological mechanisms which spark the social actions. As we can see in Part II of this anthology, it is this part of Freud's work which has inspired a number of present-day political and behavorial scientists, as well as a few historians.

On the other hand, however, philosophers of history like R. G. Collingwood would take issue with Freud. In his brilliant but perverse book, *The Idea of History*,[8] Collingwood deprecated Thucydides' work for exactly this reason: it had turned history into psychology:

> Thucydides is the father of psychological history. Now what is psychological history? It is not history at all, but natural science of a special kind. It does not narrate facts for the sake of narrating facts. Its chief purpose is to affirm laws, psychological laws. . . . Thucydides is not the successor of Herodotus in historical thought but the man in whom the historical thought of Herodotus was overlaid and smothered beneath anti-historical motives.

It is clear that, on the same grounds, Collingwood would censor Freud.

[5] Philip Rieff, *Freud: The Mind of the Moralist* (New York: Doubleday and Company, Inc., Anchor Books, 1961), p. 224.

[6] However, it must be admitted that all too often Freud leaned toward the euhemerist explanation of myth—the theory that the mythological gods were but deified mortals—and thus to an interpretation of myths as traditional accounts of historic events and figures. Cf. Rieff, *op. cit.*, p. 229.

[7] Actually, Freud hints at the cause of man's peculiar psyche—his rise to a standing position. We shall treat of this further, when we come to talk of Róheim's paper.

[8] R. G. Collingwood, *The Idea of History* (New York: Galaxy Books, 1956) pp. 29-30.

Without attempting to decide the issue here as to the correct nature of history, I should like merely to suggest that, although Freud (in his early phase, at least) all too frequently seems to have treated the psyche as developing in an inner timeless vacuum, devoid of historical circumstances, he was in his best moments aware of the *interaction* of the psychological and the historical—rather than the merging of one into the other. Thus, in *Totem and Taboo* itself, he cautions that "the understanding [as to the origin and relation of the totem organization and the incest prohibition] should be at once historical and psychological; it should inform us under what conditions this peculiar institution developed and to what psychic needs of man it has given expression." Further on, talking of religion, he points out that its development took place "under the combined influence of cultural changes, historical events, and inner psychic transformations"—a rich brew! [9]

In any case, however we conceive of it, Freud's view of man's historical evolution is rooted in, if not identical with, his belief in psychic transformations or stages. It is in this sense that we must understand the charge that man's history is his neurosis, and that historical events must be looked at merely as symptoms. In the words of James Joyce, "History is a nightmare from which I try to awake." Phrased in another way, by Rieff, "Neurosis is the failure to escape the past, the burden of one's history." The individual recapitulates ontogenetically, the phylogenic development of the race. He does this, uniquely, in his development from an unrepressed infant to a sublimated adult, and, repetitively, in his nightly dreams, where he brings out again, beside the sophisticated concerns of adult life, the primitive and childlike desires of mankind's earliest stages. There, behind and with the presentness of modern civilization, is our "archaic heritage." It is a heritage with a curse attached to it: the curse of guilt.

3

Can we free ourselves from this "curse"? In the article by Philip Rieff, we are not given an answer to this question, but rather a penetrating analysis of the terms and concepts in which Freud presented his theory. Freud's use of the "model of time"—retrospection—is considered, and the question as to the realness of the "reality" he presents to us is sharply, though sympathetically, raised and discussed. Rieff's articles, with those by Kroeber and Baron, allow us to test the validity of Freud's data and theories, and to perceive their meaning and significance.

On a different tack, a number of writers on Freud have sought recently to go beyond the master himself and to hold out the hope of mankind freeing itself from the curse of repression. One such is Herbert Marcuse, in his book, *Eros and Civilization* (1955). While attacking the neo-Freud-

[9] *Totem and Taboo* in *The Basic Writings of Sigmund Freud,* trans. and ed. by Dr. A. A. Brill (New York: The Modern Library, 1938), pp. 890 and 923.

ians (Erich Fromm, Karen Horney, and Harry Stack Sullivan), Marcuse believes with them that we need not rest content with Freud's stoical and pessimistic portrayal of the fate of civilized man; on the contrary, we can break the grip of our instinctual needs (or at least reduce them to the irreducible minimum) and, on the grounds of Freud's own theories, we can reject the identification of civilization with repression. In what seems to be an attempted reconciliation of Marx's work with Freud's, Marcuse suggests that "the very achievements of repressive civilization seem to create the preconditions for the gradual abolition of repression." Because of the involved and complex nature of Marcuse's thought—always profound and dialectical—it is inadvisable even to try to excerpt a part; the interested reader must go to the original work.

Norman O. Brown's *Life Against Death* (1959) is similar to Marcuse's book in that it seeks to go beyond Freud to a non-repressive civilization. Brown believes that "a way out of the human neurosis, a way out of history" can be obtained through psychoanalysis, which, by completing and going beyond the work of religion, and making the unconscious conscious, can "restore" to us the pre-ambivalent stage of our infancy. Indeed, we can reach a stage of unrepressed and free genital organization, according to Brown, in which play for its own sake dominates.

There are difficulties involved in reading Brown's book. He assumes a rather detailed knowledge of Freud's works, one which the average reader will not have, and then mixes up Freudian notions with a rather strange metaphysics of his own. Effecting an odd combination of religious mysticism and humanistic enjoyment of the body, he extrapolates from Freud, but without indicating the clinical evidence which supports the new structure of thought. Nevertheless, in spite of the weird and erratic aspect of the work, Brown's book is highly suggestive. I myself find Part V, "Studies in Anality," most interesting and recommend that it be read in connection with, say, Erikson's *Young Man Luther,* or with various studies revolving around the relationship of Protestantism, the rise of capitalism, and a type of "capitalist" personality, often referred to as "anal."

It is with the work of men like Marcuse and Brown in mind that Meyerhoff, an astute commentator on psychoanalysis and history, wrote his article on "Freud and the Ambiguity of Culture." Holding fast to the original Freudian position, Meyerhoff re-asserts the view that we cannot escape from the discontents inherent in civilizing ourselves: they are the price we pay for our cultural achievements. Accepting the characterization of man as necessarily ambivalent, and of culture as necessarily ambiguous, he stoically embraces the tragic view of humanity. The result is a re-affirmation and a restoration of the original Freudian position.

The work of Géza Róheim stands apart from the issue above, and leads us in another direction. It is, I believe, the most difficult of the pieces reprinted in Part I. It demands not only a detailed knowledge of psychoanalytic concepts, but a grasp of anthropological data and notions as well; to complicate matters, Róheim's "Hungarian" style does not allow for easy reading. But the effort is worth making. Róheim picks up Freud's attempt to explain the origin and evolution of man as a cultural animal; instead, however, of relying primarily on a "scientific myth," as Freud does, Róheim seeks to marshal the latest anthropological evidence—the empirical data—in this fundamental investigation. In short, he seeks to go from philosophy of history to a form of history per se: a history based on psychoanalytic and anthropological findings.

Without attempting to summarize Róheim's article, we may profitably touch on a few essential points. The initial question for Róheim is, "What is the structure of the super-ego in a really primitive community?" Taking as his "really primitive community" only the Australians, and adding that this description "may apply on the basis of the meagre data we find in anthropological books also to the Pygmy tribes"—in other words, to food gatherers—he suggests the following: 1) "That in primitive conditions a whole group of well-known phenomena are conspicuous by their absence. Although sadistic and masochistic tendencies form a part of primitive life, sadistic or masochistic perversions are completely absent; that is, we do not find that coitus or sexual pleasure is connected with punishment and suffering, or, more exactly, with imaginary punishment and imaginary suffering"; 2) "Romantic love, which invests the love object with all the qualities of the super-ego and in which the ego feels guilty because of its erotic strivings directed towards the revived Oedipus objects, is unknown to primitive mankind. . . . Also among real primitives unhappy marriages are unknown"; and 3) "In a primitive society there are no individuals who are oppressed or despised, nobody whose will is not in harmony with public will, none who live a life under the compulsion of an endopsychic 'need for punishment.' " (Clearly, this is a different picture from Freud's primal horde; as we shall see, Róheim is describing a later stage.) In short, guilt and guilt-laden love, dominance and exploitation, are not the charges sparking primitive mankind, as they are for his more civilized brethren.[10]

According to Róheim, what changes a society of equals into a society of superiors and inferiors is the shift from a genital to an anal character formation. This shift appears to be linked with the change from a food-gathering economy to an agricultural one; and it is tied up with the introduction of money (i.e., dentalium money) or wealth (i.e., magic power.)[11] For Róheim, the root of money is in the psyche, and he makes

[10] In a way, this seems to be Norman Brown's life without neurosis—only at the beginning of man's evolution rather than at the end.

[11] Róheim also suggests a related characteristic of this second phase in the evolution of human society and culture, the prominent emergence of the heroic myth. This emergence mirrors the new psychological necessity of achieving rather than merely being. As Róheim puts it: "Heroic myth is therefore a mirror of the infantile situation: the hero is the little boy, and the imago [image of authoritative person] of the mother is represented both by the heroine and by the dragon." To use historical terms, it is only at this stage that the great man in history—the doer—comes upon the world.

the suggestive comment that "originally people do not desire money because you can buy things for it, but you can buy things for money because people desire it." Elsewhere, in a monograph called the *Origin and Function of Culture* (New York, 1943), he describes this same mechanism in relation to the Duau tribe exchange system, where A gives to B because he wants (psychologically) to receive things from B—and vice-versa: "We love those who love us; i.e., we love because we yearn for love." In part, then, what Róheim has done is to set up a model of capitalist character structure: anal man.

All of Róheim's complicated handling of anthropological materials is directed toward depicting "the psychological history of mankind, how displaced libido transforms society and thus from the point of view of the individual transforms environment." According to Róheim, if I read him correctly, the displacement of the libido from the id, to the service of the ego (individual character) and thence to the super-ego (culture) and back again to the formation of the ego, was undergone by the race just as it is by the individual. Or, in other words, "ancestors became human just as the child grows up today, by a psychic elaboration of infantile traumas." The conclusion which Róheim reaches, to take the phrasing of his *Origin and Function of Culture,* is that "defence systems against anxiety are the stuff that culture is made of and that therefore *specific cultures are structurally similar to specific neuroses* [my italics]." Instead, therefore, of history itself being a neurosis, it is the *process* by which specific neuroses—cultures—and their attendant "psychotics"—individual character structures, such as the primitive genital and the "capitalistic" anal—come into being.

At this point, I should like to suggest that what is vague, shadowy, and even arcane in Róheim becomes clearer if we look at some recent work: work which, more or less, follows in Róheim's footsteps without being overtly psychoanalytic in interpretation. I am referring to two articles which appeared in *Scientific American* (September 1960). In the first of these, "Tools and Human Evolution" by Sherwood L. Washburn, the following theses are sustained: 1) that changes in human structure—teeth, bones, brain, pelvis and upright posture—occurred in an intertwined cause and effect relationship with the developing human use of tools and in accordance with Darwinian natural selection: the result was human evolution; 2) that just as the use of tools is, among the primates, unique to humans, so is the mother-child relationship, where prolonged infantile dependence and slow maturation prevents the mother from hunting, and, by throwing this task completely on the father, leads to a social organization of the human species. In this social organization, "a family exists that controls sexual activity by custom, that takes care of slow-growing young, and in which—as in the case of primitive human societies—the male and female provide different foods for the family members."

Róheim, too, in the article we reprint, stresses (as did Freud) both the importance of the prolongation of infancy for the evolution of human culture, and the control of sexual activity by custom. In Marshall D. Sahlins' *Scientific American* contribution, "The Origin of Society," these ideas are developed further. Sahlins' basic question is "How did the primate horde evolve into the human band?"; and his basic thesis is that "human society required some suppression, rather than a direct expression, of man's primate nature. Human social life is culturally, not biologically, determined." The key to human social life is sex: year-round sex in the higher primates means year-round heterosexual social life. Sex, however, while bringing society together can also render it asunder, and competition over partners can lead to anarchic struggle. As Sahlins puts it: "It was this side of primate sexuality that forced early culture to curb and repress it. The emerging human primate, in a life-and-death economic struggle with nature, could not afford the luxury of a social struggle." Thus, custom came into being to regulate sex; and the biological record shows that, progressively, through the primate order, sex has been emancipated from hormonal control and placed under the intellect, the cerebral cortex. In this condition, it is subordinated to moral rules and to higher, collective ends.

From here on, Sahlins develops his hypothesis in detail, till he reaches primitive man per se. Two points command our attention. The first is that the primate horde is pre- or sub-human: although it has risen from promiscuous mating to exclusive permanent heterosexual partnerships, it is not a "society" but only a "horde," typically grouped around a dominant male, and in enmity to all other such "hordes." When we come to human hunting and gathering groups, "bands," we find the institution of kinship and the cultural regulation of sex and marriage. "Among all modern survivors of the Stone Age," Sahlins tells us, "marriage with close relatives is forbidden, while marriage outside the band is at least preferred and sometimes morally prescribed. The kin ties thereby created become social pathways of mutual aid and solidarity connecting band to band." The description offered by Sahlins of these "bands": the lack of true government and law; the lack of warfare and thus of heroic achievement; and the lack of romantic love, is quite close to Róheim's description of primitive man, the Australians.

If this part of Sahlins' work corresponds to Róheim, his comment regarding the repression of primate sexuality applies to Freud directly. Sahlins says, and this is the second point we wished to stress in his work, "The repression of sex in favor of other ends is a battle which, while won for the species, is still joined in every individual to this day. In Sigmund Freud's famous allegory, the conflict between the self-seeking, sexually inclined id and the socially conscious superego re-enacts the development of culture that occurred in the remote past."

Now, I have reprinted Róheim's article, and spent so much time in this introduction on Washburn's and Sahlins' work, in order to suggest the possible extrapolations—some already undertaken—from Freud's philosophy of history.[12] Freud sought to explain the origin and development of human culture. He started from what he knew of the physiological and biological data of mankind—after all, Freud's original work was in neuropsychology; added an idea from Darwin—the primal horde—which stood at the brink between biology and anthropology; worked up this idea in terms of the latest anthropological evidence available to him—the work of Frazer, Robertson Smith, etc.; contributed his own empirical findings in clinical psychoanalysis—i.e., his knowledge of the individual psyche as it recapitulates in its dreams the infancy of the human race; and emerged with a psychological history of mankind.

Whatever its shortcomings and its particular errors of theory and data, Freud's philosophy of history is a powerful searchlight, turned on the tunnel of human development, both individual and social. Starting as a scientific myth, it has lent itself to empirical correction and development. Combined with biological, archeological, anthropological, and economic insights and data, it gives, I believe, a coherent picture of the evolution of human culture from the primate stage to the emergence of primitive human society: a complex of material and psychoanalytic factors. In this form, it marks, in the best sense of that word, an *historical* rather than a *mythical* explanation of man's past: and that, after all, is the triumphal point to which all explanation called "historical" seeks to raise itself.

4

It must be clear from the above that I believe the Freudian philosophy of history to be a most suggestive and useful account of human genesis. As developed by men like Washburn and Sahlins, and by the scholars whose work they join to their own, it gives us insight into what is really man's *pre-history*. But what of that which we shall now call man's actual history: the period when we find him living in complex societies which we call civilizations? What help does Freudian psychoanalysis give us in relation to "recent" history, i.e., the period stretching from, say, the time of the first historians, Herodotus or Thucydides, to the present?

Obviously, the psychoanalytic is only one thread in the woven explanation we call history. As we see in Part I, it must be studied, in pre-history, in connection with many other kinds of knowledge: biology, archeology, anthropology, etc. These disciplines, however, when we come to history per se lend themselves, alas, less readily to our purposes. The biological force is too long-ranging and gross in its results for our purposes here.

---

[12] Washburn and Sahlins do not go beyond the time of primitive man; Róheim seeks to give in more detail the actual psychological operation of early society and to suggest how the later history of man works itself out in psychological terms. It is, of course, the actual details treated by Róheim which are most difficult to get at and most subject to controversy; I myself, from an untrained position, find much of Róheim's work hard to accept.

The archeological no longer alone supplies us with its materials: instead of its blessed paucity of data, we are inundated with "contemporary" and all too available documents and other evidences. As for the anthropological, that, too, with its welcome microcosms, its small, more or less sharply delineated and self-contained societies, often numbering as few as fifty members, seems far removed from the historical leviathans of our time. These nets—the biological or the anthropological—are too large or too fine for the quarry we seek.

Instead, we turn to the disciplines of economics and sociology, to the concerns of political science, and to the traditional methods used by historians. How do the insights of psychoanalysis relate to these approaches? How does psychoanalysis illuminate the history of modern man, and help us to understand the mechanism, or the process, by which historical change takes place? Does the Freudian philosophy of history, for example, assist us in this matter?

On first glance, the answer to the last question seems "no." There is a complete gap, it might appear, between the concern of men like Freud, with his "archaic heritage," and Róheim, with his primitive man, and the student of modern events. Freud's eyes are either on the remote past or on the single individual of the present: the matter in between—the modern civilized group and its experiences—seems to escape his vision. To read his *Group Psychology* is to realize that he is still talking about the primal horde and its survival in the modern man who is part of a crowd, and that the latter is really only the witness to a murder mystery re-enacted again and again.

And yet, if we look more closely at Freud's work, we see that there is a thread which may help lead us through the complex maze of history. It unwinds from Freud's initial clinical experience with individuals (including his own self-analysis) to the reconstructed primal horde—to cultural genesis, in short—and then back to an understanding of the individual in the light of this newly revealed history; the next turn must be once again from the individual, seen from the view of this heightened clinical psychoanalysis, to the group, but this time to the modern, "historical" group. This last unwinding is what concerns us in Part II; it is an unwinding which has barely begun.

Most of the work which has been done in this area has been by political scientists. As Lucian Pye points out in his review-essay of Erikson's book, political scientists, with their interest in understanding the "connections between individual and group behavior," have turned more and more to the insights of clinical psychology, and the list of references at the end of his article is impressive testimony of this fact. Will these same insights, he asks, help the student of history?

One immediate answer is that, willy-nilly, the future historian of present-day history will *have* to deal with psychoanalytic studies simply because the political scientists of today have approached their subjects—

Nazi Germany, the Soviet Union, etc.,—in this fashion. *No* historian of
the Soviet Union who is worth his salt, will, ten or twenty years from now,
be able to ignore fundamental researches, such as Leites' *Study of Bolshevism* or, say, *The Authoritarian Personality,* ed. by Adorno *et al.,* in
writing up his work. He will have to deal with them, and a host of related
studies, simply as part of the scholarly literature on the subject.

Instead, however, of merely yielding to this *fait accompli* imposed on
him from the outside, the historian is now also faced with the grand
prospect of learning, or at least sympathetically supporting, a new method
which promises to illuminate old areas of traditional historical interest.
The historian has always been interested in individuals—in "great men in
history"; psychoanalysis is an invaluable aid here. The historian has always been interested in the behavior of groups, whether they be rebellious
peasants, East India Company men, or court cliques; here, too, he can
learn from psychoanalytic studies. And the key problem, the interaction
of the individual and the group, cries out for all the knowledge we
can get from the combined insights of sociology, economics, political science, psychoanalysis, and history.

The difficulties in the way are enormous. Anyone working in the field,
in relation to either individual or group behavior, must learn not only his
own historical discipline but the very involved theory and data of this
"foreign" study, psychoanalysis. It is all too easy to make crude, mis-
guided "analogies"; and parlor-room Freudian analysis, like hypnotic
stunts in an earlier day, can bring discredit to legitimate investigation.
More, the application of psychoanalytic methods to "patients" who are
dead and no longer subject to verification by clinical processes, and whose
"analysis" must proceed in terms of a one-way Socratic dialogue with their
remaining documents is fraught with dangers, some pointed out by
Freud himself (who nonetheless occasionally fell victim to them.)[13]

When to this we add the fact that, in its existing state, psychoanalysis
offers very little theory to guide our efforts in relating the individual to
the group, i.e., to modern psychoanalytical history, we perceive how
courageous must be our historical pioneers—Nietzsche-like supermen,
who rush in where angels fear to tread. Most of us will not be such historical pioneers. What can be expected from us is sympathetic reading, as

---

[13] Thus, when asked to interpret the famous dream of Descartes, Freud replied that
with the dreamer dead and unable therefore to supply a context for the symbols present
in the dream, its psychological analysis was barred to him. [See Maxime Leroy, *Descartes, le philosophe au masque,* 2 vols. (Paris, 1929), vol, I, pp. 89-90.] However, Freud
appears to have shown less restraint concerning material surrounding the life of
Leonardo da Vinci. See his *Leonardo da Vinci: A Psychosexual Study of an Infantile
Reminiscence,* trans. A. A. Brill (New York: Dodd, Mead & Co., 1916) and the criticism
of this work by Meyer Schapiro, "Leonardo and Freud: An Art Historical Study,"
Journal of the History of Ideas (April, 1956.) Recently, K. R. Eissler, in *Leonardo da
Vinci: Psychoanalytic Notes on the Enigma* (New York: International Universities
Press, 1961), has sought to revindicate Freud in this matter.

informed as we amateurs can make it. For the effort involved on both sides, by the psychoanalytic historians and by the readers of their work, is one related to a problem of the utmost importance: the understanding of our history, and thus of ourselves. In the words of Freud: "We cannot do without men with the courage to think new things before they can prove them."

5

If we accept the injunction, to know ourselves in this way, what concrete assistance does psychoanalysis afford to the historical understanding? What might emerge from a reading of the articles reprinted in Part II? First, I should like to point out the bearing on historical method of the psychoanalytic method per se. Both are, in their ability to predict from premises, gross and uncertain compared to the natural sciences, and both have been attacked as, therefore, offering non-valid knowledge. What is at stake, however, is a "new model" of scientific explanation, subtle, different, and more or less unto itself. We see it in Freud's comment that "from a knowledge of the premises we could not have foretold the nature of the result . . . We never know beforehand which of the determining factors will prove the weaker or the stronger. Hence it is always possible by analysis to recognize the causation with certainty, whereas a prediction of it by synthesis is impossible." Without going further into this important topic we can say that while history has far greater difficulty, if not an impossibility, in recognizing the causation with "certainty," the similarity of method with psychoanalysis is clear.[14]

On another plane, much more specific, there is a similarity between the findings of psychoanalysis regarding individual symptoms, and the documentary evidence about crowds and individuals with which history works. Thus, in the light of psychoanalytical research we can now see that the symptoms exhibited during demonic possession in the Middle Ages are the same as those manifested today by hysterical patients: in short, Freud's work can be used to "analyze" past group phenomena, and to bring us heightened historical awareness. Freud, himself, had stumbled on this fact, and was properly elated. In a letter to his friend Fliess, he burst out: "By the way, what have you got to say to the suggestion that the whole of my brand-new theory of the primary origins of hysteria is already familiar and has been published a hundred times over, though several centuries ago? Do you remember my always saying that the medieval theory of possession, that held by the ecclesiastical courts, was

[14] For a critical discussion of this topic, see, for example, *Psychoanalysis, Scientific Method and Philosophy*, a symposium ed. Sidney Hook (New York: New York University Press, 1959). W. H. Auden, in "The History of an Historian," *The Griffin*, vol. 4 no. 11 (November, 1955), a review of the second volume of Jones' *Life and Work of Sigmund Freud*, also has some interesting comments apropos of this problem. Of especial interest, too, is Hans Meyerhoff, "On Psychoanalysis and History," *Psychoanalysis and the Psychoanalytic Review*, vol. 49, no. 2 (Summer, 1962).

identical with our theory of a foreign body and the splitting of consciousness? . . . Why were the confessions extracted under torture so very like what my patients tell me under psychoanalytical treatment? . . . I read one day that the gold which the devil gave his victims regularly turned into excrement. . . . I have ordered a *Malleus Maleficarum*. . . . In connection with the dances in witches' confessions you will recall the dancing epidemics of the Middle Ages. E's nurse was a dancing witch of that kind." [15]

Basically, it is this sort of comparative psychology which Langer is calling for in his article on "The Next Assignment." Yet, if I read him correctly, it is actually not for psychoanalytic techniques per se but more for a social psychology on a rather low level of theory that Langer is mainly appealing: awareness by the historian of the effect of such things as famines, plagues, overcrowding, and epidemics on mass psychology. Thucydides' report on the great plague of Athens in 430 B.C. is one example; various treatments of the effects of the Black Death of the fourteenth century is another. What is needed, according to Langer, are more analyses of the psychic content of mass phenomena, such as the chiliastic movements depicted by Norman Cohn in his *The Pursuit of the Millennium* (New York, 1957), the Lisbon Earthquake, or the threats of death and destruction existing at any and all times. Langer's address is a bold call to the historian to look in a more informed and aware way at materials which otherwise are usually slurred over or simply ignored.

The really fundamental challenge that psychoanalysis trumpets forth to historians is: "Interpret the documents." It says to the historian, you cannot simply pass over or ignore the "facts" presented to you in your evidences. If you, like Ranke, want to know *wie es eigentlich gewesen,* how it actually happened, you must learn to ask the right questions of existing documents; and, indeed, this will lead you to seek new documents—details about individual and group behavior—which you had previously overlooked as unimportant and without significance. And further, as Erikson points out in the chapter, "The Meaning of 'Meaning It' " in *Young Man Luther,* the historical figure must be understood as meaning what he says not only in the overt and manifest content of his words but at a much deeper, more latent, level of psychoanalytical meaning. Hence, perhaps its most important contribution, psychoanalysis insists that the historian pay critical, i.e., analytic, attention to the documents and to what the voices talking through his documents "really mean."

Thus, in the article on Machiavelli by Sereno, we see the author asking

---

[15] *The Origins of Psychoanalysis: Letters, Drafts and Notes to Wilhelm Fliess, 1887-1902* (Garden City, New York: Doubleday & Company Inc., Anchor Books, 1957), pp. 190-192. The *Malleus Maleficarum* was a manual, prepared in the fifteenth century, to aid inquisitors of the church in finding witches.

the right questions of his document. Before him, the eminent Machiavelli scholar, Villari, had merely presented the document in question "for what it is, or, rather, for what it seems to be—a meaningless exercise or a little divertisement of the Florentine secretary who, when in Rome in the fall of 1503, copied the circular letter." Sereno, however, is aware that the really important questions have not been asked of the document: "Why Machiavelli felt compelled to copy the letter in his own handwriting, faithfully reproducing the form and the pattern of the original; why he kept and preserved this absurd exercise among his papers; why he painstakingly imitated Caesar's signature, are queries that Villari does not formulate." Having raised the right queries, Sereno then proceeds to give an answer, which, though obviously psychoanalytically informed, is phrased in ordinary, everyday language. Whether one judges his explanation correct or not, one cannot help seeing that he has pointed out an important new approach to the problem, especially when he concludes, "Once we look at Machiavelli and his work—as so many others have done—not merely philologically or historically but with an effort at seeing *what he really meant* [my italics], we may also look in a novel way not only at his writings but at the science he created."

Brodie's review-essay on the Georges' book about Wilson points up the overtly psychoanalytic aspects of their work, which they felt constrained to conceal in a footnote. It is a beautiful treatment of their important book, bringing out into the open some of the implications for historians of their work. Subtitled "A Personality Study," the Georges' book abjures the task of telling *what* Wilson did—the subject of so many historical treatments—and seeks to understand "the logic of his actions, . . . his behavior." It is a *developmental* biography, and as such studies the all-important interaction of personality and situational (i.e., historical) factors: Wilson's "driving, essentially autocratic leadership" was acceptable because the times in which he operated "favored political reforms and strong leadership." Dr. and Mrs. George do not leave this as a mere generalization, however, but illustrate it in the detail of their subject. Like Erikson, they are concerned with the riddle of the relationship of the individual to the masses that follow him: how does his personal psychology interplay with the psychological desires and fears of large groups of people? In succinct and clear form, Brodie summarizes and suggests the nature of this interaction.

With Flügel's treatment of Henry VIII, we give up the effort to relate the man to his circumstances in a particularly meaningful way, but we gain (if one is sympathetic to this approach) a systematic and overt application of Freudian techniques and terminology to an historical figure. Flügel, of course, was a practicing psychologist; he was not, by professional training, an historian. I suspect that his paper illustrates the advantages and the limitations of this situation. It is representative of a number of such attempts, undertaken especially in the early days of psychoanalysis, but still occasionally found today.[16] Attention ought especially to be paid to the last paragraph, which suggests the way in which historical material may validate psychoanalytical findings: a nice, and unexpected, repayment of the debt of history to psychoanalysis. What is most important in Flügel's paper, however, is its attempt to explain Henry's rather strange matrimonial behavior in a more *meaningful* way than that usually offered by historians.

I have reserved for the last the latest important attempt to relate psychoanalysis to history: Erikson's *Young Man Luther*. This book, incidentally, has the great advantage for the reader who is uninformed about psychoanalytic theories and terminology, of developing as it goes along its own theory of ego identity, a modified Freudian position. It is, I believe, along with the Georges' book, the most fecund attempt to supply the link between individual psychoanalysis and group psychology; enormously suggestive, it combines the training of a practicing psychoanalyst, the sharp awareness of a knowledgeable student of history, and the deep and warm sympathy of an appealing human being.

Our attempt to get at this book—which I earnestly recommend for full reading—is through two essays. The review-essay by Donald Meyer, though sometimes crabbed in its writing, is a penetrating, often brilliant, effort to take up the questions posed for historians by Erikson's work, and to suggest the directions from which answers must come. It poses the challenge to historians directly, of what Meyer calls "the most radically historical psychology." At once critical of Erikson's psychoanalysis and of the traditional historical method, it is critical in a detached and helpful way.

Pye's review-essay of the same subject offers a clear précis of Erikson's work and a remarkable synthesis of its results with those of other investigators in the field. Master of the materials in this area, Pye reviews the existing literature—almost all by political scientists—concerning the application of psychoanalytical methods to the study of individual and group behavior and relates them to Erikson's effort.

The articles reprinted in Part II point a rather cryptic finger. They indicate a problem rather than a solution. They are like the figure of Virgil in Dante's *Divine Comedy*, indicating the way to the circles of men's underground life. It is not for nought that W. H. Auden, in his poem "In Memory of Sigmund Freud," conjures up the image that

> . . . he went his way,
> Down among the Lost People like Dante, down
> To the stinking fosse where the injured
> Lead the ugly life of the rejected.

[16] Cf. Ludwig Jekels, "The Turning Point in the Life of Napoleon I," *Selected Papers* (New York: International Universities Press, Inc., 1953). (First published in *Imago*, Vol. 111, 4, 1914.)

Freud himself had recognized the comparison. At one point he remarked in a mood of deep pessimism to his friend Fliess, "it will be a fitting punishment for me that none of the unexplored regions of the mind in which I have been the first mortal to set foot will ever bear my name or submit to my laws." Then, later, defiantly, he said of his psychoanalytic work: "It is an intellectual hell, layer upon layer of it, with everything fitfully gleaming and pulsating; and the outline of Lucifer-Amor coming into sight at the darkest corner." [17]

In the light of this fitful gleaming we can see that only by man's pushing on to the "darkest corner" of his being, by experiencing the "divine comedy" of his past, can he rise to the heights of his noblest aspirations. This is the promise held out to us by the union of psychoanalysis and history. At the moment, we stand, at best, "Nel mezzo del cammin di nostra vita . . . per una selva oscura."

[17] *The Origins of Psychoanalysis,* pp. 320 and 324.

Introduction to the Revised Edition

Since 1963, and the original edition of this book, work in psychoanalysis and history has somewhat emerged from the "selva oscura"—the dark forest—in which it stood. Because of this development, there has been increased, rather than decreased, interest in the collection of pieces gathered together then, and *Psychoanalysis and History,* fallen out of print, has become almost a collector's item. As a result, many scholars, students, and interested readers have prodded me to seek a new edition. Happily, Grosset & Dunlap has agreed with this view, and the consequence is the present volume.

In this edition, I have kept all the original pieces and made one addition: Erik H. Erikson's path-breaking inquiry into the ways in which the psycho-historian—the new term for workers in this new field of psychoanalysis and history—becomes involved with his materials and subject. In this piece, "On the Nature of Psycho-Historical Evidence: In Search of Gandhi," treating of the historian's own transferences and countertransferences, Erikson makes highly important methodological contributions to the "doing" of history. Moreover, the article puts in succinct form the problems that are dealt with at length in Erikson's brilliant, full-length study, *Gandhi's Truth.* It is not too much to say that one fundamental way in which the latter book goes beyond Erikson's earlier work, *Young Man Luther,* is by making as conscious as possible the historian's unconscious involvement with his subject. No one, I believe, can press on effectively in psycho-historical work without taking profound notice of Erikson's insights and admonitions as to method.

Part I

FREUD'S PHILOSOPHY
OF HISTORY

The Meaning of
History and Religion
in Freud's Thought[1]

Philip Rieff

It may perhaps seem to you as though our theories are a kind of mythology. . . . But does not every science come in the end to a kind of mythology?—FREUD, "Why War?" in Collected Papers, V, 283.

This study is part of a larger attempt to elucidate the two organizing models of Freud's thought, in order to approach the total attitude controlling that thought. The first controlling model is called, here, the "model of time"; the second, the "model of analogy." This is to say, Freud's thought is, on the one hand, retrospective, historical, and, on the other, analogical. The more important of the two models as these order the Freudian interpretation of the meaning of religion, history, and politics—the model of time—is the subject of this essay. After this introduction outlines the alternative organizing models of Freud's historical thought, Section I undertakes to understand the Freudian psychology of history and the temporal relation between history and its religious dynamic, Kairos. Section II analyzes the instrumentation of Kairos as religious tradition. Section III is a statement on the methodological significance of the model of time as Kairos in Freud's thought. Section IV is a concluding explication of Freud's Kairos concept as he used it to inter-

"The Meaning of History and Religion in Freud's Thought." Reprinted from *The Journal of Religion*, XXXI, No. 2 (April 1951), 114-131, by permission of The University of Chicago Press.

[1] I have to thank for their instruction in Freud, and in other matters, my friends, Professor H. H. Gerth, of the Department of Sociology, the University of Wisconsin, and Professor James Luther Adams, of the Federated Theological Faculty, the University of Chicago.

pret the history of the Jewish and Christian religions and the nature of politics.

The guiding assumption of this study is contained in its motto. Freud's myth constructions, his metapsychological speculations, are not decorative to his insight. Rather, they are essential to it, a necessary base for it. "Without metapsychological speculation and theorizing—I had almost said 'phantasy'—we shall not get a step further." [2] A critical exposition and analysis of Freud's major conceptual models, including the myth frames of his total insight, may disclose, in some degree, the whole of Freud's outlook, the intimate substructure of his insight.

The organizing models of Freud's analysis, in its import for religious, historical, and political thought, may exist in two alternative interpretations. First, Freud may be considered a late child of the Enlightenment. Religion, history, and politics are seen, in this view, as a unilinear sublimational process, characterized, not as for some later types of humanist liberalism (W. F. Ogburn), by technological advances, the superstructural epiphenomena of the progress struggle, but primarily by ethical and moral elevation as the controlling value. In this first interpretation, Freud is in the main line of humanist religious liberalism, whose perspective does not depend, as it does for a dominant strain of contemporary secular liberalism, on an estimate of the technological constellation, but upon the constantly increasing power of the controlling ethical values. In these terms, Freud saw history as the unilinear movement from barbarism to civilization, from Id to Superego, from killer-man to humanist-man. The immediate objection to this interpretation, of Freud as humanist-liberal, as optimist, is that he is deeply concerned with the barbarism of war, as a type of event crucial to the understanding of religion, history, and politics. But, in this view, Freud's thoughts on war may be located in terms of war as a temporary regression, a setback to the unilinear, progressive movement of societies.

Second, Freud may be considered to have understood the "setbacks" to civilization not on a unilinear level, but as cyclical returns to earlier types of action from which man moves out again only to return. War becomes, in this second view, not a "setback," temporary and unfortunate, but an integral element in the circular motion of human history. The example of war gives a clue to an interpretation of the model of time contrary to that provided by the first: here, time is seen as the cyclical return of the ever-same; there, as the unilinear, unidirectional line of progress. The images of the circle and the ascending line, the moods of pessimism and optimism—these express Freud's basic attitudes and characterize its fertile contradictions. However, it is an object of this study to indicate, on the evidence of Freud's writings as clinician and moral philosopher, which of these polar orientations is a more adequate approximation of the basic posture informing Freud's thought.

[2] S. Freud, *Collected Papers* (London: Hogarth Press, 1950), V, 326.

I

"Our hysterical patients suffer from reminiscences." Freud italicized the passage. He intended the model of time to become of central importance to his readers. The emphasis is all on reminiscence. History, the memory of existence in time, is the flaw. Neurosis is the failure to escape the past, the burden of one's history. Neurotics "cannot escape from the past." [3]

Freud was fascinated and horrified by the power of the past. The whole uniqueness of man, the cause of his agony, his anxiety, is that man is a historical person, the mask of his history. Beginning with the concept of man as time-bound, Freud's major scientific achievement is his systematic insight into the life history of the individual and the social process in history. Particularly at the end of his life, he was preoccupied with the problem of time-bindedness in man and society as it expressed itself in the most interesting of neuroses—indeed, the primal neurosis—religion.

Like his great anticipator, Nietzsche, Freud was fascinated by history in the same degree as he attached a negative valuation to it. The end of the psychoanalytic process, both valuationally and chronologically, is to emancipate the patient from the burden of his history.[4] Neurosis is an "abnormal clinging to the past." "Fixation" on the past, the arrestment of the necessary development, is the most "significant characteristic of the neurosis." [5]

The first thing to say about history is that it is never, properly, past. That is, the past is never dead. It lives in the mind, never to perish. The past, indeed, operates "alongside the latest." [6] The contemporaneity of the uncontemporaneous is time's essential characteristic.[7] In a facetious moment, Freud was even inclined to doubt whether dragons are really extinct.[8] However, it is not the entire history of an individual or group that lives, just as it is not the latest. All history is not equivalent. On the contrary, the history that lives, that cannot be destroyed (except perhaps by psychoanalysis), is precisely the most remote, the earliest.

It is the *"remoteness of time"* that is the "really decisive factor" in the experience of the unconscious.[9] Yet it is not enough even to say that it is

[3] S. Freud, "The Origin and Development of Psychoanalysis," in *Social Science 2: Syllabus and Selected Readings* (Chicago: University of Chicago Press, 1949), I, 50.

[4] This point is taken up again in Section II. The term "end" has two senses, as noted by Aristotle in the *Physics* ii. 2. 194a: first, the "end" as the conclusion; second, the "end" as the highest value. Freud uses the first sense of "end" to mean the conclusion of the therapy, the second to mean the highest value of psychoanalytic thought.

[5] "The Origin and Development of Psychoanalysis," *op. cit.*, pp. 51-52.

[6] S. Freud, *Civilization and Its Discontents*, trans. Joan Riviere (Chicago: University of Chicago Press, n.d.), p. 17.

[7] K. Mannheim, *Rational and Irrational Elements in Contemporary Society* ("Hobhouse Memorial Lecture," No. 4 [London: Oxford University Press, 1934]), p. 4. Note Mannheim's spatialization of the concept of time.

[8] S. Freud, *Collected Papers*, V, 331.

[9] S. Freud, *Moses and Monotheism*, trans. Katherine Jones (London: Hogarth Press, 1949), p. 200. (My italics.)

the remotest history that continues. There is, according to Freud, an over-determination in history, as much in individual experience as in collective. A certain event, or events, necessarily in remote rather than near history—indeed, at the beginning—becomes determinative of all that must follow. Freud is a monocausalist. His method destroys multiple causation and thus the full truth of manifold understanding. Reducing change to constancy, Freud collapses history into nature, religion and politics into psychology.

It is in the master doctrine not only of the conservation of the past but of its determinativeness that Freud psychologizes religion, history, and politics out of existence. If Freud accused Marx of profaning "the grandiose multiformity of human life" by the monocausal recognition of "material needs" as the "sole motives" of history, then the accusation ought to become as much a self-accusation. The Freudian reductionism to "psychic needs" is perhaps an even more grandiose profanation of human multiformity than the Marxist.[10]

For Freud, a given life history, even as a given group history, must be examined in terms of the experience of crucial events occurring necessarily at a specific historical time. What is crucial needs have happened early. There had to be a *Kairos,* that crucial time in the past that is decisive for what then must come after. Kairos may be thought of as antinomical to *Chronos,* mathematical time in which each unit is qualitatively identical. Kairotic time, on the other hand, is not qualitatively identical —rather the reverse. Thus, for Freud, memory time is always kairotic. For example, the kairotic time of childhood may overwhelm vast stretches of later chronological time. This identifies Kairos with traumatic event, as we shall see in detail below.

As historian of the meaning of social existence, Freud, like the ancient Jews, the early Christians, Marx, and others, subscribed to the doctrine of the crucial time, the right time, the "moment rich in content and significance," [11] the time of "decisive importance" [12] in history. This is Kairos. However, the Freudian understanding of Kairos is antithetical to the dynamic theological understanding. For Tillich, for example, Kairos is the break into a radically different future, into the fullness of time, providing new opportunity. But, for Freud, Kairos is, at most, the renaming of the past. The kairotic event has already happened; while, in the radical theological understanding, Kairos is past only so far as it has

[10] *Ibid.,* p. 85.
[11] Paul Tillich, *The Protestant Era,* trans., with a concluding essay, by James Luther Adams (Chicago: University of Chicago Press, 1948), pp. 33 ff., and, further, pp. 155-56. See also, among Tillich's English writings, *The Interpretation of History* (New York: Scribner's, 1936), pp. 123-75. This, of course, is not the place to attempt even a résumé of the meaning and uses of Kairos thinking in its various classical expressions: Plato, Paul, Augustine, *et al.*
[12] *Moses and Monotheism,* p. 162.

been manifest as a hint—even a proclamation—of the future. Kairos is to come, however much it has proclaimed its coming.

Freud's cyclical, organic model of Kairos is best understood polarized against the unilinear, time-directed model of radical religious and secular thought. The second model performs a revolutionary function: God has still more to break forth. What is broken forth may well reverse what is. God is not bound. The future is a promise of new things and of good news.

The Freudian conception, however, is, in formal terms, close to one type of Christian thought: the Augustinian. Like the Augustinians, Freud locates the crucial time totally in the past. Augustinians locate Kairos as the transformative event creating Christ's church. Freud's conception is equally static, if differently located. Thus, it would be an oversimplification to understand the Freudian conception of Kairos as an inversion of the Christian. Freud, like Augustine and other sacramental thinkers, used Kairos to mean the principle of the moment of transformation in history. To that extent, his is identical with all Kairos thinking. Kairos is history, whether it radicalizes history or fixates it. The polarity is in the location of the transformation. Freud and conservative religious thinkers locate the transformation in the past. Radical thought locates the possibility of transformation in the future. The difference is the clue to Freud's politics as much as it is to Augustine's. History is predestination. Freud locates the instrument of predestination in the structure of the unconscious, however, rather than in the structure of the church. Kairos has access to the unconscious, as chronological time, Chronos, the measuring of time into equivalent, quantitative components, does not. Kairotic history is the content as well as the dynamic of the unconscious. Nothing other than Kairos, and its consequences, is, properly, history and personality. It is in this sense that Freud has assimilated the concept of predestination to his psychology.

The immediate impact of the Freudian Kairos concept, however, may be said to be the confrontation of academic faculty psychology by crisis psychology. Crisis psychology, muted in Pascal and Montaigne, extended by Kierkegaard and Nietzsche, was deepened by Freud to challenge the whole intent and operation of faculty psychology. After Freud, Pascal and Montaigne seem more modern and interesting, and Kierkegaard and Nietzsche more relevant, than the faculty psychologists. Who does not think Kierkegaard is more relevant than Ebbinghaus? The chromatic time of experimental testing (e.g., of reaction speeds) ignored man at his most definitive, as a crescive psychic structure. Nineteenth-century psychology conceived of the nature of man in terms of a summation of compartmentalized faculties, accessible in "natural science" experiments in terms of the model of mechanical reactions. This is the history of memory-testing experiments from William James, who began it, to Ebbinghaus, who brought it to its famous pinnacle. For the latter, finally, "pure" memory could be represented as a container of rote-learned nonsense syllables, measurable by speed and amount. The insights of faculty psychology say little or nothing about human nature. In the case of reaction speeds, for example, the insights are relevant only to the fetishized operations of alienated labor (e.g., a telephone operator) in modern occupational roles. Given a socially imposed task, faculty psychology may report strain thresholds but report nothing of the crescive quality of human nature. On the other hand, what matters for Freud is the spontaneous elements of human nature. Memory, in crisis psychology, is not an empty container, storing equally crucial nonsense syllables. Memory is, substantively, Kairos.

It is essential to the determinative power of Kairos that it has been, at some time, repressed. Repression supplies private and public history its dynamic. Both histories are too significant to be remembered simply, directly. But to be forgotten, of course, is not to be abolished. For Freud, as for Nietzsche, forgetting is an action (repression), not the absence of action, something dropped out of the container-mind. The unconscious, the historical origin, retains. The forgotten is not impotent because it is covert. History, as we shall see, can contain no surprises. The known does not arise from new experience, but from the remembered. Like prehistory, the unknown is only the forgotten. In this sense, according to Freud, men "have always known." Kairos needs to be forgotten, at least to be screened, but it is always potentially known; it does not cease to operate in human affairs. Contemporary events are, at most, the action-screen of kairotic history. Life history and public history, in Freud's view, are repetitions, compelled by the power of the repressed Kairos.

The dynamic thrust of Kairos is always from unconscious knowledge to conscious. Knowledge is recall; history, re-enactment. What has been given in time past as Kairos becomes thereafter pregnant with future. Every "pathogenic experience" implies a "previous one," the later one "endowed" with the earlier's "pathogenic quality." If for Marx the past is pregnant with the future, with the proletariat as the midwife of history, for Freud the future is pregnant with the past, with the psychoanalyst as the abortionist of history.

By his collapse of future into past, Freud came close to a Platonic theory of reminiscence, however naturalistic his model. Men seek to do what they have already done, as, for Plato, men's insight into the new is an idea beheld in the past. For Freud, men can only do what they have once done. History, understood at the level of the unconscious, holds no surprises. Neither does it brook any surprises. It is "in this particular way," Freud concluded, "that men have always known . . . that once upon a time they had a primeval father and killed him." [13] The Freudian Kairos is the primal crime. The history that follows is repetition.

[13] *Ibid.*, p. 161.

The Freudian idea of knowledge as reminiscence—of history as recurrence—does not depend, as it does for Plato, on the myth of the preexistence of the soul. Rather, Freud, like Nietzsche, to whom he acknowledged a debt and feared to read for that reason,[14] is Lamarckian. For both, the most crucial inheritance is of character, and character is transmitted through tradition. Tradition, then, is understood as the transformation of history into personality. The resemblance between Freud's thought and a major strain in Nietzsche is, plainly, close.[15] For both, the man most highly valued is the one who transcends history, thus escaping the burden of it. For both, it is not the most recent history, but the most remote, that is transmitted. And, for both, the recapitulation of the past in the individual is a "remembering" of the basic past, a reimbodiment of kairotic history.[16]

There is evidence, however, that Freud did not try to avoid the indirect influence, at least, of Plato.[17] Bernfeld writes[18] that Freud in 1879, at twenty-three, translated the twelfth volume of a collected edition of the writings of John Stuart Mill. The volume included Mill's essay on Grote's *Plato*, in which Mill comments on the Platonic theory of anamnesis.

[14] *Collected Papers*, I, 297.

[15] For a brilliant systematic analysis of the assimilation of Freud and Nietzsche see H. H. Gerth, "Moderne Psychologie," in *Die Welt im Fortschritt* (Berlin: F. A. Herbig Verlag, 1936), pp. 91-105.

[16] On Nietzsche's use of the idea of knowledge as reminiscence see George Allen Morgan, *What Nietzsche Means* (Cambridge: Harvard University Press, 1941), p. 70. This is not the place to discuss the alternative models of historical reflection in Nietzsche's thought. I refer here to the Nietzsche of *Zarathustra*, not to the Nietzsche of *The Use and Abuse of History*.

[17] See, on the Platonic idea of knowledge as reminiscence, the *Meno*. Freud's love of Hellenic culture leads to the conjecture that he had read the *Meno*, however much he protested that he despised philosophy as dangerous to his creativeness. It is quite naïve, as we shall see, to suppose that Freud was simply a physician who stumbled upon his discoveries in the course of his medical researches.

[18] Siegfried Bernfeld, "Freud's Scientific Beginning," *American Imago* (Boston), VI, No. 3 (September, 1949), 188. There is another sense in which Freud owes indirectly at least to the early Plato. Civilization, for Freud, is the growing "omnipotence of thoughts" (*Moses and Monotheism*, p. 179), the subordination of the senses to the ethical instruments. As humanity develops, "the world of the senses becomes gradually mastered by spirituality" (*ibid.*, p. 186). That this development is at the same time neurotic is not doubted by Freud. The "omnipotence of thoughts" is as characteristic of the individual neurosis as it is of civilization and of Platonic philosophy. Plato might be said to have raised what Freud would call his "flight from reality" to the status of a methodological principle. Freud might have made something of the following passage: "I decided that I must be careful not to suffer the misfortune which happens to people who look at the sun and watch it during an eclipse. For some of them ruin their eyes unless they look at its image in water or something of the sort. I thought of that danger, and I was afraid my soul would be blinded if I looked at things with my eyes and tried to grasp them with my senses. So I thought I must have recourse to conceptions and examine in them the truth of realities. That is the way I began" (Plato, *Phaedo*, trans. H. N. Fowler [London: Loeb Classical Library, 1913], pp. 99 ff. and 342; see also *ibid.*, 79 D, p. 277).

Bernfeld writes that Freud is reported to have said that he had been "greatly impressed by the theory of anamnesis and that he had, at one time, given it a great deal of thought." However, the young student Freud, who went into medicine rather reluctantly, preferring to read myth and history, is very different from the older Freud, the natural scientist, who treated Plato quite severely.

II

What defines the impact of Kairos upon men is their reaction to it, against it. Freud characterized the meaning of history as repressive and sublimative Kairos must, in the first instance, operate as a great repressive event The reaction to the event is, of course, unconscious. History, as the trail of Kairos, becomes a process of the "return of the repressed," [19] distorted extensively but nevertheless eternally recapitulating the Kairos.[20]

Freud then raised the question: "In what form" does Kairos live on? His answer is that Kairos lives as "tradition." [21] Finally, tradition is defined as the historical content of the mass unconscious. The definition came reluctantly, even though Freud thought it common knowledge. Even Jung knew it. Jung, as Freud wrote, did nothing by introducing the idea of the collective unconscious. The "content of the unconscious is collective anyhow." [22]

But "it was not easy," Freud tells us, "to introduce the conception of the unconscious into mass [e.g., social] psychology." [23] However, there was no more adequate theoretical alternative. Without the hypothesis of the mass psyche, Freud finds the dynamic as well as the achievements of tradition—the substance of history—incomprehensible. Tradition, finally, must be treated "as equivalent to repressed material in the mental life of the individual." On the conscious, cultural surface of a social structure, tradition, the repressed content of the past, is something "vanished and overcome in the life of a people." [24] But it is simply the hidden spring of personal and collective history—hidden as latency.

Freud conceptualizes tradition as latency, and latency not as potency but as fixation. This is "the intrinsic nature of a tradition." [25] The present, and the future, is that latent in the past. The future, like the present, in Freud's view, is pre-empted by the past. The future is only the latent past. The inner core of history is circular, as much for Freud, with his biologistically cyclical time model, as for the Greeks. The future is simply that which is overtaken by the past. In contrast to utopian and

[19] *Moses and Monotheism*, pp. 200-201.
[20] On the distortion of the Kairos see Freud's clinical papers on the function of screen-memories *et al.*, especially the *Collected Papers*, V, 47-69.
[21] *Moses and Monotheism*, p. 150.
[22] *Ibid.*, p. 208.
[23] *Ibid.*, p. 200.
[24] *Ibid.*, p. 208.
[25] *Ibid.*, p. 85.

eschatological Jewish, Christian, humanist, or Marxist thought, in Freud's view the future has no power over the past. History is a closed system. There are no unknown probabilities. What will happen is what has happened, granted a shift in context. History, Freud concludes, loves restorations. Above all, history loves "faithful reproduction." [26] Time is the order of reduplication.

Finally, for Freud, as contrasted with utopian thought, man cannot become what he wishes to be. He can only become what he has been. The future is not an open disposition. Rather, men can only hope to be made conscious of what they must be by learning what they have been. Freud possessed an almost total disdain of the future. His well-known pessimism as a social thinker must be understood in terms of his model of recurrent time against the openness and opportunity of a qualitatively different future.

Freud proposes an anti-eschatology, an anti-utopianism. There is nothing qualitatively different beyond this life and this way of life. His answer to any failure of the future to be qualitatively different from the past must be the great gibe of all disdain of the future: not "I told you so!" but, more quietly, "I could have told you so!" All observable presents point to the past. In so far as there is a future, it is a spurious future. The future is, at most, spurious because it is inescapable as the latent past.

Finally, Freud's model of time makes his basic attitude antitheodical. There is no hope, no promise. Nor is there justification. This is the best of all possible worlds, as it is the only possible world. The future is an illusion. And as the future is an illusion, life ideals and qualitative progress are illusions. The only end of life is life, living. One can only hope to survive. Freud's temper is stoical. The content of the rationality of man is to face up to the comfortless world as it is and will be. The basic posture of Freud is as stoic.

This does not disqualify the prophetic element in Freud's basic posture. Rather the prophet compounded the stoic to create Freud's orientation. Both prophet and stoic have as their chief life duty and social function the maintenance of self-identity in the face of threatening forces. Both live in a permanent crisis state, and the function of the crisis psychology is the maintenance of self-identity.

Freud's orientation is close to the crucial social element in the prophetic temper. The function of the crisis psychology of prophets is to heighten the sense of threat and fear in the face of uncontrolled changes, and to offer a control: hope as the psychic state supplied by adhering to tradition, with the prophet as instructor. Freud is, in one sense, on the side of tradition. He seeks to remind people of it and of its importance. He is the instructor revealing the meaning of the past to his listeners. But his prophetism must not be labored too far. To be a prophet is to assert that there is no way out of tradition, not to try systematically to abort it. And

[26] *Ibid.*, pp. 61-62.

Freud's end, processionally and valuationally, is to abort tradition, for
the sake of a type of progress unknown to history thus far, left unde-
scribed beyond the ideal image of the psychoanalyzed personality emancipated by rational analysis from commitments to the kairotic past.

In the view of humanist liberalism, social progress is thought capable of
being effected. Progress has come to mean, in this sense, the overcoming
of history, a break with tradition. This view of progress is simply naïve,
according to Freud. The paradox of "progress" as it has been made is that
it is always reactionary. No "progress" has been possible, Freud thought,
without the operation of tradition. To leave the present is to call up the
repressed past, to erupt underneath the present. The eruption of tradition
is the eternal return of the repressed. In this "resides its peculiar power,"
in this its power to "subjugate individuals and peoples." [27]
The role of the prophet illustrates most concretely the return pattern of
"progressive" action. The prophet, who is the archetypal progressive personality, is revolutionary at the same time and in the same sense that he
is reactionary. That is, a prophet is a revolutionary in so far as he is a
traditionalist. Against the main currents of his time, he "preached the
old Mosaic doctrine." [28] His role is to sound the call back, to shout "Remember." To be a prophet is to be the mouth of the tradition, thus re-
newing tradition among the masses, from the midst of whom Freud
thought the prophet arose to laicize them. The power to speak the tradition is the prophet's precisely because the prophet is a traditionalist. That
is, he is especially sensitive to the repressed material, and thus becomes a
temporal instrument of the tradition, "seized" by it.
However, as Freud writes, a whole people may be especially sensitive to
the repressed historical material that is their tradition. It is proof of the
power of tradition among the Jewish masses, of their "special psychical
fitness," according to Freud, that they produced so many prophets,[29] all
come to renew that tradition that is the Mosaic religion. (Freud does not
find it necessary to explain the undoubted traditionalism of the Asiatic
masses, despite the fact that Asiatic culture lacks prophetism as a social
role.) Indeed, Judaism "exercized influence on the Jewish people only

---

[27] *Ibid.*, p. 85.
[28] *Ibid.*, p. 82. For a study of the conservative political call of the prophet by an
English scholar see Canon W. J. Phythian Adams, *The Call of Israel: An Introduction
to the Study of Divine Election* (London: Oxford University Press, 1934). The finest
sociological interpretation of the personality type and role of the prophet is in Max
Weber, *Gesammelte Aufsätze zur Religionssoziologie*, Vol. III: *Das antike Judentum*
(Tübingen: Paul Siebeck, 1921), pp. 281-357; see esp. pp. 329 ff.: "Die positive eu-
phorische Wendung seiner Gefühlslage aber musste er in die Zukunft projizieren: als
Verheissung. Das bestimmte die Auslese der prophetischen Temperamente." Weber's
sociology of prophetism indicates how frequently the Jewish prophet arose not from
the "midst of the people" but was of upper-class origin, with a high cultural level.
[29] *Moses and Monotheism*, p. 176.

when it had become a tradition." [30] The kairotic "mental residue" which has become a "heritage" of that great time "needs only to be awakened." [31] The role of the prophet is always to shout: "Sleepers awake!"

Kairos, Freud came to think, is such an important experience that it must have "produced, or at least prepared . . . far-reaching changes in the life of man." "I cannot help thinking," he concludes, that "it [the primal crime] must have left some permanent trace in the human soul —something comparable to a tradition." [32]

The tradition is a constant. But it is a constant that makes history and politics meaningless. The primal event, Kairos, cuts the cord of nature. But, having cut that cord, the sequence of historical events that follow upon Kairos again lose their autonomy. Whatever qualitative change occurs is reduced by Freud to its real, true meaning: a shifting context of the ever-recurrent.

III

The consequence of Kairos, according to Freud, is an "archaic heritage" in the psychic structure of man that *"corresponds to the instincts in animals."* [33] So far as men have instincts, these are historical: Kairos is to the human what instinct is to the animal. Both reign supreme, one in man, the other in beast.

Freud's theory of Kairos as instinctual may be understood as an equivalent of his definition of instinct as rooted in history, as history-bound. An instinct may be defined as an inner (e.g., biologically rooted) urge to reinstate some earlier condition. An instinct is conservative, its function restoration. In the face of change, which is a regression (archaic model) or repression (sublimational model), instinct attempts to force a return to the *status quo ante* in the face of the self-clarificatory insight of the event or of the psychoanalytic process. Kairos, as the psychological equivalent of instinct, functions in a similar way; reason, and the ethic it demands, are threatened. It is almost as if, for Freud, instinct and Kairos alone have the historical function of reinstatement. The historicizing of instinct and the instinctualizing of history allow Freud to understand the life and historical process in Hellenic terms: as cyclical. As life has forgotten death before life, there must be a death instinct to remind life of its genesis and to reinstate into history the pattern of eternal recurrence.[34]

However, the identities of instinct and Kairos do not destroy the differences. The consequence of Kairos, "the archaic heritage of mankind,"

[30] *Ibid.*, p. 201. For a systematic Freudian treatment of ritual technology see Theodor Reik, *Ritual* (London: Hogarth Press, 1931) .

[31] *Moses and Monotheism*, p. 208.

[32] *Ibid.*, pp. 204-5.

[33] *Ibid.*, p. 161. (My italics.)

[34] On Freud's theory of instincts as a clue to his cosmology see Richard Sterba, "The Cosmological Aspect of Freud's Theory of Instincts," *American Imago*, VI, No. 3 (September, 1949), 157-61.

includes "not only dispositions, but also ideational contents, memory-traces of the experiences of former generations." [35] If Kairos differs from instinct so far as it has ideational content, though it is for that reason of difference no less permanent, the question of the generations still remains to be answered in detail. How is the ideational content of the past transmitted? That is, how is tradition possible?

Plainly, there is culture. Freud said as much and turned to what he considered to be more profound continuity. Here Freud's Lamarckianism became central. He had to deal with the individual and the group as analogous.[36]

Freud had decided that in the case of the individual the past survives in the unconscious. But it was not enough to know, as he knew with the social scientist, that the social structure of a civilization is a mirror of its history. That did not interest Freud so much. He was no Marxist, nor even a Revisionist. Nor is it simply that ideational contents are preserved esoterically, in priesthoods, or exoterically, in enlightened, publicly oriented intelligentsias, or in coteries, or in all manner of class, caste, and status formations. It is not enough to say that the higher status groups, because of their status, conserve the culture. Unknown to themselves, it is the masses who are the real conservatives. Therefore, Freud writes, there must be "something also in the ignorant mass of the people akin to this knowledge on the part of the few." [37] The difference between the masses and the classes, the many and the few, is that the latter are reflective, rationally aware. The many are unreflective, irrational, and unaware. It is as carriers of only feeling awareness, not of rational consciousness, that Freud disdains the masses (cf. G. H. Mead, *Mind, Self, and Society,* where the *I* is equated with the *Id* as unknowable).

Freud presumes, as we have said before, that there is almost complete "concordance between the individual and the mass." As the individual so the masses, too, "retain an impression of the past in unconscious memory traces." [38] These memory traces exist permanently in the Id. Therefore, "there probably exists in the mental life of the individual not only what he has experienced himself, but also what he brought with him at birth," ideational "fragments of phylogenetic origin, an archaic heritage." [39]

Thus, as individuals differ in respect of their inheritance of psychic as well as physiological dispositions, so must groups. For Freud, there seemed to have been differential stakes in the primal crime, Kairos. Our "archaic inheritance includes these differences." Some actions "can only be under-

[35] *Moses and Monotheism,* p. 159. See also *ibid.,* p. 196.
[36] A major problem raised by this point will be treated in a forthcoming paper, "The Analogy of Religion in Freud's Thought."
[37] *Moses and Monotheism,* p. 151.
[38] *Ibid.*
[39] *Ibid.,* p. 157.

stood phylogenetically, in relation to the experiences of earlier generations." [40] Freud thought the difference between inherited and acquired characteristics constructed by biological and social science had been exaggerated. There was no antithesis. "What was acquired by our ancestors is certainly an important part of what we inherit." [41]

Modern biological science may express amusement, even indignation. But Freud could not imagine social or biological science proceeding without taking this point into account. Accepting a type of Lamarckianism for purposes of his own metapsychology, now Freud could bridge the gap between "individual and mass psychology." He could treat "peoples" as he did "the individual" and religion as he did neurosis. Social movements become macrocosms of individual movements. The dynamic that moves the many is analogous to the dynamic that moves the one. Freud's Lamarckianism is "bold, but inevitable." Without it, neither social nor psychoanalytic psychology can advance together "one step further." [42]

Faced with the problem of how to understand religion as a mass neurosis, and history as a psychic burden transmitted through the generations, Freud thought he discovered in the Kairos concept the hypostasis that would permit him to understand both history and religion as exemplary modes of psychic Lamarckianism. Given the dominance of the Kairos concept, Freud's Lamarckianism itself became methodologically inevitable. Thus, his Lamarckianism, like other more explicit elements in his analytical structure, was itself a reflex of the idea of Kairos that informs the meaning of history and religion in Freud's thought.

IV

Now, Freud was prepared to illustrate his idea of history by the metapsychological history of the Judeo-Christian tradition. Kairos, for Freud, was, of course, the "primeval experience in the human family," [43] the killing of the primal father. Moses is the "tremendous father imago" of the Jews. [44] The forgotten kairotic event in Jewish history is the killing of Moses. Had not Freud picked up this "suggestion concerning Moses' end, the whole treatise [*Moses and Monotheism*] would have [had] to remain unwritten." [45] Fortunately for Freud's treatise, the Jews, "who

[40] *Ibid.*, pp. 157-59.
[41] *Collected Papers*, V, 343.
[42] *Moses and Monotheism*, pp. 160-61. Cf. the remarkable, curious Lamarckianism of Samuel Butler. To quote from his notebook of "entertaining literary" speculations: "The connection between memory and heredity is so close that there is no reason for regarding the two as generically different." And, further, "all forms of reproduction . . . are based directly or indirectly upon memory" (*The Notebooks of Samuel Butler*, ed. Henry Festing Jones [London: A. C. Fifield, 1912], pp. 57-59; see also Samuel Butler, *Life and Habit* [London: A. C. Fifield, 1910], esp. chap. xi: "Instinct as Inherited Memory").
[43] *Moses and Monotheism*, p. 204.
[44] *Ibid.*, p. 174. The Jewish masses are "his dear children."
[45] *Ibid.*, p. 95.

even according to the Bible were stubborn and unruly towards their
lawgiver and leader, rebelled at last, killed him," [46] suffered remorse, and
so became religious and Jews. The history and religion of Jewry is an
outwork of the Jewish Kairos, the teaching struggle and death[47] of the
man Moses.

The Jewish historical Kairos created the Jews, as Jews. It gave to them
their permanent national character. Freud does not doubt that the Jews
have a national character and that it is now what it was in antiquity. It
is expressed by their "unexampled power of resistance" [48] (cf. Nietzsche,
on how the Jews, "the little people of the great prophets," have been
able to maintain themselves). The national character of the Jews is a
consequence of the "special character" of their Kairos. The Jewish Kairos
is the advent of the Mosaic idea of chosenness.

Freud insisted that it was the Egyptian, Moses, who chose the Jews,
rather than the Jews who chose Moses. Moses stamped the Jewish people
with its special character: "It was one man, the man Moses, who created
the Jews." At Sinai the chosenness of the Jews was "through Moses anchored in religion; it became a part of their religious belief." [49] As God
had chosen his people, so Moses "had stooped to the Jews"; they were his
"chosen people." [50] To Moses, then, the Jews owe their character, their
"tenacity," their moralism, and the hostility that their tenaciousness and

[46] *Ibid.*, p. 98.
[47] The Teacher is, for Freud, the universal martyr image—characterized by his
charisma and wisdom, suffering the resentment of his students and public, who are his
children. There is no doubt that Freud, as a Great Teacher, identified himself with
Moses. Although he considers himself no art connoisseur, Michelangelo's "Moses," in
the Church of S. Pietro in Vincoli in Rome attracts him irresistibly. "It always delights
[me] to read an appreciatory sentence about this statue. . . . For no piece of statuary
has ever made a stronger impression on me than this. How often have I mounted the
steep steps of the unlovely Corso Cavour to the lonely place where the deserted church
stands, and have essayed to support the angry scorn of the hero's glance! Sometimes I
have crept cautiously out of the half-gloom of the interior as though I myself belonged
to the mob upon whom his eye is turned—the mob which can hold fast no conviction,
which has neither faith nor patience, and which rejoices when it has regained its illusory idols" (*Collected Papers*, IV, 249-60). Perhaps this is the most intimate self-image
the new Moses ever wrote, to the unconvinced, faithless, impatient, illusion-ridden,
idolatrous mob that is the public.
Freud at first concealed his authorship of *Moses*, and his "inner misgivings" during
the composition of the essays involved not simply the consequences of his outer situation, a refugee in London at eighty-two. The "inner difficulties" were not to be eased by
the freedom of England. Freud was still "uneasy." He was wrestling with the problem
with which he had closed grips a quarter of a century before, in *Totem and Taboo*:
religion. Now, with *Moses*, as he wrote, he felt like a bad dancer, balancing on one toe.
But he found the problem, to the end, "irresistible" (see *Moses and Monotheism*,
p. 164).
[48] *Moses and Monotheism*, pp. 166-67.
[49] *Ibid.*, pp. 168-69.
[50] *Ibid.*, p. 73.

moralism had met, if not wholly created. Moses first and thereafter "definitely fixed . . . the Jewish type." [51]

Freud had first to emphasize the historicity of the Kairos and its dynamic of repression. The Mosaic religion "exercised influence on the Jewish people *only* when it had become a tradition." [52] The point is the necessity of the event, and the establishment of a historical tradition—the creation of the Jews by the giving of the Law and the occasion of the primal murder—as a psychic constant in the Jewish generations. Kairos created the Jews. It gave them their history. The inner meaning of kairotic history remains true and operative to this day, according to Freud. It is in this sense that the Jews may be said to have kept a tradition, and tradition may be said to have kept the Jews. Freud thinks it did not matter that the Jews once renounced their religion, the teaching of Moses. Renunciation confirmed the religion, "the tradition remained." [53]

Freud understood the historicity of the idea, however, in a very specific way. Meaning is polarized as inner and outer. All meaning is historical. But inner meaning is the psychological pole; outer meaning is contextual, eventual. Outer meaning "reproduces" inner in an infinite variety of events. The eventual reproduces the psychological. The outer process, deprived of its autonomy, documents the inner.

If for the great historians of the nineteenth century, it is ideas that work themselves out as events, for Freud it is psychic states that work themselves out as events. A comparison of the systems of social causation of Freud, Marx, and Weber may be useful at this point. If we may list the levels of causation as (1) *idea,* (2) *psychic state,* (3) *event,* Freud may be said to locate the genesis of both ideas and events in psychic states. A famous example of this location might be taken from the Freudian literature on culture history and religion, from one of the most brilliant and perhaps the most relevant of Freud's epigoni, Erich Fromm. For Fromm, prior to Protestantism as both idea and event is Anxiety. The former is finally reducible to a symptom of the latter, as for Freud prior to Christianity as both idea and event was the psychic state of guilt.

It would be unfair to say that Marx locates the genesis of both ideas and psychic states in concrete events. The early Marx, at least, reconciled all three levels of historical causation in the dialectical unity of consciousness and existence. Nevertheless, Weber alone clearly rejects an ontological emphasis. He is a causal pluralist, asserting the autonomy of the three levels. Ideas may be said to be autonomous, for Weber, as they may originate as the spontaneous insight of a charismatic man. In turn, once having located the autonomy of ideas in the existence of a

[51] *Ibid.,* p. 69.
[52] *Ibid.,* p. 201. (My italics.)
[53] *Ibid.,* p. 81.

genius, Weber notes that ideas may become premium systems for the selection of useful psychic states, out of the multiple psychic states available in a culture. The event, in turn, has a logic of its own, turning ideas and psychic states to unforeseen uses. Thus Weber arrives at his most delicate evasion, in a lifetime of delicate evasions, in the problem of social causation: the irony of history, the surprising thrust of the unintended consequence, so much ignored and despised by other sociologists but nevertheless crucial to Weber.

For Freud, there is nothing that is eventual except as it is the outer meaning of the psychological. Outer meanings are to be subsumed under inner. This is to say, history operates, in the first instant, in terms of its inner, psychological articulation. It is only in this sense that Freud could write of "historical truth." The eventuality of the suffering Redeemer, for example, is, as event, quite secondary to the inner meaning of the redemptory role. Psychologically, the Redeemer is always the same tragic hero, "the chief rebel and leader" against the Primal Father. "If there was no such leader [historically], then [e.g.] Christ was the heir of an unfulfilled wish-phantasy." If, on the other hand, the hero was an event, then [e.g.] Christ was one of a number to take the role, the "successor" to it, the "reincarnation" of it.[54] Thus, social action is ambiguous. It expresses itself as an action myth. To understand an action, one must understand its "inner source," the "secret motives"[55] that are the psychological meaning informing it.

There are other evidences of the elaboration of historical meaningfulness into primary inner-psychological, and secondary outer-eventual, a distortion and disguise of the inner. Whole structures of institutions are projections of psychic states. Freud called institutions such as the "institution of remembrance festivals," and totem feasts, collective "screen-memories."[56]

The history of religions gives Freud further evidence of the dynamic interplay of inner and outer meaning. Christianity, for Freud, is a "Son religion." Judaism is a "Father religion." Christianity, in terms of its inner meaning, is the institutionally organized remembrance and recurrence of the deposing of the father by the son. In Freud's construct, Judaism stands for the true Father, against the spurious assumption by the Christians of his Son. The Christian tradition is the recurrent filial revolt, "just as in those dark times every son had longed to do."[57] But the fate of Christianity is that it cannot escape Judaism, any more than the son can escape the father.

[54] *Ibid.*, p. 140. Here is Freud's basic insight into the structure of myth. A myth may be defined as an action narrative, containing, in interrelation, both the elements of meaning, the inner-psychological and the outer-historical. *Moses and Monotheism* is in this sense a study in the structure and meaning of myth.

[55] *Ibid.*, p. 18.

[56] *Ibid.*, p. 133.

[57] *Ibid.*, p. 141.

In the inner beginning, then, was the primal crime, reproducing itself historically in the persons of Moses and Jesus. Why not then a Moses or Jesus every generation if Christ is the "resurrected Moses and the returned primeval father"? [58] We must turn, therefore, to the doctrine of the psychic trinity—Father, Son, and People—according to Freud.

Both Moses and Christ are vessels of ambivalence in the mythos of history. Thus Christ is constructed, in one sense, as the Incarnate God, Father of the rebellious sons (the People—who must kill him), thus recapitulating the primal crime. In another sense, equally true, Christ is the Son of Man, facing and suffering the Father God. Here the Father of the people becomes as well the Son, dying by the wish of the Father. This is the double role of all tragic heroes, Oedipus and Hamlet as well as Moses and Christ: to die the representative deaths of both sons and fathers. This is, for Freud, the most profound meaning of the scapegoat mechanism, and thus, for example, of anti-Semitism.

The question of a continuous reproduction of the Kairos remains. Freud, indeed, believed the Mosaic Kairos to have a special inner meaning for Western culture. It reproduced the model crime (the killing of the primal father), for the historical consciousness of Western culture. It is safe to conclude, then, that there can be but one Kairos. Each subsequent Kairos is epigonal (e.g., Moses, Christ), and thus more and more spurious, inauthentic, at least unrevealing of any new psychic states. (Here the idea of epigonal Kairoi may be assimilated to the Marxist understanding of history as repetition, first as tragedy, then as farce. See the great opening passages of *The Eighteenth Brumaire*.)

On the other hand, each Kairos is new and unique in its contextual mask. Calvary is not Sinai, even if the inner meaning is the same and Christ is simply a resurrected Moses. It is more important to emphasize, however, that every Kairos is a recurrence, the return of the repressed, the latest return of the ever-same. Returning "from the forgotten past," the primal crime "produces an incomparably strong influence on the mass of mankind, and puts forward an irresistible claim to be believed." [59] Freud is not interested in the truth of the claim. Rather, the truth of the claim is the power of the claim itself.

Religion itself, for Freud, is something quite different from Kairos. It is a neurotic elaboration of the power of Kairos, much like the impact of a charismatic leader among the masses. Within its liturgy and dogma, religion, like mass politics, seeks to routinize Kairos by reproducing it ritualistically. Freud seemed to believe that religions and significant political movement cannot originate except in Kairos, nor live except off its kairotic capital in terms of ritualist manipulation of interest in the Kairos. (Thus, Henry Wallace attempted to manipulate what he thought to be a Rooseveltian Kairos.) The capital of the Kairos must serve the invest-

[58] *Ibid.*, p. 145.
[59] *Ibid.*, p. 136.

ment of the epigone in it. If, in Marxian terms, one wishes to translate Freudianism into a bourgeois thought form, capital may be said to be fetishized in a psychological form. Kairos is funded capital, in bourgeois categories, or, in feudal terms, an entailed estate. It is in this sense that Weber thought of the grace manufactured by the Catholic saints as the church's investment for the future. The problem of salvation may well be discussed in terms of the economics of grace.

Kairos, coming up out of the past, breaks with revolutionary power against the present. Freud recognized the past as true, as Marx recognized it as only ideologically true, and only true for the revolutions before the proletarian. Freud recognized the conservative character of all revolutions, as Marx recognized their progressive character. In Freud's "shortest formula," the dialectically conservative character of revolutionary movements, like the traditionalism of the prophets, illustrates again "the well-known *duality* of . . . history." [60] Freud is far from astonished that in revolutions, particularly the most recent, for him the Russian and the Nazi, "progress has concluded an alliance with barbarism." It is only the resurgence of the past that pre-empts the present for the spurious future.[61] The starting points of progress are always at the return, in shifting contexts, of the repressed.

Then, the Christian revolution, for example, is reactionary, if the term is understood correctly, at the same time and for the same reason that it is progressive. Christianity advanced beyond Judaism precisely so far as Christ was the surrogate, not alone of the resurrected Moses, but also of the returned Father. Paul, when he developed the doctrine of original sin as the "murder of the Father who later was deified," [62] and the doctrine of guilt and salvation in the Son who was also scapegoat,

[60] *Ibid.*, p. 84. Freud's image of history as almost a Manichaean ambivalence is clearest in this passage: there are always "*two peoples* who fuse together to form one nation, *two kingdoms* into which this nation divides, two names for the Deity in the source of the Bible." And to this he must add two new dualities, discovered by himself: "the founding of *two* new religions, the first one ousted by the second and yet reappearing victorious, *two* founders of religions, who are both called by the same name Moses and whose personalities we have to separate from each other. And all these dualities are necessary consequences of the first": the presence or absence of Kairos. "One section of the [Jewish] people passed through what may properly be termed a traumatic experience which the other was spared." (Freud's italics.)

[61] *Ibid.*, p. 89. Here Freud provides the sociology of revolution with its most penetrating insight: that revolution is precisely that event which allows the most archaic to bisect the most recent accumulations in the psychic state of man. Freud thought the Bolshevik and Fascist revolutions examples of this dialectical unity between progress and retrogression, though perhaps he was too naïvely impressed with notions that Mussolini had "educated," however regressively, the Italians to run their trains on time and that the Bolsheviks had truly deprived their subjects of "the anodyne religion" and had been "wise enough to grant them a reasonable measure of sexual freedom" (see *Ibid.*, p. 90), however primitively cruel had been the coercion to freedom.

[62] *Ibid.*, p. 139.

advanced Christianity beyond Judaism to the extent that he executed a greater regression. Here Freud has made the role of the regressor-prophet Paul the most crucial to the dynamization of Christianity into a socially significant tradition. The Christian doctrine of salvation is fundamentally Paul's own ideological screen of regression. To the extent that Freud believed there was in Judaism no idea of salvation by the admission of guilt, to that extent Freud seemed to show more sympathy for that neurosis than for its inherently hostile child. [63] Like the dominant schools of modernist sociologists of religion, including Weber and Klausner, Freud identified Christ as a Jewish revival. The break, he believed, is located in Paul, as the figure who pushed the regression beyond the revival.

It is a further illustration of his location of inner meaning in history that Freud concludes that the Christian tradition must be anti-Semitic. Freud develops a specific analysis, in *Moses and Monotheism,* of the necessary anti-Semitism of the Christian tradition. It will be summarized here as further illustration of the constructs described above.

The irresistible claim of the Christian Kairos to be believed is to be understood rightly as the claim of the original killing of the primal father, of which all Kairoi are outworks. Anti-Semitism is the process of resentment by those personalities influenced by the Christian Kairos. It is a resentment against those who will not admit their guilt and thus seem somehow outside of and dangerous to a community held together in some significant measure by guilt. The Jews, Freud observed, refuse to admit their guilt. "The poor Jewish people, who with its usual stiff-necked obduracy continued to deny the murder of their 'father' [i.e., the inner meaning being equivalent to the primal father, the outer meaning to Christ], has dearly expiated this in the course of centuries. Over and over again they heard the reproach: You killed our God." Freud con-

---

[63] *Ibid.*, pp. 141-42. Freud's debt to the modernists is plain. What early theological training he had in the Jewish community was not very useful. "My youth was spent in a period when our free-minded teachers of religion placed no value on their pupils' acquisition of knowledge in the Hebrew languages and literature" (quoted by A. A. Brill, *Freud's Contribution to Psychiatry* [New York: W. W. Norton & Co., 1944], pp. 195-96). Freud considered himself as "little an adherent of the Jewish religion as of any other." Like Weber, he considered himself religiously unmusical. "I consider them all most important as objects of scientific interest, but I do not share the emotional feeling that goes with them." Freud's religious unmusicality, however, did not contradict his community with Jewry. A famous passage in the literature of consolation of secular Jewry reads: "I have always had a strong feeling of kinship with my race and have always nurtured the same in my children" (quoted from a letter to the editor of the *Jüdische Presszentrale* [Zurich], February 26, 1925). Nevertheless, his "scientific" passion for religion was great. As early as 1911, in a letter quoted by Brill (*op. cit.*, p. 192), Freud declared he "was extraordinarily absorbed in the study of the psychology of religion." The absorption lasted a lifetime. His last book was *Moses and Monotheism.* In another school of analysis, older than Freud's, Freud's concentration on the meaning of Fatherhood and the Father-God-Son triad would have been interpreted as a well-known expression of a religious type, the "God-intoxicated man," the famous phrase used by Novalis to describe the excommunicate Jew Spinoza.

cludes: "And this reproach is true, if rightly interpreted. It says in reference to the history of religion: 'You won't *admit* that you murdered God'
(i.e., the archetype of God, the primaeval Father and his reincarnations)."[64]

Thus, he concluded, Christianity, in its inner meaning, is anti-Semitic.
A major cause of anti-Semitism is not, as some would have it, the resistance of Christians to Christianity. Rather it is the acceptance of the inner
meaning of Christianity, of its essence, that works anti-Semitism.

However, Freud's construction of psychoanalytic truth allows him to
assert that the reverse is equally true. He conceives of the rebellion against
both Father and Son, Judaism and Christianity, to be a dynamic of anti-
Semitism. The pagan character, never thoroughly restructured by a religion that was missionized politically, has always sought to unburden itself
of Christianity by the displacement of anti-Semitism. Thus one can understand in Freudian terms that the spearhead of anti-Semitism in Germany
developed as a cultus of Teutonic paganism. If the Christians did not
powerfully resist anti-Semitism, the most active anti-Semites were those
seeking a regression to pagan culture, or at least a compromise of Christianity as a Son religion by rechristening Christ a Nordic.

There are important weaknesses in the Freudian reconstruction of the
genesis of political society. These will be discussed in another study. Here
the chief critical point to be made is at the problem of the concept of
Kairos as meaning the primal-father murder. Freud has picked and chosen
without regard to all the data. The father-murder myth is but one theme
in myth literature. In the myth material available—and myth was for
Freud the link between social and life history, social and individual psychology—the fratricide image stands beside the parricide image. It is difficult to choose the one to the exclusion of the other. If the images of
the parricide theme—Oedipus and the other regicide characters of the
drama—stride so movingly across the universal stage, the images of the
fratricide theme—the sons of Oedipus, Joseph and his brothers, Cain
and Abel, Arthur and his Knights, the Trojan peers, the *Niebelungen*—
indeed, all the brothers and sisters who have been so fatal to one another,
stride across the same stage, equally moving in the myth mind.

A third myth rises to complicate the Freudian selection: the Abraham
myth (cf. Kierkegaard, *Fear and Trembling*). In it, it is the father who
kills the son, not the son who kills the father. And, as we have noted
before, the propitiatory sacrifice of the Son of God (Moses, Christ), on
behalf of his sinful people, must be viewed as much a Son-killing as a
Father-killing. That the killing of the Son of Man by his own brothers,
the masses, may be viewed as commanded by a more primary Father, God,

---

[64] *Moses and Monotheism*, p. 145.

appears only as a sublimated solution of the scapegoat mechanism as a fratricide.

The great murder myth of the Old Testament is the killing of the primal brother by the primal brother. The first moral question of Western politics, as expressed in the story of Cain and Abel, seems to have been not, as Freud insists, "Am I my father's son?" Rather, the primal question was: "Am I my brother's keeper?"

In terms of the primal-murder myth, it is the war of brothers, not the revolt against the tyranny of fathers, that is the psychological origin-condition of man's social existence.[65] *Hamlet* can perhaps be read, psychoanalytically, in a way neither Freud nor Ernest Jones considered. After all, it is the killing of the brother that is the demiurge of the plot. Claudius himself instructs Hamlet, in their first scene, that nature's most "common theme is death of fathers . . . from the first corpse till he that died today." But the first corpse was a brother. The primal curse is the usurpation of the throne by fratricide. Hamlet sees the horror of brother against brother. The ghost—the dead father who is, more important, the brother —bids Hamlet: "Remember me." What the ghost reveals is the fratricide, and fratricide is what is rotten in the state of Denmark. Freud seems to have been deaf to the meaning of fratricide, although it fairly shouted at him in his brilliant analysis of *Lear* and of the ninth of Grimm's Fairy Tales, *The Twelve Brothers*. Instead he writes as he rarely wrote, belaboring the obvious: the symbolism of death as dumbness in myth literature.

But the primal war of brothers is accounted for in Freud's basic myth of the origin of the polity. He was led to assert, finally, a "sort of . . . social contract" theory.[66] The contract, he thought, came out of a Malthusian calculation of the value of scarce resources and the necessity of restraint, in this case the value of the female commodity in a scarcity situation. But even the hard light of the economic-sex calculus cannot spoil the grandeur of Freud's myth of the origins of society. In the social contract of brothers there came into being the first true society—that based on the renunciation of instinctual gratification. The establishment of man came through an act of renunciation.

The act of renunciation is at once the establishment of man in society and of the Father as God. The war of the generations ends in the deification of the dead Father, and in the socializing guilt of the brothers. Men, as a band of brothers, stand at the genesis of society when they renounce

---

[65] However, for a presumption of the equivalence of the father and the brother murder myth and totem supporting the Freudian presumption cf. Freud's mentor in these matters, Sir J. G. Frazer, *Creation and Evolution in Primitive Cosmogonies* (London: Macmillan, 1935), pp. 17-18. According to Frazer, in primitive cosmogonies the subject of the myth and the totem animal may be, evidently indifferently, either father or brother.

[66] *Moses and Monotheism*, p. 132.

their aspirations to become, each above all, the supreme Father. Renounc-
ing the promise of being the godlike Father on earth, they worship the
Father they have murdered (e.g., the primal father, then, Moses, Christ,
et al.) as God in heaven. God, according to Freud, is the positive projection of the act of renunciation. Then man is by nature, at his origins, a
killer, and religion is the history of his guilt. Freud aimed to cure man of
his guilt and thus to abolish the history of it.

Totem and
Taboo in Retrospect

A. L. Kroeber

Nearly twenty years ago I wrote an analysis of *Totem and Taboo* —that brain child of Freud which was to be the precursor of a long series of psychoanalytic books and articles explaining this or that aspect of culture, or the whole of it.[1] It seems an appropriate time to return to the subject.

I see no reason to waver over my critical analysis of Freud's book. There is no indication that the consensus of anthropologists during these twenty years has moved even an inch nearer acceptance of Freud's central thesis. But I found myself somewhat conscience-stricken when, perhaps a decade later, I listened to a student in Sapir's seminar in Chicago making his report on *Totem and Taboo*, who, like myself, first spread out its gossamer texture and then laboriously tore it to shreds. It is a procedure too suggestive of breaking a butterfly on the wheel. An iridescent fantasy deserves a more delicate touch even in the act of demonstration of its unreality.

Freud himself has said of my review that it characterized his book as a *Just So* story. It is a felicitous phrase, coming from himself. Many a tale by Kipling or Andersen contains a profound psychological truth. One

"Totem and Taboo in Retrospect." Reprinted from *The American Journal of Sociology*, XLV, No. 3 (November 1939), 446-451, by permission of The University of Chicago Press.

[1] "Totem and Taboo: An Ethnologic Psychoanalysis," *Amer. Anthropologist*, XXII (1920), 48-55.

does not need, therefore, to cite and try it in the stern court of evidential confrontation.

However, the fault is not wholly mine. Freud does speak of the "great event with which culture began." And therewith he enters history. Events are historical and beginnings are historical, and human culture is appreciable historically. It is difficult to say how far he realized his vacillation between historical truth and abstract truth expressed through intuitive imagination. A historical finding calls for some specification of place and time and order; instead of which, he offers a finding of unique cardinality, such as history feels it cannot deal with.

Freud is reported subsequently to have said that his "event" is to be construed as "typical." Herewith we begin to approach a basis of possible agreement. A typical event, historically speaking, is a recurrent one. This can hardly be admitted for the father-slaying, eating, and guilt sense. At any rate, there is no profit in discussing the recurrence of an event which we do not even know to have occurred once. But there is no need sticking fast on the word "event" because Freud used it. His argument is evidently ambiguous as between historical thinking and psychological thinking. If we omit the fatal concept of event, of an act, as it happens in history, we have left over the concept of the psychologically potential. Psychological insight may legitimately hope to attain to the realization and definition of such a potentiality; and to this, Freud should have confined himself. We may, accordingly, properly disregard any seeming claim, or half-claim, to historic authenticity of the suggested actual happening, as being beside the real point, and consider whether Freud's theory contains any possibility of being a generic, timeless explanation of the psychology that underlies certain recurrent historical phenomena or institutions like totemism and taboo.

Here we obviously are on better ground. It becomes better yet if we discard certain gratuitous and really irrelevant assumptions, such as that the self-imposed taboo following the father-slaying is the original of all taboos, these deriving from it as secondary displacements or distortions. Stripped down in this way, Freud's thesis would reduce to the proposition that certain psychic processes tend always to be operative and to find expression in widespread human institutions. Among these processes would be the incest drive and incest repression, filial ambivalence, and the like; in short, if one likes, the kernel of the Oedipus situation. After all, if ten modern anthropologists were asked to designate one universal human institution, nine would be likely to name the incest prohibition; some have expressly named it as the only universal one. Anything so constant as this, at least as regards its nucleus, in the notoriously fluctuating universe of culture, can hardly be the result of a "mere" historical accident devoid of psychological significance. If there is accordingly an underlying factor which keeps reproducing the phenomenon in an unstable world, this factor must be something in the human constitution—in other words, a psychic factor. Therewith the door is open, not for an acceptance *in toto* of Freud's explanation, but at any rate for its serious consideration as a scientific hypothesis. Moreover, it is an explanation certainly marked by deeper insight and supportable by more parallel evidence from personal psychology than the older views, such as that familiarity breeds sexual indifference, or recourse to a supposed "instinct" which is merely a verbal restatement of the observed behavior.

Totemism, which is a much rarer phenomenon than incest taboo, might then well be the joint product of the incest-drive-and-repression process and some other less compelling factor. Nonsexual taboo, on the other hand, which rears itself in so many protean forms over the whole field of culture, might be due to a set of still different but analogous psychic factors. Anthropologists and sociologists have certainly long been groping for something underlying which would help them explain both the repetitions and the variations in culture, provided the explanation were evidential, extensible by further analysis, and neither too simplistic nor too one-sided. Put in some such form as this, Freud's hypothesis might long before this have proved fertile in the realm of cultural understanding instead of being mainly rejected or ignored as a brilliant fantasy.

What has stood in the way of such a fruitful restatement or transposition? There seem to be at least three factors: one due to Freud himself, another jointly to himself and his followers, the third mainly to the Freudians.

The first of these is Freud's already mentioned ambiguity, which leads him to state a timeless psychological explanation as if it were also a historical one. This tendency is evident elsewhere in his thinking. It appears to be the counterpart of an extraordinarily explorative imagination, constantly impelled to penetrate into new intellectual terrain. One consequence is a curious analogy to what he himself has discovered in regard to the manifest and the latent in dreams. The manifest is there, but it is ambiguous; a deeper meaning lies below; from the point of view of this latent lower content, the manifest is accidental and inconsequential. Much like this, it seems to me, is the historical dress which Freud gives his psychological insight. He does not repudiate it; he does not stand by it as integral. It is really irrelevant; but his insight having manifested itself in the dress, he cannot divest himself of this "manifest" form. His view is overdetermined like a dream.

A second factor is the curious indifference which Freud has always shown as to whether his conclusions do or do not integrate with the totality of science. This led him at one time to accept the inheritance of acquired traits as if it did not clash with standard scientific attitude. Here again we have the complete explorer who forgets in his quest, or represses, knowledge of what he started from or left behind. In Freud himself one is inclined not to quarrel too hard with this tendency; without it, he might have opened fewer and shorter vistas. Of his disciples, however, who have so largely merely followed, more liaison might be expected. I recall Rank, while still a Freudian, after expounding his views to a critically sympathetic audience, being pressed to reconcile certain of them to the findings of science at large and, after an hour, conceding that psychoanalysts held that there might be more than one truth, each on its own level and independent of the other. And he made the admission without appearing to realize its import.

A third element in the situation is the all-or-none attitude of most avowed psychoanalysts. They insist on operating within a closed system. At any rate, if not wholly closed, it grows only from within; it is not open to influence from without. A classical example is Ernest Jones's resistance to Malinowski's finding that among the matrilineal Melanesians the affects directed toward the father in our civilization are largely displaced upon the mother's brother, the relation of father and children being rather one of simple and relatively univalent affection. Therewith Malinowski had really vindicated the mechanism of the Oedipus relation. He showed that the mechanism remained operative even in a changed family situation; a minor modification of it, in its direction, conforming to the change in given conditions. Jones, however, could not see this, and resisted tooth and nail. Because Freud in the culture of Vienna had determined that ambivalence was directed toward the father, ambivalence had to remain directed to him universally, even where primary authority resided in an uncle.

The same tendency appears in Roheim, whose "Psycho-analysis of Primitive Culture Types" [2] contains a mass of psychological observations most valuable to cultural anthropologists, but so organized as to be unusable by them. None have used it, so far as I know. This is not due to lack of interest on the part of anthropologists in psychological behavior within cultures, for in recent years a whole series of them have begun avowedly to deal with such behavior. Nor is it due to any deficiency of quality in Roheim's data: these are rich, vivid, novel, and valuable. But the data are so presented as to possess organization only from the point of view of orthodox psychoanalytic theory. With reference to the culture in which they occur, or to the consecutive life histories of personalities, they are inchoate. The closing sentence of the monograph—following immediately on some illuminative material—is typical: "We see then, that the sexual practices of a people are indeed prototypical and that from their posture in coitus their whole psychic attitude may be inferred." Can a conclusion be imagined which would appear more arbitrarily dogmatic than this to any psychologist, psychiatrist, anthropologist, or sociologist?

The fundamental concepts which Freud formulated—repression, regression and infantile persistences, dream symbolism and overdetermination, guilt sense, the affects toward members of the family—have gradu-

[2] *Internat. Jour. Psycho-analysis*, XIII (1932), 1-221 (Roheim Australasian Research number).

ally seeped into general science and become an integral and important part of it. If one assumes that our science forms some kind of larger unit because its basic orientation and method are uniform, these concepts constitute the permanent contribution of Freud and psychoanalysis to general science; and the contribution is large. Beyond, there is a further set of concepts which in the main have not found their way into science: the censor, the superego, the castration complex, the explanation of specific cultural phenomena. To these concepts the several relevant branches of science—sociology, anthropology, psychology, and medicine alike—remain impervious about as consistently as when the concepts were first developed. It may therefore be inferred that science is likely to remain negative to them. To the psychoanalysts, on the contrary, the two classes of concepts remain on the same level, of much the same value, and inseparably interwoven into one system. In this quality of nondifferentiation between what the scientific world accepts as reality and rejects as fantasy, between what is essential and what is incidental, the orthodox psychoanalytic movement reveals itself as partaking of the nature of a religion—a system of mysticism; even, it might be said, it shows certain of the qualities of a delusional system. It has appropriated to itself such of the data of science—the cumulative representations of reality—as were digestible to it and has ignored the larger remainder. It has sought little integration with the totality of science, and only on its own terms. By contrast, science, while also of course a system, has shown itself a relatively open one: it has accepted and already largely absorbed a considerable part of the concepts of psychoanalysis. It is indicative of the largeness of Freud's mind that, although the sole founder of the movement and the originator of most of its ideas, his very ambiguities in the more doubtful areas carry a stamp of tolerance. He may persist in certain interpretations; he does not insist on them; they remain more or less fruitful suggestions. Of this class is his theory of the primary determination of culture. As a construct, neither science nor history can use it; but it would seem that they can both accept and utilize some of the process concepts that are involved in the construct.

I trust that this reformulation may be construed not only as an *amende honorable* but as a tribute to one of the great minds of our day.

Book Review of
Moses and Monotheism
Salo W. Baron

If a thinker of Sigmund Freud's stature takes a stand on a problem of vital interest to him, the world is bound to listen. If the work so produced is also a remarkable human and historical document, if unwittingly it is a reflection of the profound changes in the entire mental atmosphere of Central Europe during the last decade, the reader's intellectual curiosity will receive stimuli in fields transcending the vast and ramified subject treated therein. Its first two—smaller—sections, which merely adumbrated the major theme, were published in 1937 in the German journal *Imago*. But the main Part III, which in the author's words "reduces religion to the status of a neurosis of mankind and explains its grandiose powers in the same way as we should a neurotic obsession in our individual patients" (p. 85), appeared too full of dynamite for an author living under the Catholic regime of Dollfuss and Schuschnigg. Its final composition had to await the conquest of Austria by Hitler, the subsequent persecution of Freud on ideological as well as racial grounds, and his escape to England, which, although far more Christian than either Austria or Germany, bears with much greater composure a psychoanalytical critique of the Christian dogma. To be sure, this unusual genesis of the work has resulted in considerable technical short-

"Book Review of Moses and Monotheism [New York: Alfred A. Knopf, Inc., 1939. Pp. vi-218] by Sigmund Freud." Reprinted from *The American Journal of Sociology*, XLV, No. 3 (November 1939), by permission of the University of Chicago Press.

comings and endless repetitions. Freud himself, hitherto a master of literary presentation which but a few years ago had rightly earned for him the major Goethe prize in contemporary German literature, deeply deplores these shortcomings, which make his discussion "as ineffectual as it is inartistic" (p. 162). Inartistic, yes—but far from ineffectual. If anything, the constant hammering of a few *leitmotifs* helps to impress upon the reader's mind those views of the author which at first appear to him farfetched or even repugnant, and to evoke the impression of certainty and logical cogency where, by the very nature of the subject, everything is so profoundly uncertain and hypothetical.

The subject of Moses and the origins of monotheism lends itself, like few others in the history of religion, to extensive, analytical treatment. The availability of a fairly large body of biographic and ethnological material, principally in the Bible, is enhanced by the great chronological gap between the events narrated therein and their record in its present form which makes it open to an endless variety of interpretation. A great deal of further folkloristic material, some of it doubtless also containing a kernel of historical truth, has been preserved in the more articulate, but still younger rabbinic and patristic, literatures, of which Freud—perhaps to his credit—has made but little use. The well-known lack of agreement among modern biblical scholars and anthropologists on some of the most fundamental issues likewise equips the analytical investigator with a mass of alternative suggestions from which he may choose those which best fit into the pattern of his theory. "The more shadowy tradition has become," says Freud, "the more meet is it for the poet's use" (p. 112). Nevertheless, perhaps as a result of being too much earth-bound and source-bound, the present reviewer feels that he cannot quite follow the author into this rarefied atmosphere of pure speculation.

In this new work Freud elaborates and illustrates, by the specific example of Moses, his main thesis on the development of religion which he had first advanced in 1912 in his striking volume on *Totem and Taboo*. In its bare essentials the theory assumes a parallelism between the evolution of mankind from its prehistoric stages to contemporary civilization and the individual growth of man from childhood to adult life. Just as in individual life the first five years after birth leave permanent impressions which, carried through a period of sexual latency to the age of pubescence, definitely condition adult psychic life and lay the ground for all human neuroses, so is mankind at large carrying in its subconscious mind the heritage of its all-important formative stage. Although forgotten during the long subsequent period of latency, the impressions of this prehistoric stage time and again come to the fore in the consciousness of civilized man. Following suggestions made by Darwin and Atkinson, Freud has long advocated the hypothesis that mankind had begun its career as a father horde, in which one strong male was the master and father of the whole horde. Unlimited in his power, he appropriated all females and banished all males outside the horde. At last a group of such exiled brothers "clubbed together, overcame the father, and—according to the custom of those times—all partook of his body" (p. 128). Of course, each of these brothers deeply desired to inherit the mantle which had thus fallen from the revered father's shoulders, but unable to overcome the resistance of the others and realizing that internecine fights were as dangerous as they were futile, compromised upon a new form of a social organization based upon the recognition of mutual obligations. These were the beginnings of morality and law. Instead of each appropriating the women of the horde to himself, the brothers renounced them altogether and established exogamy as their guiding principle. They also found a substitute for the father in a totem, usually an animal, revered as the father of the tribe which, in memory of what had happened to the primeval father, no one was allowed to kill, but which on a stated occasion was consumed in a sacrificial repast. The new leaders of the brother-horde thus

> undid their deed by declaring that the killing of the father substitute, the totem, was not allowed, and renounced the fruit of their deed by denying themselves the liberated women. Thus they created two fundamental taboos of totemism out of the *sense of guilt of the son,* and for this very reason these had to correspond with the two repressed wishes of the Oedipus complex. Whoever disobeyed became guilty of the two only crimes which troubled primitive society.[1]

Animal worship was subsequently replaced by human deities, just as socially the matriarchate gave way to a re-established patriarchal organization. But the dim memories of that early eventful revolution, after a period of latency, came back to haunt man, who by that time had attained a high degree of material and intellectual civilization.

For reasons which cannot fully be explained, in the fourteenth century B.C., under the reign of the Egyptian king, Ikhnaton, these memories blossomed out into the first, and perhaps purest, form of a monotheistic creed. The details of Ikhnaton's memorable reform, its antecedents in the doctrines of the priests of the Sun Temple at On, the influences emanating from Syria, perhaps through the king's Syrian wives, and the impact of Egyptian imperialism can no longer be ascertained, because the successful opposition after 1350 B.C. destroyed nearly all pertinent records. In any case, however, it apparently would have remained but an interesting historical episode were it not for the work of one of Ikhnaton's Egyptian disciples, named Moses. Freud, after repeating many older arguments in favor of Moses' Egyptian origin, adds an interesting psychoanalytic explanation of the Moses legend. As Otto Rank had shown some thirty years ago, this legend closely corresponds to a very widespread type of hero

[1] *The Basic Writings of Sigmund Freud,* trans. A. A. Brill (New York, 1938), p. 917.

myth, except in one essential point, viz., that here the hero actually came from the noble rather than from the humble family in the story. Some time after 1350 B.C. this Egyptian prince, perhaps also governor of the province of Goshen, where a large number of Israelites had been living under Egyptian domination, tried to salvage the suppressed teachings of Ikhnaton by creating a new following among these Semitic settlers, taking them out of Egypt and leading them to Palestine. In southern Palestine the new arrivals, as yet unprepared for the high spirituality of the new religion, murdered their leader—Freud takes here a clue from a fantastic "discovery" of Ernst Sellin—and joined a number of closely related tribes which had settled there before. Together the two groups soon came under the sway of another leader whom we may conveniently designate as the Midianite Moses. This dualism of two religions and two founders, like the other dualities of Jewish history—two peoples forming one nation, its breaking up into two kingdoms, and the two names of the Deity—is the necessary consequence of the fact that "one section of the people passed through what may properly be termed a traumatic experience which the other was spared" (p. 79). After the Egyptian Moses' death this, so to say, childhood experience of the Jewish people entered once more a period of relative latency, during which only a small minority of Levites, descendants of the original small circle of native Egyptians around Moses, carried on the tradition of the lawgiver. Several centuries later, under the stimulus of the Israelitic prophets, the original Mosaic religion was reestablished as the national religion of Israel. This monotheistic creed thus became the revived memory of the primeval father. "The great deed or misdeed of primeval times, the murder of the father, was brought home to the Jews, for fate decreed that they should repeat it on the person of Moses, an eminent father substitute." With their new belief in God, the Father, went the expectation of the return of the lawgiver, as the Messiah —Freud could have used here another hypothesis of Sellin, since abandoned, that the expected Messiah of early Israelitic prophecy was Moses redivivus, a belief held long after by Samaritan schismatics—the conviction.of Israel's chosenness, and most of the teachings of ancient Judaism, including imageless worship, ritualism, growth of spirituality, and circumcision. The latter custom, clearly of Egyptian origin, was unwittingly taken over by Moses because of its inherent connection with the castration complex originating from the relations between the primeval father and his sons. This Mosaic restoration of the primeval father still left some parts of the prehistoric tragedy unrecognized, however. Operating underground for several more centuries, they gradually generated that widespread feeling of guilt which characterized both the Jewish people and the entire Mediterranean world at the beginning of the Christian era. This sense of guilt once more resulted in the murder of a leader, but this time it was the Son who died in expiation for the primeval murder of the Father. This is, according to Freud, the underlying motif for Paul's doc-

trine of the original sin, just as the Christian communion is but a resurgence of the bodily partaking of the primeval father and its derivative,
the sacrificial repast of the totem cults. Through the Crucifixion, on the
other hand, the Christian religion truly became but a Son religion, and
hence its triumph "was a renewed victory of the Ammon priests over the
God of Ikhnaton." The Jewish people who, "with its usual stiff-necked
obduracy," continued to deny the murder of their "father," consequently
suffered severe persecution. The accusation of Christ-killing really means
"You won't admit that you murdered God" (the primeval father and his
reincarnations), whereas "we did the same thing, but we admitted it, and
since then we have been purified" (p. 142).

This bold and ingenious reconstruction of the history of religion, of
which a bare, and in many respects incomplete, outline has been presented
here, is supported by a great many detailed, no less bold and ingenious,
observations which make the book worthwhile reading even for one who
will ultimately disagree with its main thesis. Methodically, however, the
work is open to most crucial objections. The extreme liberties admittedly
taken by Freud with available biblical material is illustrative also of his
utilization of the findings of modern anthropological and historical research.

> When I use Biblical tradition here in such an autocratic and arbitrary
> way, draw on it for confirmation whenever it is convenient, and dismiss its
> evidence without scruple when it contradicts my conclusions, I know full
> well that I am exposing myself to severe criticism concerning my method and
> that I weaken the force of my proofs. But this is the only way in which to
> treat material whose trustworthiness—as we know for certain—was seriously
> damaged by the influence of distorting tendencies [pp. 37, n. 5, and p. 164 f.].

Many of us, unfortunately, will have to disagree. No, this is not the only
way; it is not even the way of authors such as A. Allwohn who, with the
help of psychoanalysis, has tried to reconstruct the subconscious erotic motivations of the prophetic career of Hosea, a subject, it may readily be
granted, much more promising than that of the austere figure of Moses in
the biblical tradition. This limitless arbitrariness in the selection and use
of the little existing evidence renders the entire factual basis of Freud's
reconstruction more than questionable. The primeval-father horde and
the murder of the primeval father are considered by almost all contemporary anthropologists as a figment of imagination. The explanation of
the subsequent rise of totemism, based upon a suggestion once made by
W. Robertson Smith, is here upheld by Freud even though he knows that
"more recent ethnologists have without exception discarded" Smith's theories (p. 207). For the career of the historical Moses, he quotes outstanding modern scholars—Meyer, Gressman, Sellin, Breasted—of whom he
speaks with greater awe than of the original biblical sources and ancient

monuments. But he selects from these writers some of their most fantastic views, often timidly advanced and sometimes later revoked by the authors themselves, drags them out of their context, and combines them into a new artificial entity. The factual evidence for the Egyptian origin of Moses largely reduces itself to the etymology of the name, but this proof appears no more conclusive than would be a parallel attempt to deduce from the name Zerubbabel, the leader of another exodus of Jewish exiles, that he was a native Babylonian. The Jews have probably then, as ever after, adopted the names prevalent among the national majorities in the midst of whom they chanced to live. Wholly untenable is Freud's attempt at identification of the divine name, *Adonai,* in Israel's credo with the Egyptian Aton. The Deuteronomic source has, of course, *Yahwe.* The substitute, *Adonai,* and its Greek equivalent, *kyrios,* are first clearly indicated in the Hellenistic period, a millennium after Moses. Neither is the violent death of Moses more than a farfetched hypothesis, largely given up by its author and shared by no other biblical scholar. Similar objections could easily be raised also against many other essential links in the Freudian reconstruction. Even if the entire factual background were proved beyond peradventure, however, as it is not, the old question would still remain as to whether the Freudian parallelism between individual and mass psychology (assuming the correct interpretation of the former) can be scientifically upheld. The period of latency, particularly, which in the case of the lapse of time between the alleged murder of the primeval father and the appearance of Ikhnaton would extend over countless generations, presupposes an extent of transmission of memories through some sort of heredity which, Freud himself admits, is unequivocally rejected "by the present attitude of biological science." In short, the cause of psychoanalytical interpretation of the history of religion, brilliantly initiated by Freud and his disciples several decades ago, seems to the present reviewer to have received a setback rather than to have made further progress through its present application to the historical career of Moses.

These considerations will probably carry little weight with "that minority of readers familiar with analytical reasoning and able to appreciate its conclusions" (p. 7) to which the author, notwithstanding his sincere efforts at popularization, primarily addresses himself. To many of these initiates, the present work, despite its scientific argumentation, will appeal as the pronunciamento of a revered prophet and sectarian leader, entirely immune from the so-called rational, but essentially psychically conditioned and hence prejudiced, attacks by outsiders. To the outsiders (and the present reviewer professes to be one of them), however, much as they may admire the author's erudition and dialectical prowess, this ingenious structure will appear as but a magnificent castle in the air.

Freud and the
Ambiguity of Culture

Hans Meyerhoff

If nothing else is gained from the re-evaluation of Freud in the series of celebrations at the occasion of the one-hundredth anniversary of his birth, it may be the correction, long overdue, of what can only be called a scientific myth: to wit, that he neglected or disregarded cultural factors in the analysis of psychological phenomena. This was said of a man who began with, and invariably returned to, the basic proposition that the drama of the self, depicting the vicissitudes of the libido, is always acted out against a family background; who as early as 1908 wrote a long essay on the effect of cultural repression upon mental illness; who in his later writings addressed himself almost exclusively to cultural problems and insisted that all psychology was group psychology (i.e., the psychology of "interpersonal relations"); and who, in the last great summary and revision of his thinking (*New Introductory Lectures on Psychoanalysis*), stated flatly that there were only two branches of science, the human sciences, i.e., "psychology, pure and applied," and the natural sciences. "Whatever he may mean to the people who deal professionally with culture," Trilling (*Freud and the Crisis of Our Culture*) observes correctly, "for the layman Freud is likely to be the chief proponent of the whole cultural concept. . . . His psychology involves culture in its very essence—it tells us that the surrogates of culture are established in the

"Freud and the Ambiguity of Culture." Reprinted from *Partisan Review*, XXIV, No. 1 (Winter 1957), 117-130, by permission of *Partisan Review*. Copyright 1957 by *Partisan Review*.

mind itself, that the development of the individual mind recapitulates the development of culture."

Psychoanalysis, however, is a cultural discipline in a more specific sense: Freud was also a philosopher of culture; and there is a more or less articulate philosophy of culture, history, and man behind the scientific structure of psychoanalysis. Freud turned to these philosophical reflections late and reluctantly; but it is precisely these philosophical issues which were responsible for the differences between himself and the post-Freudian dissenters of various persuasions. It was an odd delusion on their part to charge a thinker more deeply steeped than themselves in the heritage of history with blindness to the effect of social influences upon human life. The charge, I think, was a form of self-delusion; for the "cultural schools" have either overlooked or concealed the fact that their deviations involved, not a rediscovery, but a reinterpretation of culture. It was a reinterpretation of the meaning of culture, the nature of man, the function of religion, and the place of morality along traditional and inspirational lines.

Dissent and defection, therefore, always involved what Stanley Edgar Hyman calls "philosophic disagreement" ("Freud and the Climate of Tragedy," *Partisan Review,* Spring 1956). Freud himself saw this and said so in response to the first modifications of the libido theory by C. G. Jung. As in the case of any scientific system, it is only natural to expect that the basic concepts of psychoanalysis will be revised in the light of logical adequacy and experimental tests; and many workers in the field are constantly engaged in this task of improving the scientific status and validity of psychoanalytic theory. I suspect, however, that, despite these improvements, the final judgment about psychoanalysis will not be rendered on scientific grounds alone; for as a system of ideas about man's fate and history, psychoanalysis is more than a scientific system. A response to such a system depends, not only upon the logical status and experimental verification of its theoretical concepts, but also upon one's personal estimate of the philosophical, moral, and social implications of the system. In short, one's total response includes an ineluctably subjective element: cognitive and emotive factors, reason and character, are jointly engaged in the process of verification. And that, for better or worse, is philosophy—not in the academic sense of making a living, but in the old-fashioned sense of providing a *Weltanschauung.*

I

Ambiguity, I believe, is an essential category in the philosophy of psychoanalysis. It refers to what Ernest Jones, in the second volume of his new biography, has called Freud's "constant proclivity to dualistic ideas —the interaction of opposites, the synthesis and dissolution of antithetical concepts." But this "obstinate dualism" is of a dynamic kind; it is, as Hartmann says, "a very characteristic kind of dialectical thinking." The "interaction of opposite powers" involves a constant, dynamic process. And any resolution of this dynamic interaction in history and in man is always temporary, tentative, and precarious—in short, ambiguous.

Riesman has analyzed the dialectical ambiguity of work and play, freedom and authority, heroism and weakness "in the structure of Freud's thought" (*Selected Essays from Individualism Reconsidered*). Trilling's essay, mentioned above, is a literary commentary upon "the interaction of biology and culture in the fate of man." Hyman's recent article in the *Partisan Review*, which must be applauded as a brilliant tribute to the centennial celebrations, proceeded from the same premise to develop the thesis that "the writings of Sigmund Freud once again make a tragic view possible for the modern mind." Herbert Marcuse's book, *Eros and Civilization*,[1] is perhaps the most exhaustive and penetrating study yet undertaken of the tragic "dialectic of civilization."

Culture, according to Freud, is a product of three independent variables: (1) necessity (*Ananke*) imposed by nature; (2) the instinctual polarity in man: love and death (Eros and Thanatos) ultimately fused in the "seething cauldron" of the id; and (3) the institutions and ideals developed by society. The "dialectic of civilization" is a function of the interaction of these three variables. Culture—like the individual ego—is a precarious, unstable, compound because the process of synthesizing and reconciling these three components is never complete, final, and successful. If, as Géza Róheim has said, in *The Origin and Function of Culture*, "civilization is a series of institutions evolved for the sake of security," then this security system is constantly threatened by explosive and destructive tendencies in the three partners. Nature imposes harsh necessities which may never be completely mastered. The instincts may break out in open or subversive revolt against the repressions imposed by society. And the ideological superstructure may crush man because it is unbearable and unworkable.

More specifically, Freud envisaged the dialectical struggle as "a battle between the Titans" Eros and Thanatos, or as a result of the insoluble quest to press these two "heavenly forces" into service on behalf of a satisfactory and lasting social adaptation against the background of a neutral or hostile environment. This quest is never-ending; for Eros is reluctant to complete the cultural task which it has begun in the family, and Thanatos always threatens to destroy the cultural achievements wrested from a reluctant Eros. Worse: in the process of acculturation, Eros loses ground against the forces of destruction. For culture must transform both instincts; it must domesticate them (by displacement and sublimation) to achieve both a greater mastery over nature and a more secure gratification of the instincts in interpersonal relations. Unfortunately, it can accomplish this task only at a price; and the price we pay

[1] Beacon Press, 1955.

for the cultural achievements accounts for the feeling of "discontent" running through the history of civilization. In Freud's own words (*Civilization and Its Discontents*): "The price of progress in civilization is paid in forfeiting happiness through the heightening of a sense of guilt."

The sense of guilt is "the most important problem in the evolution of culture." Its origins lie in the perennial revolt against the mythical father and in the establishment of the first taboos in the primitive society of the brother clan. This mythical prototype of the origin of civilization served Freud as the basis for the crucial assertion that "that which began in relation to the father ends in relation to the community." In other words, all cultural systems reflect "the conflict of ambivalence, the eternal struggle between Eros and the destructive instinct," originally felt toward the mythical father image. Culture has devised a precarious resolution of this ambivalence. It checks the destructive impulse by turning it inward, where it is then discharged, as a sense of guilt or moral anxiety, against the individual himself. As the libidinal ties were extended "from the group of the family to the group of humanity," a process for which the impossible moral command, "Love thy neighbor as thyself," is the most conspicuous symbol in Western culture, the cycle of repression, guilt, and anxiety was repeated through countless generations. And "the feelings of guilt . . . were reinforced" by each successive resolution of the original conflict, or by the increasing need to internalize aggressive and destructive tendencies in the form of a vigilant conscience. Thus the superego is progressively strengthened in the course of history; and the destructive elements, in man and society, gain at the expense of Eros.

Culture, then, is both a blessing and a curse; and it is both throughout the history of civilized man. Human history is a record of this ambiguity: a repetitive cycle of progress and regression, revolt and repression, achievement and failure, stability and upheaval, security and insecurity, liberation and enslavement. And unless we bring the unconscious "ambivalence" behind the cultural process into full consciousness and design appropriate precautionary measures to deal with it adequately, Freud was inclined to think—this is his pessimistic, tragic view of life— that man's fate was likely to be sealed by the "immortal adversary" of Eros.

Culture occupied so dominant a place in Freud's mind that he not only assigned to it—all "cultural" dissenters to the contrary—a crucial part in the causal analysis of neuroses, but even compared it (like Plato) to an "organic process" of its own, independent of all the factors contributing to it. Along these lines, he envisaged the ideal of a "true social science" which would "show in detail how these different factors—the general human instinctual disposition, its racial variations, and its cultural modifications—behave under the influence of varying social organization, professional activities and methods of subsistence" (*New Introductory Lectures*). Moreover, he raised the interesting question of whether we could not study the "cultural superego" as an independent social agency and thus apply psychoanalysis to the pathology of whole cultures. He presently warned, however, that such an undertaking would encounter serious difficulties. For in the case of an individual neurosis, we have a fixed, though arbitrary and conventional, standard of "reality" by which we are guided in the therapeutic situation. It is the cultural pattern itself "which we assume to be 'normal.'" No such standard of comparison would be available in dealing with the neurosis of a whole culture.

II

This hint thrown out at the end of *Civilization and Its Discontents* has produced a spate of studies on the pathology of cultures—German, Russian, Japanese, English, French, and American. None of them, I think, has been able to avoid the danger against which Freud warned wisely. All of them have blithely proceeded on the doubtful assumption that there is a *cultural* standard of "normalcy" against which we can measure and evaluate deviations. The latest study in this direction is Erich Fromm's book *The Sane Society*.[2] In *Escape from Freedom*, Fromm attempted to diagnose the pathology of totalitarianism; *The Sane Society* is his contribution to the pathology of democratic capitalism. There is much in this analysis, particularly in the long fifth chapter called "Man in Capitalistic Society," which is first-rate social psychology; but in this survey I wish to concentrate only upon the over-all philosophical perspective from which the book is written. For *The Sane Society* is a most instructive document for clarifying, once and for all, (1) the differences between the "cultural schools" of psychoanalysis and Freud's approach to culture, and (2) the social and philosophical implications of these differences.

Fromm's concept of culture is in the tradition of Marx and Freud. Only instead of using terms like "ideological superstructure" or "cultural superego," he introduces the notion of a "social character," which he has used in previous books. It is the characterological counterpart of the cultural superego in that it refers to those character traits and attitudes which people have in common by virtue of the fact that they live in the same society. Similarly, Fromm's explanation of neurosis, whether individual or social, is quite traditional. A neurosis is, roughly speaking, the result of a severe conflict between the social character (i.e., cultural superego) on the one hand, and basic human drives on the other. What is new in Fromm's system is the nature and function of these drives. Instead of Eros and Thanatos, Fromm postulates five basic needs: the need for freedom, the need for rootedness, the need for transcendence, the need for identity, and the need for a frame of orientation and devotion. Next, the dynamic principles according to which these needs interact with nature and culture are highly simplified as compared with the complex dynamic

[2] Rinehart, 1955.

processes by which Freud tried to account for the bewildering viscissitudes of the libido. In fact, instead of dynamic interaction, we find a simple, static polarity. Each drive has a dual goal—sacred and profane. Thus there are five ideal goals: love; freedom; brotherhood; individuality; and a rational religion. They represent a way of life through which man realizes himself and finds health and happiness. Correspondingly, there are five negative goals; they represent a way of life through which man falls into alienation and neurosis. The ideal goals, of course, are good; the negative goals, evil. These are the psychological foundations for what Fromm has called "normative humanism."

It is obvious that Fromm does not introduce a new cultural perspective; but he does replace Freud's psychological apparatus, its topological, dynamic, and economic principles, by a different psychological theory. And he does this for a normative purpose—i.e., to lay down specific rules for "good" and "bad" solutions of the human situation. A good solution corresponds to a "sane society." In such a society, the ideal goals of human needs and the social structure are so adjusted to each other that they produce mental health. *Per contra*, a society which thwarts and perverts man's inherent striving for mental health is "insane," even though its members may not know it. Mental health "is the *same* for man in *all* ages and *all* cultures" (italics mine). It consists of a remarkable composite of virtues in line with the ideal goals; for it "is characterized by the ability to love and to create, by a sense of identity based on one's experience of self as the subject and agent of one's powers, by the grasp of reality inside and outside of ourselves, that is, by the development of objectivity and reason." It is obviously not easy to enjoy mental health; but citing numerous authorities from Ikhnaton to Jesus, Fromm believes that his own definition "coincides essentially with the norms postulated by the great spiritual teachers of the human race"—as if they had ever been able to agree with each other.

Thus we get a sharp, clear-cut division between light and darkness, between good and evil, between normalcy and neurosis, between health and disease, between happiness and misery, between self-realization and alienation. And we have achieved the objective of eliminating the concept of ambiguity from Freud's analysis of the interaction of culture and personality. Culture is not necessarily Janus-faced; according to Fromm, it may well smile on all of us with a benign and benevolent face. Instead of doubt, we get reassurance; instead of ambiguity, inspiration; and Freud's subtle irony makes way for the voice of prophecy.

It must be said that Fromm's voice is one of the sanest in the siren songs of neo-Freudian revisionists. There is much that is attractive in his blueprint for a sane society, which he calls "communitarian socialism"; but these are details which, again, must be set aside. In general, the reforms he advocates are in the tradition of humanitarian socialist thinkers as set

forth, say, in Buber's *Paths in Utopia*. Yet, curiously enough, the elaborate psychological apparatus yields results which, on the whole, are rather
commonplace or ideological. They are commonplace in that they ultimately amount to saying something like this: if only we go to work and
set our house in order—i.e., improve and reform social institutions and
ideologies—the world will be a better place to live in. They are ideological in that the justification for this faith does not, or need not, come
from any psychological knowledge in depth, but from an acceptance of
the traditional wisdom of religious prophets. "Fromm," as Marcuse puts
it sharply, "revives all the time-honored values of idealistic ethics as if
nobody had ever demonstrated their conformist and repressive features."
Fromm[3] has objected to this charge: if "ideal goals" like love, integrity,
maturity, etc. are said to be ideological, would the critic also rule out
terms like hate, destructiveness, sadism as ideological language? This
defense does not meet the issue head-on, for the crucial point is what the
ideal goals mean in Fromm's vocabulary. And, as we shall see presently,
they mean what they have always meant in religious and moral discourse.
Hence the psychological foundations which Fromm employs for his critique of society cannot go beyond the traditional interpretations of these
ideal goals.

This is not true of Freud. Even a brief indication of his thinking on
reform, revolution, and conservatism helps to throw his approach to these
problems into sharp contrast with Fromm's. Freud spoke in favor of "reforms" at least along three general lines: (1) sexual morality; (2) economic injustice; and (3) technological progress. But in addition to these
reformist tendencies, Freud's thinking is "revolutionary" at least in two
respects: First, he believed that reforms were patchwork "without alter-
ing the foundations of the whole system." Secondly, he believed, rightly
or wrongly, that any culture can and must always be weighed against
the demands made on behalf of man's libidinal life—the gratifications
and frustrations of which constitute man's inalienable rights against the
demands imposed by society. Both of these revolutionary aspects of
Freud's thought are conspicuously absent in Fromm's system, as they are
in any other system of inspirational psychoanalysis. *Per contra,* one can
search far and wide in Freud's works and will not find that he leans on
the authority of scripture—whether religious, moral, or political. That
Freud remained a "conservative" despite these revolutionary implications
of his thought is well known. Aside from temperament, he was conservative because he was deeply convinced (a) that an intractable Adam
dwelt in the instinctual life of man, (b) that the instincts obeyed a "conservative" principle of their own, and (c) that they were called upon to
perform impossible and insoluble tasks on behalf of human culture.

[3] See the controversy between Fromm and Marcuse conducted in the pages of *Dissent*
(Summer and Autumn 1955, Winter 1956).

III

The theme of Marcuse's *Eros and Civilization* is the instincts at war with culture. It is called "a philosophical inquiry into Freud," which will cause misgivings in circles distrustful of philosophical speculation divorced from clinical experience and practical therapy. Others more open to their metaphysical commitments may agree with Kluckhohn's judgment that, with the exception of the two volumes by Ernest Jones, Marcuse's book is "the most significant general treatment of psychoanalytic theory since Freud himself ceased publication." The treatment is "orthodox" in that Marcuse accepts Freud's "dialectic of civilization" and outlines his own solution of the problem against the background of Freud's metapsychology. Thus, in content and spirit, this approach differs sharply from any variety of neo-Freudian revisionism.

The contrast is particularly striking when we consider the different meanings which Fromm and Marcuse assign to the same terms. Both use "alienation" as their point of departure—thus indicating that both bring the influence of Hegel and Marx to a study of Freud. But the two men mean very different things by the same concept. For Fromm "alienation" means that man living in a capitalistic society is debased in his "true" nature, his essential humanity, which refers to the realization of the ideal goals and spiritual values mentioned above. Marcuse, on the other hand, takes Freud's hint that alienation means "alienation from instincts," and that the reconditioning of our machines, both cultural and personal, should begin and end with a liberation and transformation of the instinctual life. Similarly, they assign entirely different meanings to the crucial concepts believed to lead beyond alienation. For example, "freedom" in Fromm refers to a highly sublimated and special kind of "inner" freedom, as it did, say, for Spinoza. Marcuse uses the term with reference to the instincts unfolding without repression by social customs and norms. Again, "love" in Marcuse's vocabulary designates Freud's Eros with a full and unequivocal recognition of the manifold sexual components of the instinct. Fromm uses the word again in a highly attenuated, aim-inhibited sense: "productive love" is a composite of care, responsibility, respect, and knowledge—but does not include sex. It is well to remember in philosophical controversies[4] that two writers can use the same words and speak an entirely different language.

Yet, despite these differences, Marcuse's essay marks another attempt to resolve the ambiguity which Freud read into the history of human culture. Marcuse, too, is a utopian thinker; he, too, envisages a realm of freedom in which the most distinctive features of Freud's thought, the precariousness, openness, insecurity, and tragedy of man's fate in culture are laid to eternal rest. In contrast to Fromm and other neo-Freudian

---

[4] See note, p. 62.

writers, however, Marcuse embarks upon such a utopian blueprint by accepting two basic premises of Freud's own analysis of culture: (1) the biological theory of instincts; (2) the nature of culture as an instrument of repression. If there is to be a leap into freedom, it must, therefore, be envisaged as the transcendence of the concept of culture in general, as a repudiation of *all* historical manifestations and justifications of repression, domination, and exploitation of man in society.

Such a project is "in a strict sense 'unreasonable.'" It involves two assumptions: first, that we revise the prevailing concept of reason; secondly, that we assign to Freud's analysis of culture only an historical validity. The ordinary meaning of reason in science and society is for Marcuse, as it was for Scheler, a form of *Herrschaftswissen*. Its primary function has been to gain mastery over nature and man; hence, it is a type of rationality which is itself subservient to the ideas of conquest, domination, and repression. In the name of freedom, therefore, it must be opposed by a different kind of reason, which Marcuse finds in art. Next, he believes that Freud's pessimistic diagnosis of culture reflects a historical, not a universal, necessity. To be sure, every major civilization seems to exhibit the same pattern of authority, repression, and. guilt; but these characteristics, according to Marcuse, are still historical accidents because he attributes them to the special conditions which have so far prevailed in the evolution of human culture: the need to master a recalcitrant nature and the necessary sacrifices imposed upon the reluctant instincts to perfect a system of security against want and fear. The moment these special conditions cease to operate it may be possible to reverse the inexorable march of unreason through history. This moment has arrived. Our culture has reached a level of technological perfection and material abundance which, as Marx predicted long ago, would enable us to suspend and supersede the repressive, irrational solutions of the fateful "dialectic of civilization." It has put within our grasp the prospect of a "free" and "rational" society—even though this prospect must appear utopian and unreasonable from the perspective of the ideas of freedom and reason developed by a repressive culture.

Since the leap into freedom is not forthcoming, there must be special conditions at work which prevent it. Marcuse singles out two such conditions, which he calls surplus repression and the performance principle, respectively. By "surplus repression" he means the social restrictions and forms of exploitation necessitated, not by the natural struggle for survival, but by the historical struggle for power and domination in society. By the "performance principle" he means the type of work necessitated, not by need and use, but by the competitive, acquisitive features of a capitalistic economy. Marcuse concludes that Freud's analysis of culture is predicated upon a misreading of the reality principle in the light of surplus repression and excess performance. More precisely, it is a correct reading of the historical record, but a false extrapolation from it. According to Marcuse, the historical curse can at last be lifted from man's soul because surplus repression and the performance principle are no longer necessary for survival and social adaptation.

Unlike Fromm, Marcuse does not see the vague breaking of a new dawn in political economy or religion, but in the aesthetic dimension. His prophets are Novalis, Baudelaire, Proust, Gide, Rilke, Valéry, and all the others who have chosen art as a way of life. It is their vision which has always held a mirror up to human nature—and shown it to be disfigured by a repressive, irrational reality. Marcuse invokes the mythical figures of Orpheus and Narcissus as archetypes for the aesthetic vision and as perennial reminders of "The Great Refusal" to serve reality and reason at the price of libidinal freedom and pleasure. Freud himself had specifically excluded "fantasy" from the universal reign of the reality principle in the adult ego; but, on the whole, he tended to think of the products of fantasy and imagination, in the normal adult as well as in the special case of the artist, as harmless play, as delightful escapes into an illusory world, as pleasing anodynes against the harshness and frustrations of life.

Drawing upon the humanistic idealism of Kant and Schiller, Marcuse enlarges the meaning of play and art so that they may become the tools for building a new world beyond history: *"Là, tout n'est qu'ordre et beauté, luxe, calme, et volupté."* He insists, as do other critics of Freud, that art is more than a harmless illusion or substitute gratification. The creative imagination caught in the works of art makes a *cognitive* claim upon the individual by confronting him with "truths" about life, liberty, and the pursuit of happiness which are buried under the debris of an ugly social reality and a repressive scientific rationality. Play has a reality-testing function (Riesman). Moreover, play is self-determined or self-regulative. It creates its own pattern and structure in the process of transforming intrapsychic energy. Structure, organization, and sublimation emerge spontaneously from the instinctual sources which are absorbed in playful activity; they are not imposed from the outside by social rules or natural necessity.

This argument is crucial for Marcuse's version of a libidinal aestheticism. In a long and difficult chapter called "The Transformation of Sexuality into Eros," he sets out to show that as in play, so in sex, the impulse or psychic energy behind the activity may and will develop, as part of its own dynamics, certain self-inhibiting and self-denying mechanisms—even, and especially, when the impulse is liberated from the traditional cultural superego and its repressive features. Thus checks and balances generated by the instinct itself will sustain the cultural process beyond its present liberation. Only the cultural process will then be nourished by displacements and sublimations under the aegis of a liberated id, instead of under the destructive and painful tyranny of the traditional superego. Taking a cue from Róheim, Marcuse envisages the prospect of libidinal freedom as a reversal of the traditional dynamics of the cultural process. Instead of a hostile and anxiety-ridden superego wresting valuable ground from the id, the id will, as it were, break through and flood both ego and superego with libidinal energy. The result of this great reversal will be twofold: (1) There will come about what Marcuse calls an "erotization of the total personality," i.e., a rediscovery on the mature, adult level of the polymorphous-perverse state of sexuality which Freud attributed to early infancy; and (2) there will come about an "erotization" of social relations, including the working conditions still required to maintain a state of material abundance. In both respects, Marcuse believes such an "unreasonable" project would provide genuine liberation—as against the pseudo-freedom of the inspirational schools of psychoanalysis—and the basis for resolving, once and for all, the fateful ambiguity of culture and man which Freud postulated on the grounds of the irreconcilable conflict between happiness and guilt.

IV

These ideas, obviously, represent an original and challenging contribution to the body of psychoanalytic thought. They also raise a great many questions; e.g., about the function of art, the nature of instincts, the interaction of culture and personality, and so on. We cannot discuss these problems; but we may ask in conclusion: Does this ideal of a libidinal aestheticism achieve the objective of solving the cultural equation which Freud believed to be insoluble? It is, I think, doubtful that it does; or insofar as it brings about a resolution of the ambiguity inherent in Freud's analysis of culture, it does so by shifting the problem to another level. For the problem apparently solved within the context of Freud's dichotomy between the instincts and their historical vicissitudes, between the pleasure principle and a culturally conditioned reality principle, reappears, I am afraid, as the dilemma between historical reality and utopia. All human and cultural reality is under the governance of time. Utopias, being "timeless" constructions, cannot incorporate this temporal dimension into their own system. Worse: they cannot establish a meaningful connection between their own system beyond time and the social reality in time. They cannot and do not answer the fatal question: what difference will the passage of time make to the realization of the utopian ideal? In short, any utopian vision is tainted by the spot of the transition period; and the damned spot will not rub off—not even with the help of art. Maybe time does come to a stop in the "timeless" images caught in aesthetic expression; but in this respect, at least, art reveals its illusory nature; for we cannot reify the eternal moments of art and incorporate them into the historical and social world, which is always subject to changes in time.

Thus it is inevitable that in Marcuse's essay, as in any utopian construction, the human dilemma reappears in the form of the irreconcilable gap between the historical situation, on the one hand, and the leap into freedom beyond history, on the other. In the concrete terms of our own situation, this means that the liberation of Eros would and must take place under the conditions of a highly advanced technological civilization and under the governance of a pleasure principle developed by this civilization. What this would look like is difficult to predict. But it is at least an open question, all gloomy critics notwithstanding, whether the pleasure principle is not now celebrating undreamt-of triumphs in The Brave New World of T.V. Murphy. And whatever view we take "in the long run," when, in Keynes' phrase, we'll all be dead, it is undeniable, I think, that the very technological and historical conditions which make it possible for us to envisage an age of abundance, freedom, and love will and must influence the cultural face of his future. It is surely a safe lesson of history that a great many other factors, beside the self-regulating mechanisms that may (or may not) unfold within the instincts, will condition man's passage to a new world.

Thus the aesthetic dimension cannot bridge the crucial gap either—if for no other reason than that society is not a work of art. We can never wipe the canvas clean and start all over again as much as we dream of it; we can never remake ourselves or history out of entirely new cloth. The prophetic visions of rebirth, resurrection, and the new life in eternity are, ultimately, illusory phantasms, born of an undying faith in the omnipotence of thought and nourished by the romantic longings of the perennial child in man.[5] By contrast, Freud's recognition of an ineluctable ambiguity in man's quest to master nature, social relations, and himself appears much more "realistic" in that it is based on a sober estimate of the record of human history and personal experience verifiable in our own lives. This recognition, as we have seen, did not prevent Freud from taking a stand against surplus repression and alienation; but it did save him from saying that the historical ambiguity of man and his culture would ever be resolved permanently. For that we not only know too little—but too much.

Ambiguity runs as a persistent theme through the structure of Freud's thought. Culture is an ambiguous, unstable compound just as the ego is an ambiguous, precarious organization. Mental health and normality are flexible, relative, and ambiguous terms, not clear-cut propositions dividing the children of light from the children of darkness. *A fortiori*, the notions of a "good" life or a "good" society are even more variable and ambiguous. All popular distortions of Freudianism to the contrary, there is no royal road to happiness, there is no single, unequivocal meaning that

[5] There is, of course, the phenomenon of genuine religious conversions; but their effects are notoriously neutral in the balance sheet of history. They are usually confined to the individual—in which case he is "reborn" as a new man "within," i.e., either participates in the social scene as before or becomes an outcast from society (guru, hermit, monk). On the other hand, when religious conversions have changed the course of history (as in the case of Constantine, Mohammed, or Luther), the "dialectic of civilization" has not been affected by them.

can be attached to this elusive term. It has been the objective of all inspirational schools of psychoanalysis to eliminate this disturbing note of
ambiguity from Freud's thought. It is disturbing because it is, among
other things, a blow to our personal and cultural narcissism; for (a) it
does not enable us to read the progression of history as "progress," (b)
it does not enable us to feel superior, in our own cultural superego, to
that of other periods in history, and (c) it does not provide consolation
and/or salvation. And that, as Freud wrote, is "at bottom what they all
demand—the frenzied revolutionary as passionately as the most pious
believer."

The inspirational schools of psychoanalysis have come along to supply
this demand. All of them, interestingly enough, have retained a dualistic
conceptual scheme inherited from Freud: the conflict between inferiority
and superiority (Adler); the polarities of personal and collective, in-
trovert and extrovert, anima and animus (Jung); the movements away
from, against, and toward (Horney); the distinction between existential
and historical dichotomies (Fromm). All of them, however, have maintained that there is a way out of these dichotomies, that there is an un-
ambiguous resolution of inner conflicts, or that there is an unequivocal
meaning of integration, self-realization, freedom, health, and happiness.
Thus all of them have ended up by giving moral and inspirational instruction, which is sold in a more popular and effective dosage by the Reverend
Peale. In all of them, therefore, this movement away from Freud returns
to an ideology of adjustment and salvation which is in line with the religion and ethics of a culture in despair. It is this compulsive pursuit of certainty and consolation which distinguishes their structure of thought
more radically from Freud's than any specific difference in theory or
therapy.

For Freud did not provide religious inspiration—nor did he take utopian leaps. Instead, he professed Socratic ignorance about the ultimate
issues of life and happiness and courageously adhered to a philosophical
outlook subtly poised on ambiguity and irony. If one would dare hope
for the future, he might wish that such a *Weltanschauung* might still
make an appeal to future generations when the current wave of inspirational psychoanalysis has spent itself because it is no longer necessary.

The Evolution of Culture

Géza Róheim

Prehistory may not confirm the belief of mankind in the Golden Age, but psychoanalysts will understand it as representing the happy period of our life when we could enjoy ourselves without anxiety or compulsion. Still, we suspect that in addition to the ontogenetic truth embodied in this explanation there may be something in phylogenesis in the infancy of mankind that corresponds with this myth. Perhaps the anthropologist is also actuated by such hidden motives in searching for the Isles of the Blessed somewhere in the Pacific.

Well, we must ask, what is primitive man like? How can we characterize the living representatives of so-called primitive civilizations? If we reconsider this question, we find that it really amounts to the same thing as if we were to ask, what is civilized man like? If psychoanalysis can characterize the normal, the neurotic, the psychotic, or the antisocial, it must also be able to explain psychologically what is meant by primitive man.

It is nearly twenty years ago that I was discussing the question of the psychological unity of mankind with Ferenczi and Rank. I had begun analysis with Ferenczi a short time before, and my knowledge of the subject was more theoretical than otherwise. I stood my ground, representing

"The Evolution of Culture." Reprinted from *The International Journal of Psycho-Analysis*, XV, No. 4 (October 1934), 387-418. [Approximately one-third of the original article has been deleted by the editor because of lack of space.] Copyright 1934 by *The International Journal of Psycho-Analysis*.

the classical evolutionary school of anthropology, and I held the view that human beings were essentially the same whatever race, class, or civilization they might belong to. Psychoanalysis, I thought, had only confirmed what Tylor, Bastian, and Frazer had taught us: *homo sum et humani nil a me alienum puto*. On the other hand, Ferenczi and Rank were of the opinion that popular belief and the experience of everyday life meant something, and that therefore there is evidently a quality that characterizes the mental make-up of the French as being different from the English, of the European as different from the American and Asiatic, and so on. It may not be science, but it is intuition. My answer was, give me a single instance of a myth or a custom in which psychoanalysis will find anything but universally human tendencies. This argument proved unanswerable, but nevertheless it was far from being conclusive.

Where shall we look for these differences? Not in our instinctual life, but in our ideals; not in the id, but in the analysis of the superego. It is instructive, therefore, to compare the varieties of what I have called the group ideal.[1]

Let us take as our first instance the people of Manus so excellently described by Margaret Mead. A stone-age people in a minute tropical Venice, yet with ideals so similar to those of modern civilization. Work, property, business probity are the main virtues; undischarged debts or other economic obligations the worst things in life.[2] The skulls of the dead are kept in the house, and in his everyday work man is assisted by his father's spirit. But in return the spirits demand the exercise of certain restraints and virtues. Sexual offenses, light words, careless jests and economic laxity bring down the wrath of the spirits either on the offender or on one of his relatives.[3] But there is a certain tendency toward specialization in spirit life. Spirits of those who died when they were young kill the young: adulterous spirits kill those who commit adultery. That is, they punish the sins they have themselves committed.[4] Society takes only one thing seriously, and that is *kawas* (barter, trade, exchange = Trobriand *kula*), and this is the main difference between children and adults. Children have nothing to do with *kawas*.[5] When a man speaks of his wife, he mentions the size of the betrothal payment that was made for her; when he speaks of his sister, he says: "I give her sago and she gives me beadwork." The whole of life, his most intimate relation to people, his conception of places, his evaluation of his guarding spirits, all fall under the head of *kawas* (exchange).[6] Small children have been

---

[1] Cf. "Super-Ego and Group-Ideal," *International Journal of Psycho-Analysis*, Vol. XIII, 1932, p. 175.

[2] M. Mead: *Growing up in New Guinea*, 1930, p. 9.

[3] M. Mead, *op. cit.*, p. 101.

[4] M. Mead, *op. cit.*, p. 102.

[5] M. Mead, *op. cit.*, pp. 81, 86, 92.

[6] M. Mead, *op. cit.*, p. 81.

made ashamed of their bodies, ashamed of excretion.[7] A girl has been taught that it is a shameful thing to think of her husband personally, but it is the proper thing for her to think of the dog's teeth or of the shell money which has been paid for her betrothal feast.[8] The conventional attitude is that a wife and a husband do not love each other, and a man spends a large part of his time with his sister. Here we have the fission in love life, well known to clinical analysts. A man has intercourse with his wife, loves his sister, and flirts with his cross-cousin.[9] The cross-cousin is the proper partner for all sorts of erotic games, but not for coitus; and the male cross-cousin is the orthodox partner in the exchange (*kawas*). . . .

I spent the year 1930 in Duau (Normanby Island), one of the three large islands that form the d'Entrecasteaux group. The group ideal of Duau is the *to-kune*, the man who gives or receives presents, or who is prominent in the *kune*, the interisland circulation of strings of shells (*bagi*) and of white arm shells (*mwari*), which corresponds with the *kawas* of Manus. A good girl desires marriage with an *esa-esa*, a rich or famous man. When we gave the women some sweets Doketa would say: "You are a real *esa-esa*. There is nobody like you among the whites." I objected, saying that Mr. Smith, a white trader whom he knew, was certainly much more of an *esa-esa* than I was. Oh no, Doketa said, for only somebody who like myself is always distributing things to men, women, and children alike is a real *esa-esa*.

The difference between Manus and Duau is that in Manus the whole system is more rigid, more like trade or barter, while in Duau stress is laid on the gift aspect, on the attitude of the giver as a man who is only bent on making others happy.

Kune in Duau is not only the circulation of neck strings (shell money) but also the present, the share received by each guest at the *sagari*. A *sagari* is a feast, or rather the distribution of yams, and therefore closely connected with agriculture. The *esa-esa* is not only the leader of the *kune* exploits, but the owner of the land. We are here in a typically matrilineal society based on the unconscious identification of the boy with his mother. In its institutionalized form this identification consists in the distributive function of the male as a nourishing mother. From the ego point of view this formula means more work and more food, from that of the ego-ideal it involves social prestige. As compared with the system of the people of Manus it implies a stronger genital element in character formation, for in the ritual of the garden there is not only identification with but also the fertilization of the Earth Mother. What is really repressed here is the aggressive component of male sexuality represented in society by the black magic of the *barau*. Being a *barau* is the worst

[7] M. Mead, *op. cit.*, p. 205.
[8] M. Mead, *op. cit.*, p. 57.
[9] M. Mead, *op. cit.*, pp. 161, 166, 299.

crime, and it is a terrible thing to accuse anybody in public of being
guilty of such practices. Yet, such is the fundamental hypocrisy of mankind, at the same time it is generally known that any person of social
eminence, anybody who has a big garden or who gives a big feast, must
be a *barau*. His very existence proves it. The *sagari*, therefore, really
looks like a veiled manic outbreak, a condensation of sublimated wish-
fulfillments of all kinds. The general trend in the formation of this group
ideal is regressive from the genital to the pregenital (oral and anal) position.

All this is not so very different from Europe. Property is praiseworthy,
love is antisocial. We are still in the Victorian ideology or something similar; we are still considering societies that are kept in balance by a regression of the genital to the anal organization, and by a superstructure built
upon the latter either as a reaction formation or as a sublimation. But if we
go to Central Australia we are truly in a world that differs from our own.
Our eternal search for happiness assumes a different form. Nobody ac-
cumulates riches; there is nothing to distribute.[10] Men masturbate in a
group, both in ordinary life and in ritual. In ritual the official aim of
the masturbation is to get blood from the erected penis and to use this
blood as a glue for the decoration of others. In ordinary life the "ritual"
of this group masturbation demands that everybody should talk about
the size of the other man's penis. "Yours is as big as a *muruntu* (mythical
dragon)," one man says. The other replies: "Mine is small, but yours is
as big as a gum tree!" The phallic phase of development, with stress
laid on the male genital and with the exclusion of women, is the basis
of society. The group ideal is the old man, the keeper of the *tjurunga*
(phallus), the leading actor of the ceremony (primal scene), the repository of traditional knowledge. One of the folk etymologies renders Mal-
punga (the phallic hero) as the one who knows the song very well. The
memory of an Aranda old man is really remarkable. For about four
months old Jirramba would have a new song or myth to tell nearly every
day, and it was generally believed that if I had made a start with Tnyetika,
the leader of ceremonies of the Aranda *taka,* I should have had nothing
to do but write what he sang for a whole year. The phallic hero as
owner of the song, the importance of singing and of food magic in the
phallic ritual, seem to indicate the phallic-oral orientation in the unconscious—that is, the specific attitude in which the boy identifies his own
penis with the mother's nipple and carries over the aggression mobilized
by oral frustration to the genital act.[11] "*Unta ilkukabaka*" in Aranda
(have you eaten?), when pronounced with a certain accentuation, means:
have you had intercourse? An immature girl is "raw," a nubile female

[10] A kangaroo is divided when it is brought in, but this cannot be compared to the
elaborate piling up and distribution of food in the Papuan feast.
[11] Ernest Jones: "The Phallic Phase," *International Journal of Psycho-Analysis,* Vol.
XIV, 1933, p. 10

"cooked"; while *mbanja* (marriage) really means rape. Ego-syntonic activities are based on phallic (spear as phallic symbol), oral, and aggressive (hunting) tendencies, and not on anal functions. . . .

All this shows a picture of many colors. Ruth Benedict is probably right in declaring that all possible lines of individual human behavior have been exalted in some society into typical group behavior.[12] It would appear, therefore, that our attempt to arrive at a moderately uniform description of what is primitive as distinguished from what we should call civilized or neurotic must be regarded as futile. However, on second consideration we can discover at least one uniform feature: the very existence of a certain uniformity within the limits of one social group. In clinical analysis we see how people choose a certain path in life, how their pursuits, professions and character are determined by their infancy. In a primitive tribe there is more unity in the picture, unity in the group ideal. It is therefore probable that in a primitive society there is more unity in the infantile situation, that the relation of the parents to their children is more closely determined by social patterns than it is in civilized life. Therefore psychoanalysis, when applied to the study of primitive man, cannot be a merely individualistic method, but must be combined with the analysis of custom and ritual. Custom looms forth more conspicuously in the life of the individual, and the individual is less far removed from the originators of these customary elements than in a complex civilized society.

We can now raise a question that must be of crucial importance in an attempted psychology of primitive mankind. What is the structure of the superego in a really primitive community? What are its component libidinal elements, what kind of libido has been deflected into the aim-inhibited tendencies of the superego? What is the intensity of the superego: is it lenient or severe, are the tendencies of self-punishment implacable or mild, sudden and abrupt or less perceptible but of greater depth? And, finally, what is the area of the superego, what ego and id trends come under its sway, and which tendencies still remain at the free disposal of the ego and the id? We shall see that the solution of the first problem really contains the answer to the second and third questions.

There are two different opinions regarding the origin, date, and formation of the superego. On the one hand we have the original formula put forward by Freud and accepted by the majority of psychoanalysts. First we have the fully developed Oedipus complex with castration and repression, and then the latency period and the development of the superego. On the other hand, Melanie Klein, and in general the English psychoanalysts, are inclined to use the term "superego" for much earlier phenomena. According to this latter view the child lives in an unreal world full of imaginary dangerous beings, and the origin of this phantasy sys-

[12] Benedict: "Psychological Types in the Culture of the South-West." *Proc.* XXIII. *International Congress of S. Americanists.*

tem must be sought for, not only in actual experience in the ontogenetic development of the child, but essentially in the congenital aggressivity of the infant. According to this view the even temporary loss of the nipple activates the tendency to penetrate into the mother, to take possession of, and destroy, her body. The child in search of the nipple desires to penetrate into the mother, but it identifies the nipple with its own pleasure-giving organ, the penis, and via the primal scene also with the father's penis. The dreaded retribution is the reverse side of this phantasy. The dreaded demons or giants are the parents who tear the child's body into two pieces, retribution for the phantasy provoked by the primal scene, or destroy it from the inside, because it is the child who wishes to tear out the contents of the mother's body—i.e., the father's penis, the embryo, milk or feces. All this corresponds exactly to the phantasy system of Australian demonology. . . . As I have been trying to show, the "religion" or phantasy system of demon and medicine man is a precursor of the totemistic or *tjurunga* cult and mythology. The culture heroes of the *tjurunga* religion are the phallic wild-cat ancestors, frequently mentioned in myth as the associates of the demons. Just as the demon lore is typified by the dogs stuck together in copulation, the mythical origin of the *tjurunga* cult is that of two *tjurungas* bound together, one of them being male and the other female. If we use the terminology of Melanie Klein, we might say that the devils represent the destructive penis (something that penetrates into the body, eats the body from the inside), the *tjurunga* the good penis (or the nourishing mammae), by the aid of which it is possible to multiply food-giving animals. . . .

European civilization looks at primitive man from two opposite angles. On the one hand we have romanticism with Rousseau and the theory of the Golden Age, the yearning for the freedom that was. On the other hand there is classical evolutionism with its optimistic doctrine of progress. In psychoanalysis this second view is represented particularly by Laforgue. According to him, primitive man has an extremely severe superego, is a being full of anxiety taboos and inhibitions. In fact he goes so far as to affirm that "savages" are relatively impotent.[13] The trouble is that Laforgue's conclusions are based on books. Anthropological books describe things that interest the anthropologist. They give an account of taboos and demons and witchcraft, but from books alone one cannot form an estimate of the quantitative importance of these things in everyday life. As a matter of fact, a native is much less interested in these things than an anthropologist. Life is food and women and quarrels, not mystery and reverence. It is correct to say that primitives have a "severe" superego if we mean by this the quantity of aggressivity piled up in the superego. Women who break the taboo by prying into the ceremonies are killed, and the castration complex takes the form of severe genital mutilations. The superego is aggressive but not too deeply introjected.

[13] R. Laforgue: *Libido, Angst und Zivilisation*, 1932.

The materialization of the superego in the *tjurunga,* an object that is stored away in the sacred caves, is a functional symbol of its exogenous origin. Breaking the food taboos is punished by the magic of the old men, not by an automatically functioning evil magic inherent in the food. If the food were simply grabbed by the stronger men and kept for themselves we should be nearer to the dominance system of the anthropoid apes,[14] or if the breakers of the law were troubled by their conscience this would be civilized society. In primitive society the superego is phallic, oral, and eruptive—that is, suddenly and vehemently aggressive. But it is not severe from a characterological point of view; that is, it does not keep a permanent and rigid watch on human behavior in such a manner as to endanger ego strivings, to make life more difficult. Both the dynamic quality or cathexis and the scope of the superego depend on the specific component impulses that have undergone sublimation. In Central Australia anal and urethral impulses are nearly completely free, not frustrated or sublimated into the service of the ego or superego.[15] There is no "sphincter morality."

The supernatural beings of an Australian society are not "good"; i.e., they are not ethically superior, not better than mankind. This is in direct opposition to everything that Father Schmidt believes about Australian "High Gods." The "ethical" or nonethical nature of these supernatural beings can be estimated only through personal experience in the field. If a supernatural being is qualified as "good" in Howitt or a book of a similar kind, it remains very doubtful what the word means in the original language. Thus, for instance, the Aranda *mara* or Luritja *indota* should be explained in English by three words: good, beautiful, normal. A folk-tale hero, like the Sky Being himself, is always good in this sense, but this does not mean good deeds or good will, only normality. It is the opposite of the monstrous of anxiety. Whatever or whoever is not *mara* (normal) is an *erintja* (devil). Man can be happy here because he does not try to be too good. In Central Australia human beings are all "good," because the destructive impulses are projected into the world of demons. Civilization with its unattainably good supernatural beings means endopsychical conflict.

If we compare the life of primitive mankind with the representatives of civilization as known to us in clinical analysis, we immediately notice that in primitive conditions a whole group of well-known phenomena are conspicuous by their absence. Although sadistic and masochistic tendencies form a part of primitive life, sadistic or masochistic perversions are completely absent; that is, we do not find that coitus or sexual pleasure is connected with punishment and suffering, or, more exactly, with imaginary punishment and imaginary suffering. The importance of the fact that these perversions are characteristic of civilization but absent in

[14] Cp. S. Zuckerman: *The Social Life of Monkeys and Apes,* 1932.
[15] The urethral impulse contributes a certain share to character formation.

savagery will be evident if we consider their origin and meaning. Besides the fundamental fusion of genital and aggressive strivings their real significance is to be sought for in the severity of the superego which refuses to tolerate the sexual act except with the punishments endured in infancy. The masochist is playing the part of the punished child; the sadist does to others what has been done to him. Or else the sadist identifies himself with the superego, the masochist with the ego, in endopsychical conflict. Primitive children are not punished for most things for which civilized children suffer, hence the absence of these perversions among primitive adults. Romantic love, which invests the love object with all the qualities of the superego and in which the ego feels guilty because of its erotic strivings directed toward the revived Oedipus objects, is unknown to primitive mankind. A lovesick swain who refuses to eat and sits moaning in the moonlight, raving about his pure goddess and the sinfulness of his own desires, chivalry, and the "Minnesänger"—such things would seem ridiculous in the light spread by the camp fires of the Pitchentara.[16] Women are not won by sighs, but by a strong arm and a few well-directed blows. Also among real primitives unhappy marriages are unknown. There are men who have had enough of their wives and so bring in a younger woman, and there are women who run away from their husbands, but a couple held together by mutual hatred for a lifetime is unthinkable. They lack the inclination to make pain permanent, to exalt suffering into a national institution. The same is true of criminality. Most offenses are only offenses in the eyes of those who suffer by them, and it is only they and their nearest relatives who take action against the evildoer. Social condemnation is absent. But in those few cases—incest and ritual offenses (i.e., symbolic incest)—where society feels inclined to do something, it does it thoroughly, and the offender will hardly be in a position to offend a second time. In a primitive society there are no individuals who are oppressed or despised, nobody whose will is not in harmony with public will, none who live a life under the compulsion of an endopsychic "need for punishment."

In a paper on the psychology of work Winterstein[17] uses the person of Sisyphus as a symbol of modern civilization. He says that the ideal of modern man, work and no end, was felt as a curse or punishment in the beginning of civilization in ancient Greece. The virtues of our modern citizen, of the man who provides for the future, devotes his life to work and to his family, is conscientious and punctual at his office, are the exact opposite of the easygoing ways of a savage. But we can understand the contrast still better if we think of the obsessional neurosis as a negative form of the anal-sadistic organization, or of a person whom

[16] [For a most interesting modern analysis of the troubadours and minnesingers of the Middle Ages, see Herbert Moller, "The Meaning of Courtly Love," *Journal of American Folklore*, Vol. 73, No. 287, 1960. B.M.]
[17] A. Winterstein: "Zur Psychologie der Arbeit," *Imago*, Bd. XVIII, 1932.

we should qualify as an anal character. In obsessional neurosis we find the perpetual anxiety that a certain deed or thought might cause the death of a certain person, while primitive man practices this very form of killing by magic. The savage will never rack his brain or ponder about the future, he has no care for his next meal before he feels hunger, he does not pile up excremental symbols (money) as a guarantee against a dreaded state of famine, loss of life and pleasure. He is not pedantic and certainly not clean. There is no displacement of anal libidinal energies, no sublimation of these energies into the sphere of the superego or of the ego. If we try to ascertain the libidinal basis of ego functions we find, as in the case of the superego, that ego functions are built up on a basis of deflected oral- and phallic-sadistic trends. The process of becoming civilized means that the superego and ego gain ground at the expense of the id.

This generalized statement demands a commentary. A long list of peoples and a long list of civilizations are usually called primitive, but the description given above applies with certainty only to the Australians, and it may apply on the basis of the meager date we find in anthropological books also to the Pygmy tribes—in other words, to food gatherers. In the life of the people of Duau whom I know, and also in the lives of other New Guinea and Melanesian people, money, or something that for want of a better word we must translate as "money," plays a conspicuous role. The shell money in question signifies wealth, but even more than wealth it means social prestige. I have discussed the excremental symbolism of shell money in a paper published more than ten years ago,[18] and in my field notes I find several variants of an explanatory myth which accounts for the origin of the *kune* (Trobiand *kula*) by the story that once when a pig was killed for a feast, instead of fæces *bagi* (strings of red shells) and *mwari* (white arm shells) were found in its guts. As we have already observed, the great aim in life for everybody in Duau is to own *bagis* and *mwaris,* to be great in the *kune* and in making a *sagari* (that is, in piling up and distributing yams). But however "rich" anybody may be, this makes no difference in practical life; it does not mean less work and more pleasure. The *bagi* is only "held" for a short time, like the cup won by a football team, and the yams are only piled up to be distributed to strangers. I have called this state of things *narcissistic capitalism,* and it is probably a far more general phenomenon among semiprimitive societies than we might have suspected. The libidino-economic basis of these societies is the displacement of cathexis from the genital to the anal functions. In societies of this kind wealth means magic power and magic power means wealth. "The persistence with which the Yurok desire wealth is extraordinary. They are firmly convinced that persistent thinking of money will bring it. Particularly is this believed to

---

[18] "Heiliges Geld in Melanesien," *Internationale Zeitschrift für Psychoanalyse,* Bd. IX, 1923.

be true while one is engaged in any sweat-house occupation. As a man climbs the hill to gather sweat-house wood—always a meritorious practice in the sense that it tends to bring about fulfillment of wishes—he puts his mind on dentalia. He makes himself see them along the trail or hanging from fir trees eating the leaves. When he sees a tree that is particularly full of these visioned dentalia, he climbs it to cut its branches just below the top. In the sweat house he looks until he sees more money shells, perhaps peering in at him through the door." [19]

The narcissistic value of money is shown also in its opposition to coitus. Here again the dentalium money of the Yurok agrees with the magical power of other North American tribes.[20] "The Yurok hold a strong conviction that dentalium money and the congress of the sexes stand in a relation of inherent antithesis. This is the reason for the summer mating season: the shells would leave the house in which conjugal desires were satisfied and it is too cold and rainy to sleep outdoors in winter." [21]

The linking up of cleanliness, merit, power, and dentalium money clearly shows the beginnings of anal character formation, which although still an essentially narcissistic form of gratification, is beginning to transform a society of equals into a society of superiors and inferiors. "The beautiful skins or head-dresses or obsidians displayed at a dance by one rich man excite the interest and envy of visitors of wealth whereas poor men take notice but are not stirred. Such wealthy spectators return home determined to exhibit an even greater value of property the next year. Their effort in turn excites the first man to outdo all his competitors." [22] The desire for these anal symbols comes first, the practical application afterwards. *That is, originally people do not desire money because you can buy things for it, but you can buy things for money because people desire it.* It is a long way from narcissistic to real capitalism, and none of the people who are usually called primitive have overstepped this boundary. My definition of primitive people as possessing a superego based mainly on deflected oral and genital strivings applies to the food gatherers. Wherever we have agriculture—that is, the idea of providing for the future—we must assume a certain development of anal (sphincter) character. In the form of capitalism which I have called narcissistic, urethral elements (ambition, vanity) taken over from the food-gathering stage of development (Central-Australian ritual) play a conspicuous part beside the anal-libidinal components. It would be an interesting task to sketch the psychological history of mankind, how displaced libido transforms society and thus from the point of view of the individual transforms en-

[19] A. L. Kroeber: *Handbook of the Indians of California,* 1925, p. 41.

[20] Cf. the folk-tale motive of the hero who loses his power because he prefers woman to power: G. A. Dorsey: *The Pawnee,* 1906, Part I, p. 104. *Idem, The Mythology of the Wichita,* 1904, p. 254.

[21] Kroeber, *loc. cit.*

[22] Kroeber, *op. cit.,* p. 40.

vironment. The ego is then compelled to new adaptations, and the anal-sadistic energies which first underwent transformation from id impulses into elements of the superego now enter largely into the composition of the ego itself.

If we give up our descriptive point of view and adopt a dynamic outlook, we must say that the process of becoming civilized is identical with the extension and intensification of the scope of the superego. Important ego modifications are not the direct result of adaptation to environment, but of the pressure of the superego on the ego. But if we go on with our questions and inquire into the origin of the superego, the answer will be, if we confine ourselves to a general statement and avoid controversy: from the Oedipus complex, from the infantile situation. If we compare various races, people, and phases of culture with each other, the *prolongation of infancy* proceeds *pari passu* with cultural progress. The races which play a leading part in civilization arrive at puberty much later than primitive mankind. . . .

As a matter of fact, we find both in humanity and in the animal world that prolonged infancy and higher development go together. Prolonged infancy means the prolongation of the period in which traumas must be felt as such, and it is the psychical elaboration of these traumas (aggressions, libidinal traumas, Oedipus situation, primal scene, castration anxiety), the development of the superego, which differentiates man from his animal brethren. Sexually we are mature before our body is prepared to bear the brunt of this maturity, and somatically we counterbalance this retardation in ego development by psychical defense mechanisms. The infantile situation means prolonged helplessness and explains human evolution. In other words, ancestors became human just as the child grows up today, by a psychic elaboration of infantile traumas. The process of retardation which led us from the ape to primeval man has been continuing ever since, and by prolonging infancy increases the volume of traumas that come to bear on the individual. On the other hand, it is these traumas that supply the material out of which the superego is formed. Retardation[23] therefore means an ever-increasing intensification and extension of the superego. The latency period, which is the time of full superego formation in our own civilization, is absent or only faintly indicated among the most primitive races of mankind.

"If we consider once more the origin of the superego as we have described it," says Freud, "we shall perceive it to be the outcome of two highly important factors, one of them biological and the other historical: namely, the lengthy duration in man of the helplessness and dependence belonging to childhood, and the fact of his Oedipus complex, the repression of which we have shewn to be connected with the interruption of

[23] For the biological law of retardation cp. Bolk, *Das Problem der Menschwerdung*, 1926. Sir Arthur Keith, "The Evolution of the Human Races," *Journ. Roy. Anthr. Institute*, Vol. LXIII, 1928, p. 312.

libidinal development by the latency period [24] and so with the twofold onset of activity characteristic of man's sexual life." [25] We can therefore either say that primitive man has a more superficial type of superego, or —what amounts to the same thing—that the savage represents a less retarded variety of mankind. Being human means sacrificing the present for the sake of the future, prolonging fore-pleasure at the expense of end-pleasure. It means less happiness but more security.

In an important paper on the differences in the psychology of man and woman in civilized society Karen Horney describes the situation of the male child. Every boy behaves as if he were influenced by the idea that his genital should be larger because he compares his own penis with the genital organ of the mother. Hence the typically male attitude of regarding coitus as a task that must be achieved, and the latent anxiety regarding the size of the penis and regarding potency.

> Now one of the exigencies of the biological difference of the sexes is this: that the man is actually obliged to go on proving his manhood to the woman. There is no analogous necessity for her; even if she is frigid she can engage in sexual intercourse and conceive and bear a child. She performs her part by merely *being* without any *doing*—a fact which has always filled men with admiration and resentment. The man on the other hand has to *do* something in order to fulfil himself. The ideal of "efficiency" is a typical masculine ideal.[26]

A patient who is suffering from impotence dreams of impossible feats which he has to perform, of dragons or fiery steeds as antagonists in a fight, has horrible visions of a fish with a huge jaw full of teeth about to bite off his penis and at the same time feels his hands growing to inordinate dimensions. The dragons and other monsters are the parent, the heroic deed is coitus, and the greatness of the task in phantasy or dream life shows the quantity of anxiety that has to be dealt with in analysis. Heroic myth is therefore a mirror of the infantile situation: the hero is the little boy, and the imago of the mother is represented both by the heroine and by the dragon. Heroic myth is far more prominent in relatively civilized, semibarbarous communities than among real primitives. Food gatherers have no heroes like the Polynesian Maui, the Vedic Indra, the Germanic Thor, or the Hebrew Jahwe. A characteristic feature in the life of these heroes is that they stand alone against a host of giants, dragons, or otherwise superhuman, destructive beings, and the improbability of the victory increases the thrill of the deed. . . .

Central Australia has a mythology in which this heroic element is com-

[24] This "interruption" should be regarded as a specific instance of the general phenomenon of retardation.

[25] Freud: *The Ego and the Id,* pp. 45-46.

[26] K. Horney: "The Dread of Woman," *International Journal of Psycho-Analysis,* Vol. XIII, 1932, p. 359.

pletely absent. On the other hand, however, we find this same plot or situation (one human being against a host of supernaturals), which is also the nucleus of Eurasian *Märchen*, in Central Australian folk tales. The theme of these stories is the victory achieved by the *indatoa* (normal man) against a host of cannibal phallic giants, representatives of the parental imagos. But these stories, with the functional significance of overcoming infantile anxiety, are limited to the infantile part of the population, while the proper stuff for men are the ritual songs and myths in which the heroic element is lacking. The great deed of the hero-god, the dream of semibarbarous nations, may be regarded as foreshadowing the advent of our own form of civilization. We have evolved a state of things in which everybody must be a hero, must do something, achieve something, in order to become an ordinary adult male member of society. The architect must always build new houses and outdo his rivals, the author must invent new plots for books, the business man must develop his business, the employee tries to get a better employment: everybody is rushing about in a state of feverish haste, emphatically *doing* something —that is, continually *proving* his sexual potency. Civilized adults, like children, depend on an ever-increasing number of other adults for the gratification of their wishes. The process of growing up, once a biological process, has now become an achievement.

If we argue from the viewpoint of the theory of retardation, we come to the conclusion that "humanization" and "civilization" both mean a prolonging of the infancy period: which means that the savage is more infantile than the ape and civilized man more infantile than the savage. On the face of it this sounds rather absurd. But nobody would doubt the statement if it were applied merely to our body. The fact of retardation in becoming mature can be proved both for the savage as compared to the ape and for civilized man as compared to the savage. It is also obvious that our tendency to cling to infancy grows with civilization. There is a marked change even in the behaviour of the previous as compared to that of our own generation. People simply refuse to admit that such a thing as age exists. Rejuvenation is a civilized problem, whether we consider it as it appears in alchemy, in *Faust,* or in modern movements, and finally in the experiments of Steinach and Voronoff. However, we cannot doubt that in many respects the savage is psychologically a child while we are something different. Lack of care for the morrow, an egoistic and narcissistic temperament, instability and liability to sudden outbursts, are characteristic both of the denizens of the jungle and of the nursery. We are something different, and for want of a better word we may call this state of things "being adult." By "we" I do not mean, in this case, the analytical ideal, but rather the average member of a civilized community. This form of "growing up" differs considerably from animal maturity, which is a perfect, but not easily modified, rigid adaptation to the outer world. The change that has taken place is obviously regressive, caused by an increasing development of the infantile situation. Thus the psychological corollary of the biological process of retardation is not psychical infantilism but a state of things that is brought about by a series of mechanisms evolved out of the infantile situation, and evolved in order to cope with the anxiety which is the consequence of the infantile situation.

We should therefore distinguish three forms of being adult: (1) the animal; (2) the civilized; (3) the analyzed. Type 3 is a return of type 1 on a higher plane, containing adaptation to a more complicated form of reality and the additional quality of elasticity. Type 2 contains all the peculiar forms of personality distortion which we undergo in consequence of anxiety, or rather of the defense mechanisms developed for the purpose of dealing with this infantile anxiety. Thus the real psychical parallel to the biological process of retardation lies in the sentence: we become adult (type 2) in consequence of the modifications we are subject to in the infantile situation. The prolonging of the infantile situation means an increasing weight bearing on the genital position, and the losses suffered in this battle by the latter indicate the successive phases of civilization. In my previous publications I have arrived at the theory of retardation through what I have called the ontogenetic theory of culture. This means, as indicated above, the idea of culture as conditioned by a habitual infantile trauma, and then the further conclusion that the process of becoming human in general is due to a universal infantile "trauma," to some modification in the parent-child situation. This theory explains two things: human culture in general and the specialized forms evolved in certain areas. The evolution of the latter is determined by exogenous, "historical" factors, by things that happen to the child. It seems, however, that we can also answer a question that has been asked by English psychoanalysts regarding the developmental phases of human culture.[27] The researches of Melanie Klein, Edward Glover, and others have shown that the infantile situation calls forth a series of phantasy systems and corresponding mechanisms, and the question is whether anthropology has anything similar to offer in the development of culture. Certain striking similarities between these phantasy systems and anthropological data make me believe that this question can be answered in the affirmative. If this is correct, the next conclusion would be that there are two types of modification in human culture, and that one of these is comparable to an individual neurosis, which, although it can be classified under one of the general clinical formulas, yet contains elements common to several of these systems and is built up chiefly on the early experiences of the individual. This is what we call the special forms assumed by civilization and society in different areas. The other type refers to successive phases and the corresponding typical innate mechanisms, to a series of attempts

[27] Cf. E. Glover: "Common Problems in Psycho-Analysis and Anthropology," *British Journal of Medical Psychology*, Vol. XII, 1932, p. 112.

at dealing with the same difficulties which are always ready for use and will always be made use of in the same order of succession. . . .

The various "systems" in which human culture develops may thus be viewed as a series of attempts to deal with infantile anxieties. It is probable that the part-object and body-destruction system is followed everywhere by a fully developed Oedipus system with castration symbolism. A third form of culture corresponds with the constructive games the aim of which is to rebuild the body of the mother. It uses the phantasy system of the first type of anxiety, but overcompensates and libidinizes the destructive element. In Papuan matrilinear civilization, Mother-Earth, the village, the house, and the canoe are symbols of the reconstructed and protective mother. It seems probable that all these and other systems of dealing with the fundamental problem of anxiety are utilized consecutively, and that in each phantasy system the id aims and the ego undergo modifications. But these modifications are not due to the pressure of reality. Rather we must regard them as defeats in the struggle with the superego —that is, as due to the biological fact of a prolonged infancy. The same environment which did not compel the chimpanzee to modify its ego structure could not have brought about this modification in man had it not been for the fact of our retarded development.

We have suggested that the myth of the Golden Age contains an element of truth not only in its ontogenetic but also in its phylogenetic interpretation. The following lines of Ovid's poem may serve to confirm this suggestion:

> Poena metusque aberant, nec verba minacia fixo
> aere legebantur, nec supplex turba timebat
> iudicis ora sui, sed erant sine vindice tuti.[28]

The absence of anxiety of punishment and of the "judge" (superego) are truly characteristic not only of the beginnings of the individual but also of the prehuman days of our race. It is through a series of complicated mechanisms of dealing with anxiety that our civilization has developed and is still developing. But if the Myth of the Golden Age in the past is more than a projection of human infancy to the cradle of our race, may we ascribe the same degree of reality to the utopian hopes of mankind, to the belief in a Golden Age that is to come? In these days of darkness, when the old ideal of individual liberty and happiness has nearly disappeared, can we still believe that Falstaff is not dead [29] and that the ardent desire of mankind for unhappiness, as manifested in all anti-individualistic political systems, may in the future again give way to the opposite tendency? It is difficult to reconcile the desire for an optimistic

[28] Ovid, *Metamorphoses*, Book I, 91 *seq.*
[29] Cp. Franz Alexander: "A note on Falstaff," *The Psychoanalytic Quarterly*, Vol. II, 1933, p. 592.

outlook with the view expressed in my book, *The Riddle of the Sphinx*. There I regarded the evolution of mankind as proceeding from bad to worse and a sort of inverted Couéism as the formula of human history.[30] As I maintained there, the factor which since the dawn of humanity has been at work at developing civilization at the expense of happiness is the death impulse or destructive impulse as active through the superego. It is interesting to observe that this view of history is in accordance with the myth:

> Tertia post illam successit aënea proles
> saevior ingeniis et ad horrida promptior arma.

The complicated series of attempts to deal with infantile aggression and anxiety libidinal trends and ego defense mechanisms evolved in consequence of delayed maturity or retardation are superimposed one on another, and result in all the troubles and cataclysms, in all the neurosis and unhappiness, in all the peculiar psychotic mass movements which are so characteristic of our civilization. Perhaps, however, we should again follow the lead of the myth and assume a repetition of cycles in nature, a kind of recommencement like the process started in analysis.[31] Then we might hope for an acceleration of the process of growing up, for the great effort to be made by Eros,[32] for the return of something like the Golden Age as foretold by Virgil (4th Eclogue):[33]

> Ultima Cymaei venit iam carminis aetas;
> magnus ab integro saeclorum nascitur ordo.
> Iam redit et Virgo, redeunt Saturnia regna;
> iam nova progenies caelo demittitur alto.

[30] [A system of psychotherapy, introduced by Emile Coué (1857-1926), based upon autosuggestion of health. *B.M.*]

[31] Cp. Bálint: "Characteranalyse und Neubeginn," *Internationale Zeitschrift für Psychoanalyse*, Bd. XX, 1934, S. 54.

[32] Freud: *Civilisation and its Discontents*, 1930, p. 144.

[33] On the mythological significance of this poem, see E. Vorden, *Die Geburt des Kindes* (Studien der Bibliothek, Wartburg), 1924.

Part II

THE APPLICATION
OF PSYCHOANALYSIS TO HISTORY

The Next Assignment

William L. Langer

Anyone who, like myself, has the honor to serve as president of this association and to address it on the occasion of its annual meeting may be presumed to have devoted many years to the historical profession, to have taught many successive college generations, to have trained numerous young scholars, and to have written at least some books and articles. The chances are great that he has reached those exalted levels of the academic life which involve so many administrative and advisory duties, as well as such expenditure of time and energy in seeing people, in writing recommendations, and in reading the writings of others that he is most unlikely ever again to have much time to pursue his own researches. Nonetheless, his long and varied experience and his ever-broadening contacts with others working in many diverse fields have probably sharpened his understanding of the problems of his own profession and enhanced his awareness of the many lacunae in our knowledge of the world and of mankind, both in the past and in the present. It would seem altogether fitting, therefore, that I, for one, should make use of this occasion not so much for reflection on the past achievements of the profession (which is what might be expected of a historian), as for speculation about its needs and its future—that is, about the directions which historical study might profitably take in the years to come.

I am sure to sense, at this juncture, a certain uneasiness in my audience,

"The Next Assignment." Reprinted from *The American Historical Review*, LXIII, No. 2 (January, 1958), pp. 283-304. Copyright 1958 by *The American Historical Review*. [Presidential address at the annual dinner of The American Historical Association, at the Statler Hotel, New York City, December 29, 1957.]

for historians, having dedicated their lives to the exploration and under-standing of the past, are apt to be suspicious of novelty and ill-disposed toward crystal gazing. In the words of my distinguished predecessor, they lack the "speculative audacity" of the natural scientists, those artisans of brave hypotheses. This tendency on the part of historians to become buried in their own conservatism strikes me as truly regrettable. What basically may be a virtue tends to become a vice, locking our intellectual faculties in the molds of the past and preventing us from opening new horizons as our cousins in the natural sciences are constantly doing. If progress is to be made, we must certainly have new ideas, new points of view, and new techniques. We must be ready, from time to time, to take flyers into the unknown, even though some of them may prove wide of the mark. Like the scientists, we can learn a lot from our own mistakes, and the chances are that, if we persist, each successive attempt may take us closer to the target. I should therefore like to ask myself this evening what direction is apt to lead to further progress in historical study; what direction, if I were a younger man, would claim my interest and atten-tion; in short, what might be the historian's "next assignment."

We are all keenly aware of the fact that during the past half-century the scope of historical study has been vastly extended. The traditional politi-cal-military history has become more comprehensive and more analytical and has been reinforced by researches into the social, economic, intellec-tual, scientific, and other aspects of the past, some of them truly remote from what used to be considered history. So far has this development gone that I find it difficult to envisage much further horizontal expansion of the area of investigation.

There is, however, still ample scope for penetration in depth, and I, personally, have no doubt that the "newest history" will be more inten-sive and probably less extensive. I refer more specifically to the urgently needed deepening of our historical understanding through exploitation of the concepts and findings of modern psychology. And by this, may I add, I do not refer to classical or academic psychology, which, so far as I can detect, has little bearing on historical problems, but rather to psycho-analysis and its later developments and variations as included in the terms "dynamic" or "depth psychology."

In the course of my reading over the years I have been much impressed by the prodigious impact of psychoanalytic doctrine on many, not to say most, fields of human study and expression. Of Freud himself it has been said that "he has in large part created the intellectual climate of our time." [1] "Almost alone," remarks a recent writer in the *Times Literary Supplement,* "he revealed the deepest sources of human endeavor and remorselessly pursued their implications for the individual and society." [2]

[1] "Freud and the Arts," London *Times Literary Supplement,* May 4, 1956.
[2] *Ibid.* See also Abram Kardiner, *The Psychological Frontiers of Society* (New York, 1945), p. 11; Goodwin Watson, "Clio and Psyche: Some Interrelations of Psychology

Once the initial resistance to the recognition of unconscious, irrational forces in human nature was overcome, psychoanalysis quickly became a dominant influence in psychiatry, in abnormal psychology, and in personality study. The field of medicine is feeling its impact not only in the area of psychosomatic illness, but in the understanding of the doctor-patient relationship. Our whole educational system and the methods of child training have been modified in the light of its findings. For anthropology it has opened new and wider vistas by providing for the first time "a theory of raw human nature" and by suggesting an explanation of otherwise incomprehensible cultural traits and practices. It has done much also to revise established notions about religion and has given a great impetus to pastoral care and social work. The problems of mythology and sociology have been illuminated by its insights, and more recently its influence has been strongly felt in penology, in political science, and even in economics, while in the arts almost every major figure of the past generation has been in some measure affected by it.[3]

Despite this general and often profound intellectual and artistic reorientation since Freud published his first epoch-making works sixty years ago, historians have, as a group, maintained an almost completely negative attitude toward the teachings of psychoanalysis. Their lack of response has been due, I should think, less to constitutional obscurantism than to the fact that historians, as disciples of Thucydides, have habitually thought of themselves as psychologists in their own right. They have indulged freely in psychological interpretation, and many no doubt have shared the fear that the humanistic appreciation of personality, as in poetry or drama, might be irretrievably lost through the application of a coldly penetrating calculus.[4] Many considered the whole psychoanalytic

and History," in *The Cultural Approach to History*, ed. Caroline Ware (New York, 1940), pp. 34-47; Hans W. Gruhle, *Geschichtsschreibung und Psychologie* (Bonn, 1953), p. 7; *The Social Sciences in Historical Study*, Social Science Research Council Bull. No. 64 (New York, 1954), pp. 61 ff.

[3] See the article by Henry W. Brosin, "A Review of the Influence of Psychoanalysis on Current Thought," in *Dynamic Psychiatry*, ed. Franz Alexander and Helen Ross (Chicago, 1952), pp. 508-53; Ernest Jones, *What Is Psychoanalysis?* (new ed., New York, 1948), pp. 80 ff.; Iago Galdston, ed., *Freud and Contemporary Culture* (New York, 1957). See also J. A. Gengerelli, "Dogma or Discipline?" *Saturday Review*, Mar. 23, 1957; Gardner Murphy, "The Current Impact of Freud upon Psychology," *Amer. Psychologist*, XI (1956), 663-72; A. Irving Hallowell, "Culture, Personality and Society," in *Anthropology Today*, A. L. Kroeber (Chicago, 1953), pp. 597-620; Clyde Kluckhohn, "The Influence of Psychiatry on Anthropology in America during the Past One Hundred Years," in *One Hundred Years of American Psychiatry*, ed. J. K. Hall (New York, 1944), pp. 589-618, and "Politics, History and Psychology," *World Politics*, VIII (1955), 112-23; Harold D. Lasswell, "Impact of Psychoanalytic Thinking on the Social Sciences," in *The State of the Social Sciences*, ed. Leonard D. White (Chicago, 1956), pp. 84-115; R. Money-Kyrle, *Superstition and Society* (London, 1939); Walter A. Weisskopf, *The Psychology of Economics* (Chicago, 1955); Erich Fromm, *Psychoanalysis and Religion* (New Haven, 1950); F. J. Hoffman, *Freudianism and the Literary Mind* (Baton Rouge, 1945); Louis Schneider, *The Psychoanalyst and the Artist* (New York, 1950).

[4] Raymond B. Cattell, *An Introduction to Personality Study* (London, 1950), pp. 13-14. H. D. Lasswell, *Psychopathology and Politics* (Chicago, 1930), p. 11, refers to "the

doctrine too biological and too deterministic, as well as too conjectural, and they were, furthermore, reluctant to recognize and deal with unconscious motives and irrational forces. Psychoanalysis, on the other hand, was still a young science and therefore lacked the prestige to make historians acquire a guilt complex about not being more fully initiated into its mysteries.[5] Almost without exception, then, they have stuck to the approach and methods of historicism, restricting themselves to recorded fact and to strictly rational motivation.[6] So impervious was the profession as a whole to the new teaching that an inquiry into the influence of psychoanalysis on modern thought, written a few years ago, made no mention whatever of history.[7]

This is as remarkable as it is lamentable, for, on the very face of it, psychoanalysis would seem to have much to contribute to the solution of historical problems. Many years of clinical work by hundreds of trained analysts have by now fortified and refined Freud's original theory of human drives, the conflicts to which they give rise, and the methods by which they are repressed or diverted. Psychoanalysis has long since ceased being merely a therapy and has been generally recognized as a theory basic to the study of the human personality. How can it be that the historian, who must be as much or more concerned with human beings and their motivation than with impersonal forces and causation, has failed to make use of these findings? Viewed in the light of modern depth psychology, the homespun, commonsense psychological interpretations of past historians, even some of the greatest, seem woefully inadequate, not to say naïve.[8] Clearly the time has come for us to reckon with a doctrine that strikes so close to the heart of our own discipline:[9]

---

obscurantist revulsion against submitting the sacred mystery of personality to the coarse indignity of exact investigation." Keats is said to have feared that spectrum analysis would ruin his enjoyment of the rainbow. See Jones, *What is Psychoanalysis?* pp. 12 ff.

[5] Sidney Ratner, "The Historian's Approach to Psychology," *Jour. Hist. Ideas*, II (1941), 95-109.

[6] Edward N. Saveth, "The Historian and the Freudian Approach to History," *New York Times Book Review*, Jan. 1, 1956; Gruhle, *Geschichtsschreibung und Psychologie*, pp. 116 ff.; Richard L. Schoenwald, "Historians and the Challenge of Freud," *Western Humanities Rev.*, X (1956), 99-108.

[7] Brosin, "Review of Influence of Psychoanalysis on Current Thought."

[8] Gruhle, *op. cit.*, pp. 127 ff., cites a number of instances from the writings of eminent German historians, and Max Horkheimer, "Geschichte und Psychologie," *Zeitschrift für Sozialforschung*, I (1932), 125-44, argues the complete inadequacy of the psychological concepts of the classical economists. Alfred M. Tozzer, "Biography and Biology," in *Personality in Nature, Society, and Culture*, ed. Clyde Kluckhohn and H. A. Murray (2d ed., New York, 1953), pp. 226-39, plays havoc with the simple-minded biological twist in much biographical writing.

[9] This thought is more or less explicitly expressed by Louis Gottschalk, "The Historian and the Historical Document," in *The Use of Personal Documents in History, Anthropology and Sociology*, Social Science Research Council Bull. No. 53 (New York, 1945), and in *The Social Sciences in Historical Study*. See also Sir Lewis Namier, "Human Nature in Politics," in his *Personalities and Powers* (London, 1955); Schoenwald, "Historians and the Challenge of Freud."

Since psychoanalysis is concerned primarily with the emotional life of the individual, its most immediate application is in the field of biography. Freud himself here showed the way, first in his essay on Leonardo da Vinci (1910) and later in his analytical study of Dostoevsky (1928). He was initially impressed by the similarity between some of the material produced by a patient in analysis and the only recorded childhood recollection of the Italian artist. With this fragmentary memory as a starting point, Freud studied the writings and artistic productions of Leonardo and demonstrated how much light could be shed on his creative and scientific life through the methods of analysis. No doubt he erred with respect to certain points of art history. Quite possibly some of his deductions were unnecessarily involved or farfetched. Nonetheless, recent critics have testified that he was able, "thanks to his theory and method, and perhaps even more to his deep sympathy for the tragic and the problematic in Leonardo, to pose altogether new and important questions about his personality, questions which were unsuspected by earlier writers and to which no better answer than Freud's has yet been given." [10]

The striking novelty and the startling conclusions of Freud's essay on Leonardo had much to do with precipitating the flood of psychoanalytic or, better, pseudo-psychoanalytic biographical writing during the 1920's. Almost all of this was of such a low order—ill-informed, sensational, scandalizing—that it brought the entire Freudian approach into disrepute. I have no doubt that this, in turn, discouraged serious scholars—the historians among them—from really examining the possibilities of the new teachings. Only within the last generation has the situation begun to change. The basic concepts of psychoanalysis, such as the processes of repression, identification, projection, reaction formation, substitution, displacement, and sublimation, have become more firmly established through clinical work and have at the same time increasingly become part of our thinking. Meanwhile, concerted efforts have been made to build up systematic personality and character study on a psychoanalytic basis, and the so-called neo-Freudians, advancing beyond the narrowly environmental factors, have done much to develop the significance of constitutional and cultural influences.[11]

While recognized scholars in related fields, notably in political science, have begun to apply psychoanalytic principles to the study of personality

[10] Meyer Shapiro, "Leonardo and Freud: An Art-Historical Study," *Jour. Hist. Ideas,* XVII (1956), 147-78, and other critics there cited.

[11] Fromm, "Die psychoanalytische Charakterologie und ihre Bedeutung für die Sozialpsychologie," *Zeits. f. Sozialforschung,* I (1932), 253-77, and *Psychology and Religion,* pp. 10 ff.; Karen Horney, *The Neurotic Personality of Our Time* (New York, 1937), chap. I; Franz Alexander, *Fundamentals of Psychoanalysis* (New York, 1948), chap. VI; Ralph Linton, *The Cultural Development of Personality* (New York, 1945); Kardiner, *Psychological Frontiers of Society,* esp. chap. XIV; Gerald S. Blum, *Psychoanalytic Theories of Personality* (New York, 1953); Gordon W. Allport, *Becoming: Basic Considerations for a Psychology of Personality* (New Haven, 1955); Georges Friedmann, "Psychoanalysis and Sociology," *Diogenes,* No. 14 (1956), 17-35.

types and their social role, historians have for the most part approved of the iron curtain between their own profession and that of the dynamic psychologists. It is, indeed, still professionally dangerous to admit any addiction to such unorthodox doctrine.[12] Even those who are in general intrigued by the potentialities of psychoanalysis are inclined to argue against its application to historical problems. They point out that evidence on the crucial early years of an individual's life is rarely available and that, unlike the practicing analyst, the historian cannot turn to his subject and help him revive memories of specific events and relationships. To this it may be answered that the historian, on whatever basis he is operating, is always suffering from lack of data. Actually there is often considerable information about the family background of prominent historical personalities, and the sum total of evidence about their careers is in some cases enormous. Furthermore, the experiences of earliest childhood are no longer rated as important for later development as was once the case, and the historian, if he cannot deal with his subject as man to man, at least has the advantage of surveying his whole career and being able to observe the functioning of significant forces.[13] In any event, we historians must, if we are to retain our self-respect, believe that we can do better with the available evidence than the untrained popular biographer to whom we have so largely abandoned the field.

The historian is, of course, less interested in the individual as such than in the impact of certain individuals upon the society of their time and, beyond that, in the behavior of men as members of the group, society, or culture. This leads us into the domain of social or collective psychology, a subject on which much has been written during the past twenty-five years, especially in this country, but in which progress continues to be slight because of the difficulty of distinguishing satisfactorily between large groups and small groups, between organized and unorganized aggregations, between such vague collectivities as the crowd, the mob, and the mass.[14] Much certainly remains to be done in this area, especially in the elaboration of a theory to bridge the gap between individual and collective psychology.

Freud himself became convinced, at an early date, that his theories

---

[12] Bernard Brodie, in his review of the excellent study of *Woodrow Wilson and Colonel House* (New York, 1957) by Alexander and Juliette George, notes that the authors, while using very effectively the concepts of psychoanalysis, are scrupulous not to mention the fact. "A Psychoanalytic Interpretation of Woodrow Wilson," *World Politics*, IX (1957), 413-22. [The same comment appears to hold for the article by Renzo Sereno, "A Falsification by Machiavelli," which we reprint along with the Brodie review in this anthology. *B.M.*]

[13] Gruhle, *Geschichtsschreibung und Psychologie*, pp. 127 ff.

[14] Gustave Le Bon, *La psychologie des foules*, was published in 1895. The earliest texts, those of William McDougall, *An Introduction to Social Psychology*, and of Edward A. Ross, *Social Psychology*, were first published in 1908. See M. Brewster Smith, "Some Recent Texts in Social Psychology," *Psychological Bull.*, L (1953), 150-59.

might have a certain applicability to historical and cultural problems.[15] He accepted the conclusions of Gustave Le Bon's well-known study of the psychology of crowds (1895) and recognized that a group may develop "a sort of collective mind." [16] As the years went by, his clinical work led him to the conclusion that there were close parallels between the development of the individual and of the race. Thus, the individual's unconscious mind was, in a sense, the repository of the past experiences of his society, if not of mankind.[17] In his most daring and provocative works, *Totem and Taboo* (1913) and his last book, *Moses and Monotheism* (1939), Freud tried to determine the effect of group experience on the formation of a collective group mind.

Anthropologists, like historians, will probably continue to reject Freud's historical ventures as too extravagantly speculative, but the fact remains that anthropological and sociological researches suggest ever more definitely that certain basic drives and impulses, as identified by Freud, appear in all cultures and that the differences between cultures derive largely from varying methods of dealing with these drives.[18] Furthermore, social psychologists are increasingly aware of the similarity in the operation of irrational forces in the individual and in society.[19] Everett D. Martin, an early but unusually discerning student of the subject, noted in 1920 that the crowd, like our dream life, provides an outlet for repressed emotions: "It is as if all at once an unspoken agreement were entered into whereby each member might let himself go, on condition that he approved the same thing in all the rest." A crowd, according to Martin, "is a device for indulging ourselves in a kind of temporary insanity by all going crazy together." [20] Similarly, Freud's erstwhile disciple, C. G. Jung, has characterized recent political mass movements as "psychic epidemics, i.e. mass psychoses," and others have noted that the fears and rages of mass movements are clearly the residue of childish emotions.[21]

All this, as aforesaid, still requires further exploration. It does seem, however, that we shall have to learn to reckon with the concept of "collective mentality," even on the unconscious level, and that the traits of that mentality—normally submerged and operative only in association

[15] Freud's letter to C. G. Jung, July 5, 1910, quoted in Ernest Jones, *The Life and Work of Sigmund Freud,* II (New York, 1955), 448-49.

[16] Freud, *Group Psychology and the Analysis of the Ego* (New York, 1921).

[17] Jones, *What is Psychoanalysis?* pp. 20 ff.

[18] Géza Róheim, *Psychoanalysis and Anthropology* (New York, 1950).

[19] Kluckhohn, "The Impact of Freud on Anthropology," in *Freud and Contemporary Culture,* pp. 66-72.

[20] *The Behavior of Crowds* (New York, 1920), pp. 35-36. Martin was well versed in the psychoanalytical literature of his time.

[21] Jung, quoted by Ira Progoff, *Jung's Psychology and Its Social Meaning* (New York, 1953), p. ix; Erik H. Erikson, "The First Psychoanalyst," *Yale Rev.,* XLVI (1956), 40-62; Melitta Schmideberg, "Zum Verständnis massenpsychologischer Erscheinungen," *Imago,* XXI (1935), 445-57.

with others or in specific settings—can best be studied as a part of, or extension of, individual psychology. That is to say that progress in social psychology probably depends on ever more highly refined analysis of the individual—his basic motivations, his attitudes, beliefs, hopes, fears, and aspirations.[22]

Perhaps I may digress at this point to remind you of Georges Lefebvre's long-standing interest and concern with the character and role of mobs and crowds in the French Revolution, and especially of his impressive study of the mass hysteria of 1789 known as "The Great Fear." Although Lefebvre thought Le Bon superficial and confused, he was convinced by his own researches that there was such a thing as a "collective mentality." Indeed, he considered it the true causal link between the origins and the effects of major crises.[23] Without specific reference to psychoanalytic concepts, Lefebvre arrived at conclusions altogether consonant with those of modern psychology. His truly impressive studies in a sense prefaced the more recent analyses of totalitarian movements which, in my estimation, have so clearly demonstrated the vast possibilities that have been opened to social scientists by the findings of dynamic psychology.[24]

As historians we must be particularly concerned with the problem whether major changes in the psychology of a society or culture can be traced, even in part, to some severe trauma suffered in common—that is, with the question whether whole communities, like individuals, can be profoundly affected by some shattering experience. If it is indeed true that every society or culture has a "unique psychological fabric," deriving at least in part from past common experiences and attitudes, it seems reasonable to suppose that any great crisis, such as famine, pestilence, natural disaster, or war, should leave its mark on the group, the intensity and duration of the impact depending, of course, on the nature and magnitude of the crisis. I hasten to say in advance that I do not, of course, imagine the psychological impact of such crises to be uniform for all members of the population, for if modern psychology has demonstrated anything it is the proposition that in any given situation individuals will

---

[22] See esp. Fromm, "Über Methode und Aufgabe einer analytischen Sozialpsychologie," *Zeits. f. Sozialforschung*, I (1932), 28-54.

[23] Lefebvre, "Foules révolutionnaires," in his *Études sur la révolution française* (Paris, 1954), pp. 271-87, and *La grande peur de 1789* (Paris, 1932). Philip Rieff, "The Origins of Freud's Political Psychology," *Jour. Hist. Ideas*, XVII (1956), 233-49, is equally hard on Le Bon.

[24] To mention a few titles: Nathan Leites, *A Study of Bolshevism* (Glencoe, Ill., 1953); Gabriel A. Almond, *et al., The Appeals of Communism* (Princeton, 1954); Hannah Arendt, *The Origins of Totalitarianism* (New York, 1951); the essay by Henry Pachter in *The Third Reich*, ed. M. Baumont, J. H. E. Fried, and E. Vermeil (New York, 1955) and the discussion of it by Carl E. Schorske, "A New Look at the Nazi Movement," *World Politics*, IX (1956), 88-97. See also Hadley Cantril, *The Psychology of Social Movements* (New York, 1941), for a discussion of various modern mass movements, and Raymond A. Bauer, "The Psycho-Cultural Approach to Soviet Studies," *World Politics*, VII (1954), 119-32, for a critical review of several analyses of Soviet society.

react in widely diverse ways, depending on their constitution, their family background, their early experiences, and other factors. But these varying responses are apt to be reflected chiefly in the immediate effects of the catastrophe. Over the long term (which is of greater interest to the historian) it seems likely that the group would react in a manner most nearly corresponding to the underlying requirements of the majority of its members—in other words, that despite great variations as between individuals there would be a dominant attitudinal pattern.

I admit that all this is hypothetical and that we are here moving into unexplored territory, but allow me to examine a specific problem which, though remote from the area of my special competence, is nevertheless one to which I have devoted much study and thought. Perhaps I may begin by recalling Freud's observation that contemporary man, living in a scientific age in which epidemic disease is understood and to a large extent controlled, is apt to lose appreciation of the enormous, uncomprehended losses of life in past generations, to say nothing of the prolonged and widespread emotional strain occasioned by such disasters.[25] Some exception must be made here for historians of the ancient world who, since the days of Niebuhr, have concerned themselves with the possible effects of widespread disease and high mortality on the fate of the Mediterranean civilizations. Some have made a strong case for the proposition that malaria, which seems to have first appeared in Greece and Italy in the fourth or fifth centuries B.C., soon became endemic and led on the one hand to serious debilitation, sloth, and unwillingness to work, and on the other to excitability, brutality, and general degradation. Recent researches suggest that malaria may have been one of the main causes of the collapse of the Etruscan civilization and may have accounted, at least in part, for the change in Greek character after the fourth century, especially for the growing lack of initiative, the prevalent cowardice, and the increasing trend toward cruelty. With reference to the fate of the Roman Empire, Professor Arthur Boak has recently re-examined the striking loss of population in the third and fourth centuries A.D. and has attributed it largely to the great epidemics of A.D. 165-180 and 250-280, thus reaffirming the view of Niebuhr and others that the Empire never really recovered from these tragic visitations.[26]

The literature on these and subsequent epidemics is, however, devoted largely to their medical and sanitational aspects, or at most to their economic and social effects. My primary interest, as I have said, is with the

[25] Freud, "Thoughts for the Times on War and Death" (1915), in *Collected Papers* (London, 1924-1934), IV, No. 17.

[26] W. H. S. Jones, *Dea Febris: A Study of Malaria in Ancient Italy* (n.p., n.d.) and *Malaria and Greek History* (Manchester, 1909); Jones, Major R. Ross, and G. G. Ellet, *Malaria, a Neglected Factor in the History of Greece and Rome* (Cambridge, 1907); Nello Toscanelli, *La malaria nell'antichità e la fine degli Etruschi* (Milan, 1927), esp. pp. 237 ff.; A. E. R. Boak, *Manpower Shortage and the Fall of the Roman Empire in the West* (Ann Arbor, Mich., 1955).

possible long-range psychological repercussions. To study these I think we may well pass over the great plague of Athens in 430 B.C., so vividly reported by Thucydides, and the so-called plague of Justinian of the sixth century A.D., not because they were unimportant but because there is much more voluminous and instructive information about the Black Death of 1348-1349 and the ensuing period of devastating disease.

Western Europe seems to have been relatively free from major epidemics in the period from the sixth to the fourteenth century, and it may well be that the revival of trade and the growth of towns, with their congestion and lack of sanitation, had much to do with the spread and establishment of the great mortal diseases like plague, typhus, syphilis, and influenza.[27] At any rate, the Black Death was worse than anything experienced prior to that time and was, in all probability, the greatest single disaster that has ever befallen European mankind. In most localities a third or even a half of the population was lost within the space of a few months, and it is important to remember that the great visitation of 1348-1349 was only the beginning of a period of pandemic disease with a continuing frightful drain of population. It is hardly an exaggeration to say that for three hundred years Europe was ravaged by one disease or another, or more usually by several simultaneously, the serious outbreaks coming generally at intervals of five to ten years.[28] Professor Lynn Thorndike, who thirty years ago wrote in the *American Historical Review* of the blight of pestilence on early modern civilization, pointed out that the period of greatest affliction was that of the Renaissance, and especially the years from about 1480 until 1540, during which period frequent severe outbreaks of bubonic plague were reinforced by attacks of typhus fever and by the onset of the great epidemic of syphilis, to say nothing of the English Sweat (probably influenza) which repeatedly devastated England before invading the Continent in 1529. The bubonic plague began to die out in western Europe only in the late seventeenth century, to disappear almost completely after the violent outbreak at Marseilles in 1720. But the Balkans and Middle East continued to suffer from it until well into the nineteenth century, and the pandemic that broke out in India in the 1890's was evidently comparable to the Black Death in terms of mortality and duration.[29]

The extensive records of the Black Death have been long and carefully studied, not only with reference to their medical aspects, but also in connection with the economic and social effects of so sudden and substantial a loss of population. The English population is estimated to have fallen from 3,700,000 in 1348 to 2,100,000 in 1400, the mortality rates of the

[27] Bernard M. Lersch, *Geschichte der Volksseuchen* (Berlin, 1896), pp. 52 ff.; L. Fabian Hirst, *The Conquest of Plague* (Oxford, 1953), p. 10. It is highly likely that the arrival of rats in Europe in the twelfth century had an important bearing on the spread of bubonic plague. See Hans Zinsser, *Rats, Lice and History* (Boston, 1935), pp. 195 ff.; Major Greenwood, *Epidemics and Crowd-Diseases* (New York, 1937), pp. 289 ff.

[28] [See the original article for a long list of references. *B.M.*]

[29] [See the original article for list of references. *B.M.*]

period 1348-1375 far exceeding those of modern India. While the figures for continental countries are less complete, the available data suggest that the losses were comparable.[30] Cities and towns suffered particularly, but in some areas as many as 40 per cent of the villages and hamlets were abandoned, the survivors joining with those of other settlements or moving to the depopulated towns where opportunity beckoned.[31] Although a generation ago there was a tendency, especially among English historians, to minimize the social effects of the Black Death, more recent writers like G. G. Coulton, for example, acknowledge that the great epidemic, if it did not evoke entirely new forces, did vastly accelerate those already operative.[32] The economic progress of Europe, which had been phenomenal in the thirteenth century, came to a halt and was soon followed by a prolonged depression lasting until the mid-fifteenth century and in a sense even into the seventeenth.[33]

I make only the most fleeting reference to these questions, because my chief concern, as I have said, is to determine, if possible, what the long-term psychological effects of this age of disease may have been. The immediate horrors of great epidemics have been vividly described by eminent writers from Thucydides to Albert Camus and have been pictured on canvas by famous artists like Raphael and Delacroix.[34] At news of the approach of the disease a haunting terror seizes the population, in the Middle Ages leading on the one hand to great upsurges of repentance in the form of flagellant processions and on the other to a mad search

[30] [See the original article for list of references. *B.M.*]

[31] [See the original article for list of references. *B.M.*]

[32] [See the original article for list of references. *B.M.*]

[33] So eminent an authority as Wilhelm Abel, "Wachstumsschwankungen mitteleuropäischer Völker seit dem Mittelalter," *Jahrb. f. Nationalökonomie u. Statistik*, CXLII (1935), 670-92, holds that pestilence, famine, and war were not enough to account for the enormous decline in population and that psychological forces, as yet unanalyzed, led to a reluctance to marry and raise a family. E. J. Hobsbawm, "The General Crisis of the European Economy in the 17th Century," *Past and Present* (1954), No. 5, 33-53 and No. 6, 44-65, notes that the economic crisis, which had been in process since about 1300, came to an end at just about the time the plague died out. On the general economic depression see especially M. Postan, "Revisions in Economic History: the Fifteenth Century," *Econ. Hist. Rev.*, IX (1939), 160-67; John Saltmarsh, "Plague and Economic Decline in England in the Later Middle Ages," *Cambridge Hist. Jour.*, VII (1941), 23-41; Edouard Perroy, "Les crises du xiv⁰ siècle," *Annales*, IV (1949), 167-82, who stresses the fact that the Black Death created a demographic crisis, superimposed on a food crisis (1315-1320) and a financial crisis (1335-1345); Robert S. Lopez, "The Trade of Medieval Europe: The South," *Cambridge Economic History of Europe*, II (Cambridge, 1952), pp. 338 ff.; Postan, "The Trade of Medieval Europe: The North," *ibid.*, pp. 191 ff.; and Lopez's review of M. Mollat's *Le Commerce maritime normand à la fin du moyen âge*, in *Speculum*, XXXII (1957), 386.

[34] Cf. the realistic account in Camus, *La peste* (Paris, 1947), with the contemporary account of the yellow fever epidemic in Philadelphia in 1793 in Howard W. Haggard, *Devils, Drugs and Doctors* (New York, 1929), p. 213. Recent, as yet unpublished, studies of modern epidemics by Professors James Diggory and A. Pepitone of the University of Pennsylvania bear out all the main features of earlier descriptions. Some striking plague paintings are reproduced in Raymond Crawfurd, *Plague and Pestilence in Literature and Art* (Oxford, 1914).

for scapegoats, eventuating in large-scale pogroms of the Jews.[35] The most striking feature of such visitations has always been the precipitate flight from the cities, in which not only the wealthier classes but also town officials, professors and teachers, clergy, and even physicians took part.[36] The majority of the population, taking the disaster as an expression of God's wrath, devoted itself to penitential exercises, to merciful occupations, and to such good works as the repair of churches and the founding of religious houses. On the other hand, the horror and confusion in many places brought general demoralization and social breakdown. Criminal elements were quick to take over, looting the deserted houses and even murdering the sick in order to rob them of their jewels. Many, despairing of the goodness and mercy of God, gave themselves over to riotous living, resolved, as Thucydides says, "to get out of life the pleasures which could be had speedily and which would satisfy their lusts, regarding their bodies and their wealth alike as transitory." Drunkenness and sexual immorality were the order of the day. "In one house," reported an observer of the London plague of 1665, "you might hear them roaring under the pangs of death, in the next tippling, whoring and belching out blasphemies against God." [37]

[35] Although the appearance of flagellantism and the beginnings of the Jewish pogroms antedated the Black Death, they reached their fullest development in 1348-1349. See the basic accounts by Karl Lechner, "Die grosse Geisselfahrt des Jahres 1349," *Historisches Jahrbuch,* V (1884), 437-62; Heine Pfannenschmid, "Die Geissler des Jahres 1349 in Deutschland und den Niederlanden," *Die Lieder und Melodien der Geissler des Jahres 1349,* ed. Paul Runge (Leipzig, 1900), pp. 89-218; Joseph McCabe, *The History of Flagellantism* (Girard, Kans., 1946), esp. 33 ff.; Norman Cohn, *The Pursuit of the Millennium* (London, 1957), chap. vi. See further Hecker, *Epidemics of the Middle Ages,* p. 32 ff.; Hoeniger, *Der Schwarze Tod;* Johannes Nohl, *The Black Death* (London, 1926); A. L. Maycock, "A Note on the Black Death," *Nineteenth Century,* XCVII (1925), 456-64. As late as 1884 in Italy physicians were suspected as agents of the rich to poison the poor, and in 1896 British officials in Bombay were charged with spreading the plague. See Melitta Schmideberg, "The Role of Psychotic Mechanisms in Cultural Development," *Internat. Jour. Psychoanalysis,* XI (1930), 387-418; René Baehrel, "La haine de classe au temps d'épidémie," *Annales,* VII (1952), 351-60, who analyzes the popular reaction to the cholera epidemic of 1831-32; and Ilza Veith, "Plague and Politics," *Bull. Hist. Medicine,* XXVIII (1954), 408-15.
[36] The extent of such exodus may be judged from the fact that during the yellow fever epidemic of 1878 about 60 per cent of the population fled the city of Memphis (unpublished MS by James C. Diggory.)
[37] Quoted in Walter G. Bell, *The Great Plague in London in 1665* (London, 1924), p. 222. In addition to the classic accounts of Thucydides (*Peloponnesian War,* Book II) and Boccaccio (*Decameron,* introd.), see also the notes of the great physician, Ambroise Paré, *De la peste* in *Oeuvres complètes* (Paris, 1841), Ill, 350-464; Mullett, *op. cit.,* p. 118, on the London plague of 1603; F. P. Wilson, *The Plague in Shakespeare's London* (Oxford, 1927), chap. v on the London plague of 1625. Much evidence is adduced in B. S. Gowen, "Some Psychological Aspects of Pestilence and Other Epidemics," (Winchester, Tenn., 1907; enlarged reprint from the *Amer. Jour. Psychology,* XVIII [Jan., 1907], 1-60); Karl Lechner, *Das grosse Sterben in Deutschland* (Innsbruck, 1884), pp. 93 ff.

The vivid description of the Black Death in Florence, in the introduction to Boccaccio's *Decameron,* is so familiar that further details about the immediate consequences may be dispensed with. Unfortunately neither the sources nor later historians tell us much of the long-range effects excepting that in the late nineteenth century a school of British writers traced to the Black Death fundamental changes in the agrarian system and indeed in the entire social order; the English prelate-historian, Francis Cardinal Gasquet, maintained that the Black Death, with its admittedly high mortality among the clergy, served to disrupt the whole religious establishment and thereby set the scene for the Protestant Reformation. Though this thesis is undoubtedly exaggerated, it does seem likely that the loss of clergy, especially in the higher ranks, the consequent growth of pluralities, the inevitable appointment of some who proved to be "clerical scamps" (Jessopp), and the vast enrichment of the Church through the legacies of the pious, all taken together played a significant role in the religious development of the later Middle Ages.[38]

But again, these are essentially institutional problems which may reflect but do not explain the underlying psychological forces. That unusual forces of this kind were operative in the later Middle Ages seems highly probable. Indeed, a number of eminent historians have in recent years expatiated on the special character of this period.[39] I will not attempt even to summarize the various interpretations of the temper of that age which have been advanced on one side or the other. None of the commentators, so far as I can see, have traced or determined the connection between the great and constantly recurring epidemics and the state of mind of much of Europe at that time. Yet this relationship would seem to leap to the eye. The age was marked, as all admit, by a mood of misery, depres-

---

[38] On the high mortality of the clergy in England see especially Russell, *British Medieval Population,* pp. 222 ff., 367. On the general problem see Gasquet, *Great Pestilence,* pp. xvi-xvii, 203 ff.; Augustus Jessopp, *The Coming of the Friars and Other Historical Essays* (New York, 1889), pp. 245 ff.; Coulton, *The Black Death,* p. 48, and particularly his chapter on the Black Death in *Medieval Panorama* (New York, 1938); Hoeniger, *Der Schwarze Tod,* pp. 126 ff.; Anna M. Campbell, *The Black Death and Men of Learning* (New York, 1931), 136 ff.; A. Hamilton Thompson, "The Registers of John Gynewell, Bishop of Lincoln, for the years 1349-1350" and "The Pestilences of the 14th Century in the Diocese of York," *Archeol. Jour.,* LXVIII (1911), 301-60, LXXI (1914), 97-154. According to Peter G. Mode, *The Influence of the Black Death on the English Monasteries* (Chicago, 1916), chaps. II, VI, the heads of at least 120 monasteries had died and some of those who succeeded proved to be veritable gangsters. Verlinden lays great stress on the enrichment of the Church in Spain through donations and legacies.

[39] Johan Huizinga's *The Waning of the Middle Ages* (London, 1927) was, in a sense, the counterpart to Jakob Burckhardt's *The Civilization of the Renaissance in Italy* (London, 1878). Of the more recent books the following seem to me particularly significant: Rudolf Stadelmann, *Vom Geist des ausgehenden Mittelalters* (Halle, 1929); Will-Erich Peuckert, *Die grosse Wende. Das apokalyptische Saeculum und Luther* (Hamburg, 1948); Hermann Heimpel, "Das Wesen des Spätmittelalters," *Der Mensch in seiner Gegenwart* (Göttingen, 1954).

sion, and anxiety, and by a general sense of impending doom.[40] Numerous writers in widely varying fields have commented on the morbid preoccupation with death, the macabre interest in tombs, the gruesome predilection for the human corpse.[41] Among painters the favorite themes were Christ's passion, the terrors of the Last Judgment, and the tortures of Hell, all depicted with ruthless realism and with an almost loving devotion to each repulsive detail.[42] Altogether characteristic was the immense popularity of the Dance of Death woodcuts and murals, with appropriate verses, which appeared soon after the Black Death and which, it is agreed, expressed the sense of the immediacy of death and the dread of dying unshriven. Throughout the fifteenth and sixteenth centuries these pitilessly naturalistic pictures ensured man's constant realization of his imminent fate.[43]

The origins of the Dance of Death theme have been generally traced to the Black Death and subsequent epidemics, culminating in the terror brought on by the outbreak of syphilis at the end of the fifteenth century. Is it unreasonable, then, to suppose that many of the other phenomena I have mentioned might be explained, at least in part, in the same way? We all recognize the late Middle Ages as a period of popular religious excitement or overexcitement, of pilgrimages and penitential processions,

[40] Huizinga, *op. cit.*, chap. I; Stadelmann, *op. cit.*, pp. 7, 13; Peuckert, *op. cit.*, pp. 21, 144; Willy Andreas, *Deutschland vor der Reformation* (5th ed., Stuttgart, 1948), p. 202; Otto Benesch, *The Art of the Renaissance in Northern Europe* (Cambridge, 1945), p. 10. In a broad way, Renouard (see fn. 28) and Lucien Febvre ("La peste noire de 1348," *Annales*, IV [1949], 102-103) have suggested the psychological and religious repercussions of the great epidemics. Some authors speak of hysteria, paranoia, and mental disease. See Willy Hellpach, *Die geistigen Epidemien* (Frankfurt, 1905), pp. 84 ff.; Gregory Zilboorg, *A History of Medical Psychology* (New York, 1941), pp. 153 ff.; Norman Cohn, *Pursuit of the Millennium*, p. 73.

[41] See esp. Frederick P. Weber, *Aspects of Death and Correlated Aspects of Life in Art, Epigram and Poetry* (London, 1918), pp. 157 ff.; Erna Döring-Hirsch, *Tod und Jenseits im Spätmittelalter* (Berlin, 1927), *passim*. See also Huizinga, *Waning of the Middle Ages*, chap. XI; Peuckert, *Die grosse Wende*, pp. 95 ff.; and esp. Émile Mâle, *L'Art religieux de la fin du moyen âge en France* (Paris, 1908), pp. 375 ff., 423 ff., Paul Perdrizet, *La Vierge de Miséricorde* (Paris, 1908), chap. IX. Michelangelo on one occasion wrote to Vasari: "No thought is born in me which has not 'Death' engraved upon it" (quoted in Piero Misciatelli, *Savonarola* [English trans., Cambridge, 1929], p. 103).

[42] See Mâle, pp. 477 ff.; Millard Meiss, *Painting in Florence and Siena after the Black Death* (Princeton, 1915), esp. chap. II; Crawfurd, *Plague . . . in Literature and Art*, chap. VIII. On the German painter see Joseph Lortz, *Die Reformation in Deutschland* (3d ed., Freiburg, 1940), I, 102; Benesch, *Art of the Renaissance*, pp. 10 ff.; Arthur Burkhard, *Matthias Grünewald* (Cambridge, 1936), pp. 74 ff.; Gillo Dorfles, *Bosch* (Verona, 1953).

[43] On the artistic side see Crawfurd, chap. VIII; Mâle, pp. 383 ff.; Curt Sachs, *The Commonwealth of Art* (New York, 1946), pp. 88 ff. See also Andreas, *Deutschland vor der Reformation*, pp. 206 ff.; Stadelmann, *Vom Geist des ausgehenden Mittelalters*, pp. 18 ff.; and the specialized studies of Gert Buchheit, *Der Totentanz* (Berlin, 1926); Henri Stegemeier, *The Dance of Death in Folksong* (Chicago, 1939); Wolfgang Stammler, *Der Totentanz* (Munich, 1948); and the particularly significant historical analysis of Hellmut Rosenfeld, *Der mittelalterliche Totentanz* (Münster, 1954), pp. 33 ff., 59 ff.

of mass preaching, of veneration of relics and adoration of saints, of lay piety and popular mysticism.[44] It was apparently also a period of unusual immorality and shockingly loose living, which we must take as the continuation of the "devil-may-care" attitude of one part of the population. This the psychologists explain as the repression of unbearable feelings by accentuating the value of a diametrically opposed set of feelings and then behaving as though the latter were the real feelings.[45] But the most striking feature of the age was an exceptionally strong sense of guilt and a truly dreadful fear of retribution, seeking expression in a passionate longing for effective intercession and in a craving for direct, personal experience of the Deity, as well as in a corresponding dissatisfaction with the Church and with the mechanization of the means of salvation as reflected, for example, in the traffic in indulgences.[46]

These attitudes, along with the great interest in astrology, the increased resort to magic, and the startling spread of witchcraft and Satanism in the fifteenth century were, according to the precepts of modern psychology, normal reactions to the sufferings to which mankind in that period was subjected.[47] It must be remembered that the Middle Ages,

[44] The subject is too large to permit of even a cursory analysis, but see Stadelmann, chap. III; Lortz, I, 99 ff.; Andreas, chap. III and pp. 191 ff.; and Heimpel, noted above. See also Evelyn Underhill, *Mysticism* (12th ed., London, 1930), esp. 453 ff., and "Medieval Mysticism," *Cambridge Medieval History*, VII (New York, 1932), chap. XXVI; Margaret Smith, *Studies in Early Mysticism in the Near and Middle East* (London, 1931), pp. 256-57. As long ago as 1880 the eminent orientalist Alfred von Kremer suggested the connection of mysticism (Sufism) with the great plague epidemics in the Middle East. See his "Über die grossen Seuchen des Orientes nach arabischen Quellen," *Sitzungsberichte der phil.-hist. Classe der kais. Akad. Wissenschaftern, Wien*, XCVI (1880), 69-156.

[45] James W. Thompson, "The Aftermath of the Black Death and the Aftermath of the Great War," *Amer. Jour. Sociol.*, XXVI (1920-1921), 565-72, on the continuing degeneration.

[46] Wallace K. Ferguson, "The Church in a Changing World: A Contribution to the Interpretation of the Renaissance," *Amer. Hist. Rev.*, LIX (1953), 1-18; review by Kurt F. Reinhardt of Friedrich W. Oedinger, *Über die Bildung der Geistlichen im späten Mittelalter* (Leiden, 1953), in *Speculum*, XXXII (1957), 391-92; Lortz, I, 99 ff.; Andreas, pp. 152-53, 169 ff.; and the eloquent pages on the Church in the mid-fourteenth century in Henri Daniel-Rops, *Cathedral and Crusade: Studies of the Medieval Church, 1050-1350* (London, 1957), pp. 593 ff. Norman Cohn, *The Pursuit of the Millennium*, is devoted entirely to a study of the "revolutionary chiliastic movements" in Europe from the Crusades onward. [We might also suggest here a comparison with Erik Erikson's analysis in *Young Man Luther* (1958). B.M.]

[47] On the triumph of astrology see Lynn Thorndike, *A History of Magic and Experimental Science*, IV (New York, 1934), 611 ff.; H. A. Strauss, *Psychologie und astrologische Symbolik* (Zurich, 1953); Mark Graubard, *Astrology and Alchemy* (New York, 1953), chaps. IV, V. On the re-emergence of pagan superstitions, the practice of magic, and the belief in witches as a heretical sect devoted to worship of the devil and the perpetration of evil see Thorndike, *op. cit.*, IV, 274 ff.; Peuckert, pp. 119 ff.; Andreas, pp. 28 ff., 217 ff.; Joseph Hansen, *Zauberwesen, Inquisition und Hexenprozess im Mittelalter* (Munich, 1900), pp. 326 ff.; Margaret A. Murray, *The Witch-Cult in Western Europe* (Oxford, 1921), esp. pp. 11 ff.; Harmanns Obendiek, *Satanismus und Dämonie in Geschichte und Gegenwart* (Berlin, 1928); Montague Summers, *The History of Witch-*

ignoring the teachings of the Greek physicians and relying entirely upon Scripture and the writings of the Church fathers, considered disease the scourge of God upon a sinful people.[48] All men, as individuals, carry within themselves a burden of unconscious guilt and a fear of retribution which apparently go back to the curbing and repression of sexual and aggressive drives in childhood and the emergence of death wishes directed against the parents. This sense of sin, which is fundamental to all religion, is naturally enhanced by the impact of vast unaccountable and uncontrollable forces threatening the existence of each and every one.[49] Whether or not there is also a primordial racial sense of guilt, as Freud argued in his *Totem and Taboo* (1913), it is perfectly clear that disaster and death threatening the entire community will bring on a mass emotional disturbance, based on a feeling of helpless exposure, disorientation, and common guilt.[50] Furthermore, it seems altogether plausible to suppose that children, having experienced the terror of their parents and the panic of the community, will react to succeeding crises in a similar but even more intense manner. In other words, the anxiety and fear are transmitted from one generation to another, constantly aggravated.

craft and Demonology (2d ed., New York, 1956), pp. 1 ff.; Gregory Zilboorg, *op. cit.* It may be noted, for what it is worth, that in the fifteenth century witches were accused of inhibiting human fertility: possibly a reflection of popular concern over the rapidly diminishing population. It is also interesting to observe that witch trials died out in Europe concurrently with the disappearance of the plague in the eighteenth century.

[48] God might, of course, act through natural phenomena such as comets, floods, droughts, or miasma. For a good discussion of this point see G. G. Coulton, *Five Centuries of Religion*, II (Cambridge, 1927), p. 394; Hirst, *Conquest of Plague,* chap. II; Kenneth Walker, *The Story of Medicine* (New York, 1955), pp. 71 ff.; and esp. Paul H. Kocher, "The Idea of God in Elizabethan Medicine," *Jour. Hist. Ideas,* XI (1950), 3-29. This explanation was generally accepted through the early modern period and undoubtedly presented a great obstacle to the development of medical and sanitational measures. See Mullett, *Bubonic Plague and England,* pp. 74, 88. Recent studies on modern disasters indicate that it is still widely held, despite the discoveries of Pasteur and his successors. See Martha Wolfenstein, *Disaster: A Psychological Study* (Glencoe, Ill., 1957), pp. 199 ff.

[49] The crucial problem of guilt feelings has not been much studied except by Freud and his successors. See Freud, "Thoughts for the Times on War and Death," (1915) and the succinct discussion in Jones, *What Is Psychoanalysis?* pp. 101 ff., 114. For the continuance of this feeling in modern times see Wolfenstein, *Disaster,* p. 71. Cantril, *The Invasion from Mars* (Princeton, 1940), pp. 161 ff., quotes one man as saying: "The broadcast had us all worried, but I knew it would at least scare ten years' life out of my mother-in-law."

[50] A later explanation of the sense of communal guilt, as it appears among the Jews, was advanced by Freud in his *Moses and Monotheism* (1939). Still another, quite different and quite persuasive, argument is presented by Theodor Reik, *Myth and Guilt: The Crime and Punishment of Mankind* (New York, 1957), esp. pp. 34 ff., 146 ff. Oskar Pfister, *Das Christentum und die Angst* (Zurich, 1944) has examined the relation of anxiety to guilt feelings and the magnification of communal anxieties in the face of disaster. For concrete studies of medieval mass hysteria see Louis F. Calmeil, *De la folie* (Paris, 1845); René Fülöp-Miller, *Leaders, Dreamers and Rebels* (New York, 1935); and esp. the admirable scholarly study of Cohn, *Pursuit of the Millennium,* which stresses the analogies between individual and collective paranoia.

Now it has long been recognized by psychologists that man, when crushed by unfathomable powers, tends to regress to infantile concepts and that, like his predecessor in primitive times, he has recourse to magic in his efforts to ward off evil and appease the angry deity.[51] It is generally agreed that magic and religion are closely related, both deriving from fear of unknown forces and especially of death, and both reflecting an effort to ensure the preservation of the individual and the community from disease and other afflictions.[52] Death-dealing epidemics like those of the late Middle Ages were bound to produce a religious revival, the more so as the established Church was proving itself ever less able to satisfy the yearning for more effective intercession and for a more personal relationship to God.[53] Wyclif, himself a survivor of the Black Death, is supposed to have been deeply affected by his grueling experience, and there is nothing implausible in the suggestion that Lollardy was a reaction to the shortcomings of the Church in that great crisis.[54] In this connection it is

---

[51] Jung, "After the Catastrophe," *Essays on Contemporary Events* (London, 1947). See also Johann Kinkel, "Zur Frage der psychologischen Grundlagen und des Ursprungs der Religion," *Imago*, VIII (1922), 23-45, 197-241; Henry E. Sigerist, *Civilization and Disease* (Ithaca, 1943), chap. VI; Arturo Castiglioni, *Adventures of the Mind* (New York, 1946), pp. ix, 2, 11, 19; Bronislaw Malinowski, *Magic, Science and Religion* (Boston, 1948), pp. 15, 29, 116; Charles Odier, *Anxiety and Magic Thinking* (New York, 1956), pp. 38 ff.; Melitta Schmideberg: "Role of Psychotic Mechanisms in Cultural Development"; Franz Alexander, "On the Psychodynamics of Regressive Phenomena in Panic States," *Psychoanalysis and the Social Sciences*, IV (1955), 104-11. Hirst, *Conquest of Plague*, has noted the reversion to magic during all great plague epidemics and reports that charms and amulets were never more prevalent among even educated Englishmen than during the epidemic of 1665. Jessopp, *Coming of the Friars*, p. 166, remarked that in his day the threat of any epidemic still brought on "wild-eyed panic" and resort to all kinds of superstitious practices.

[52] James H. Leuba, *The Psychological Origin and the Nature of Religion* (London, 1921), pp. 4, 81; George F. Moore, *The Birth and Growth of Religion* (New York, 1924), pp. 3, 8, 17; W. B. Selbie, *The Psychology of Religion* (Oxford, 1924), p. 32; Malinowski, *Magic, Science and Religion*, p. 29; Willy Hellpach, *Grundriss der Religionspsychologie* (Stuttgart, 1951), pp. 6 ff.

[53] In this connection the great expansion of the cult of the Virgin Mary and even more of her mother, St. Anne, is worth noting; also the fact that among the ten or twelve most popular saints of the late fifteenth century, the so-called "plague saints" (St. Anthony, St. Sebastian, St. Roch), were particularly favored. See Huizinga, *Waning of the Middle Ages*, chap. XII; Crawfurd, *Plague . . . in Literature and Art*, chap. VIII; and esp. Mâle, *Art religieux*, pp. 157 ff., 193 ff., and Perdrizet, *La Vierge de Miséricorde, passim*.

[54] *The Last Age of the Church*, written in 1356 and first published in 1840, is a violent denunciation of the depravity revealed in the time of the Black Death. It was long believed to have been the first work of Wyclif but is now attributed to an unnamed Spiritual Franciscan. See James H. Todd, *The Last Age of the Church, by John Wycliffe* (Dublin, 1840); J. Foster Palmer, "Pestilences: Their Influence on the Destiny of Nations," *Trans. Royal Hist. Soc.*, I (1884), 242-59; H. B. Workman, *John Wyclif: A Study of the English Medieval Church* (Oxford, 1926), I, 14; Robert Vaughan, *The Life and Opinions of John de Wycliffe* (London, 1928), I, 238 ff.; and, on the general problem, Coulton, *The Black Death*, p. 111, and Mullett, *Bubonic Plague and England*, p. 34.

also worth remarking that the first expression of Zwingli's reformed faith was his *Song of Prayer in Time of Plague*.[55]

Most striking, however, is the case of the greatest of the reformers, Martin Luther, who seems to me to reflect clearly the reaction of the individual to the situation I have been sketching. Luther left behind almost a hundred volumes of writings, thousands of letters, and very voluminous table talk, suggesting an unusually self-analytical and self-critical personality.[56] From all this material it has long been clear that he suffered from an abnormally strong sense of sin and of the immediacy of death and damnation. Tortured by the temptations of the flesh and repeatedly in conflict with a personalized demon, he was chronically oppressed by a pathological feeling of guilt and lived in constant terror of God's judgment. So striking were these traits that some of Luther's biographers have questioned his sanity.[57]

Here it is interesting to recall that one of our own colleagues, the late Professor Preserved Smith, as long ago as 1913, attacked the problem in an article entitled "Luther's Early Development in the Light of Psychoanalysis." [58] Smith, who was remarkably conversant with Freudian teaching when psychoanalysis was still in its early stage of development, considered Luther highly neurotic—probably driven to enter the monastery by the hope of finding a refuge from temptation and an escape from damnation, and eventually arriving at the doctrine of salvation by faith alone only after he had convinced himself of the impossibility of conquering temptation by doing penance. It may well be that Smith overdid his thesis, but the fact remains that his article was treated with great respect by Dr. Paul J. Reiter, who later published a huge and greatly detailed study of Luther's personality. Reiter reached the conclusion, already suggested by Adolf Hausrath in 1905, that the great reformer suffered from a manic-depressive psychosis, which, frequently associated with

[55] This very moving appeal for divine aid (1519) is reprinted in Georg Finsler, *et al.*, *Ulrich Zwingli: Eine Auswahl aus seinen Schriften* (Zurich, 1918), pp. 17-19. See also Pfister, *Das Christentum und die Angst*, 321 ff., according to whom Calvin was terror-stricken by the plague and, unlike Luther, was unwilling to stick at his post during severe epidemics. He firmly believed that a group of thirty-four men and women witches had for three years spread the plague in Geneva and that in their case even the most extreme forms of torture were justified.

[56] Karl Holl, "Luthers Urteile über sich Selbst," *Gesammelte Aufsätze zur Kirchengeschichte*, I, *Luther* (Tübingen, 1921); Heinrich Böhmer, *Road to Reformation; Martin Luther to the Year 1521* (Philadelphia, 1946), foreword; Karl A. Meissinger, *Der katholische Luther* (Munich, 1952), p. 2.

[57] Hartmann Grisar, *Luther* (London, 1913-1917), I, 110 ff.; VI, chap. xxxvi, discusses many of these views but Grisar takes a more moderate stand. The most recent Catholic biography is that of Joseph Lortz, *Die Reformation in Deutschland*, which is a very model of reasonableness. [Once again, a reference to Erikson's *Young Man Luther* is in order here. B.M.]

[58] *Amer. Jour. Psychology*, XXIV (1913), 360-77.

genius, involved a constant struggle with, and victory over, enormous psychological pressures. The point of mentioning all this is to suggest that Luther's trials were typical of his time. In any event, it is inconceivable that he should have evoked so great a popular response unless he had succeeded in expressing the underlying, unconscious sentiments of large numbers of people and in providing them with an acceptable solution to their religious problem.[59]

I must apologize for having raised so lugubrious a subject on so festive an occasion, but I could not resist the feeling that the problems presented by the later Middle Ages are exactly of the type that might be illuminated by modern psychology. I do not claim that the psychological aspects of this apocalyptic age have been entirely neglected by other students. Indeed, Millard Meiss, a historian of art, has written a most impressive study of Florentine and Sienese painting in the second half of the fourteenth century in which he has analyzed the many and varied effects of the Black Death, including the bearing of that great catastrophe on the further development of the religious situation.[60] But no one, to my knowledge, has undertaken to fathom the psychological crisis provoked by the chronic, large-scale loss of life and the attendant sense of impending doom.

I would not, of course, argue that psychological doctrine, even if it were more advanced and more generally accepted than it is, would resolve all the perplexities of the historian. Better than most scholars, the historian knows that human motivation, like causation, is a complex and elusive

[59] Hausrath, *Luthers Leben* (Berlin, 1905); Reiter, *Martin Luthers Umwelt, Charakter und Psychose* (Copenhagen, 1937, 1941); Wilhelm Lange-Eichbaum, *Genie, Irrsinn und Ruhm* (4th ed., Munich, 1956), pp. 375-78. See also Walther von Loewenich, "Zehn Jahre Lutherforschung," in *Theologie und Liturgie*, ed. Liemar Hennig (Cassell, 1952), pp. 119-70, and Martin Werner, "Psychologisches zum Klostererlebnis Martin Luthers," *Schweiz. Zeitsch. für Psychologie*, VII (1948), 1-18, who follows Smith's thesis closely. The argument hinges on the harshness of Luther's upbringing and the extent of his father fixation. Smith noted that on at least one occasion Luther asserted that he had entered the monastery to escape harsh treatment at home. His father's unalterable opposition to this step may have played a part in Luther's later decision to leave the monastery. According to Roland H. Bainton, *Here I Stand: A Life of Martin Luther* (New York, 1950), pp. 288 ff., Luther's decision (in 1525) to marry was at least in part due to his wish to gratify his father's desire for progeny. Recent writers tend to explain away the harshness of Luther's youth, which indeed was probably less unusual and less important than Smith supposed. See Otto Scheel, *Martin Luther* (Tübingen, 1916); Böhmer, *Martin Luther;* Meissinger, *Der katholische Luther;* Robert H. Fife, *The Revolt of Martin Luther* (New York, 1957), pp. 5, 9, 99, 117 ff.; Bainton, *Here I Stand,* pp. 23, 25, 28 and chap. xxi *passim*, who insists that Luther's psychological troubles were of a strictly religious character, due to "tensions which medieval religion deliberately induced, playing alternately upon fear and hope."

[60] Meiss, *Painting in Florence and Siena after the Black Death,* while dealing with a restricted subject and a limited period, is in my opinion a masterpiece of synthesis and one of the very few books to recognize the full and varied impact of the Black Death. See also Hans Baron, *The Crisis of the Early Italian Renaissance* (Princeton, 1955), II, 479-80.

process. In view of the fact that we cannot hope ever to have complete evidence on any historical problem, it seems unlikely that we shall ever have definitive answers. But I am sure you will agree that there are still possibilities of enriching our understanding of the past and that it is our responsibility, as historians, to leave none of these possibilities unexplored. I call your attention to the fact that for many years young scholars in anthropology, sociology, religion, literature, education, and other fields have gone to psychoanalytic institutes for special training, and I suggest that some of our own younger men might seek the same equipment. For of this I have no doubt, that modern psychology is bound to play an ever greater role in historical interpretation. For some time now there has been a marked trend toward recognition of the irrational factors in human development, and it is interesting to observe the increased emphasis being laid on psychological forces. May I recall that perhaps the most stimulating non-Marxist interpretation of imperialism, that of the late Joseph Schumpeter, which goes back to 1918, rests squarely on a psychological base? Or need I point out that recent treatments of such forces as totalitarianism and nationalism lay great stress on psychological factors? [61] Indeed, within the past year two books have appeared which have a direct bearing on my argument. One is T. D. Kendrick's *The Lisbon Earthquake,* which is devoted to a study of the effects of that disaster of 1755 upon the whole attitude and thought of the later eighteenth century. The other is Norman Cohn's *The Pursuit of the Millennium,* which reviews the chiliastic movements of the Middle Ages and comes to the conclusion that almost every major disaster, be it famine, plague, or war, produced some such movement and that only analysis of their psychic content will help us to explain them.

Aldous Huxley, in one of his essays, discusses the failure of historians to devote sufficient attention to the great ebb and flow of population and its effect on human development. He complains that while Arnold Toynbee concerned himself so largely with pressures and responses, there is in the index of his first six volumes no entry for "population," though there are five references to Popilius Laenas and two to Porphyry of Batamaea.[62] To this I might add that the same index contains no reference to pestilence, plague, epidemics, or Black Death. This, I submit, is mildly shocking and should remind us, as historians, that we cannot rest upon past achievements but must constantly seek wider horizons and deeper insights. We find ourselves in the midst of the International Geophysical Year, and we all know that scientists entertain high hopes of enlarging through cooperation their understanding as well as their knowledge of the universe. It is quite possible that they may throw further light on such problems as the influence of sunspots on terrestrial life and the

---

[61] See, for example, Hannah Arendt, *The Origins of Totalitarianism,* and Boyd C. Shafer, *Nationalism: Myth and Reality* (New York, 1955).

[62] Huxley, *Tomorrow and Tomorrow and Tomorrow* (New York, 1956), p. 221.

effects of weather on the conduct of human affairs.[63] We may, for all we know, be on the threshold of a new era when the historian will have to think in ever larger, perhaps even in cosmic, terms.

[63] Fully a generation ago a Soviet scientist thought he could establish an eleven-year cycle of maximum sunspot activity and that these periods were also those of maximum mass excitability as revealed by revolutions and other social disturbances. Furthermore, his correlation of periods of maximum sunspot activity with cholera epidemics in the nineteenth century seemed to reveal a remarkable coincidence. See the summary translation of the book by A. L. Tchijevsky, "Physical Factors of the Historical Process," as read before the American Meteorological Society, December 30, 1926, and now reprinted in *Cycles* (Feb., 1957). Of the many studies of climatic, nutritional, and similar influences on human affairs, see Ellsworth Huntington, *Civilization and Climate* (New Haven, 1915); *The Character of Races* (New York, 1924); *Mainsprings of Civilization* (New York, 1946); Willy Hellpach, *Geopsyche* (5th ed., Leipzig, 1939); Louis Berman, *Food and Character* (Boston, 1932); C. C. and S. M. Furnas, *Man, Bread and Destiny* (Baltimore, 1937); E. Parmalee Prentice, *Hunger and History* (New York, 1939); Josué de Castro, *The Geography of Hunger* (Boston, 1952).

A Falsification
by Machiavelli

Renzo Sereno

The encounters between Caesar Borgia and Niccolò Machiavelli, and their influence on the latter's thought and writing, are still shrouded in vagueness and uncertainty. This is due not to lack of positive documentation or to scarcity of evidence, but rather to a plethora of interpretations and fancy. Instances of this vagueness and fancy may be found in interpretations of a document written in Niccolò's own hand, which is preserved in the Central National Library of Florence.[1]

On May 3, 1503, a certain Troches or Troccio, until then one of Caesar's

"A Falsification by Machiavelli." Reprinted from *Renaissance News*, XII, No. 3 (Autumn 1959), 159-167. Copyright 1959 by *Renaissance News*.

[1] Biblioteca Nazionale Centrale di Firenze, Carte Macchiaveli, i, 1. From the Ricci collection. "Perche havemo intesco che troches è partito de la Santita de N.S. Sanza sua et nostra licentia a tutti nostri vaxalli comandamo sotto pena derebellion et disgratia che in qualunque loco si trovasse sia subito retenuto finche a nostra notitia pervenisse: Et si site vassalli o amici de la Maesta cristianissima ve exortamo et pregamo che per quanto esso troches va per cose che sono contro l'honor de sua Maesta simiemente lo vogliate retener protestando de tutti li danni et interesse della Maesta cristianissima che faciendo locontrario poteranno venire Datum Rome xix Maij M.D. iij Cesar." ("Since we have heard that Troches has left the Holiness of our Lord without His or our license, we order, under pain of rebellion and disgrace to all our vassals that wherever Troccio is he has to be held at once until we are given notice. If the recipient is a vassal of His Most Christian Majesty we exhort and beg His vassals to hold him as he (Troccio) is engaged in affairs contrary to His Majesty's honor, cautioning them that they are to be held responsible for all damages that would come to His Majesty if action is not taken. Given in Rome, xix May 1503.")

most trusted bravos, fled from Rome. Caesar at once despatched a circular letter to his vassals ordering them to seize the fugitive, alleging that he had fled the city without license of His Holiness. Apprehended and confined to a tower in the Trastevere section, Troccio was interviewed by Caesar, who then withdrew to a room from which he could spy on the prisoner, whereupon his chief assassin, Don Micheletto, entered the cell and strangled the unlucky Troccio under the gaze of his unseen master.

The document mentioned above is a holograph copy by Machiavelli of the circular letter sent by Caesar to his vassals. The Florentine, after having copied the text in his own handwriting, carefully and skillfully imitated the Spaniard's signature. The document is so interesting and so intriguing that it has caught the attention of a number of people. It was published by Count Passerini,[2] who stated that the letter was a convincing and final proof of the intense friendship and intimacy which had bound writer and ruler. Caesar Borgia, according to Count Passerini, had actually dictated the letter to Machiavelli, or had asked him to write it and then had signed it with his own signature. But this hypothesis was proved to be a bit fanciful by a contemporary of Count Passerini, Nitti,[3] who rightly observed that the date of this letter makes this explanation untenable and unacceptable, because not only at that very date but throughout the spring of 1503 Machiavelli was in Tuscany, and he had had no contact whatever with Caesar or his court. But having gathered impressive and final evidence to prove this point, Nitti was unwilling to give up the appealing fancy of crafty counselor and ruthless prince plotting together new courses of history. Nitti surmised that the letter was written by Niccolò in Tuscany upon Caesar's command and then sent to Rome for Caesar's signature.

This hypothesis, however, is as nonsensical as the former one, and, like the former, seems to be based on the intense desire of some historians to discover what would be a unique document in order to deck history and political theory with romantic claptrap. Of the impossibility of either hypothesis the historian Villari gives incontrovertible evidence[4] and presents the document for what it is, or, rather, for what it seems to be— a meaningless exercise or a little divertissement of the Florentine secretary, who, when in Rome in the fall of 1503, copied the circular letter. It would have been unreasonable, in fact downright insane, to waste precious time in journeys from Rome to Florence and back to Rome only to secure Machiavelli's penmanship to draft the text of a short police order in which urgency mattered far more than style or judgment. Nor was there any reason to engage his diplomatic style, at that time far from famous, to write, not a message to a prince or a brief to a chancellor, but a routine

[2] *Opere di Nicolò Macchiavelli* (Firenze: Cenniniana, 1873), IV, 298.
[3] *Macchiavelli nella vita e nelle opere* (Napoli, 1876), pp. 223-224, n. 1.
[4] Villari, *The Life and Times of Niccolò Machiavelli* (London: T. Fisher Unwin, 1892), I, 344-345.

communication to a few secondary vassals. And these vassals were as near to Caesar's court as they were removed from the Ten of Balia, all this in a matter wholly alien to Niccolò. Villari, an outstanding paleographer and handwriting expert in his own right, states that no doubt exists about the handwriting being Machiavelli's own; yet, having ascertained this point, which more recent inquiries prove undeniable, he goes no further. Why Machiavelli felt compelled to copy the letter in his own handwriting, faithfully reproducing the form and the pattern of the original, why he kept and preserved this absurd exercise among his papers, why he painstakingly imitated Caesar's signature, are queries that Villari does not formulate. Yet there is no other evidence of a close friendship between Caesar and Niccolò than Machiavelli's own word in his writings, and of positive documents all that exists is this falsification.

But if, seeking some explanation, we look at this nugatory and seemingly pointless caprice of Machiavelli, we reach a double order of conclusions that may help us to understand not only the document but the Florentine's manner of thinking as well. This quest is not undertaken in an apodictic mood; it is an attempted voyage in a most extraordinary mind.

The first concerns the idea that Machiavelli had of the Borgia. The relations between the two were by no means as close and as intimate as Machiavelli wanted his friends, the Signoria, and perhaps posterity, to believe. To start, Niccolò made his debut in public life and in history in 1499, and Caesar left public life and history in 1503, when, a lackland king, he returned to Spain to die, still a young man, in obscurity. During this brief span of four years their meetings were few, perhaps three at the most, and there is nothing to suggest that they were of particularly intimate nature. Leaving aside moral considerations, Niccolò's judgment of Caesar is so grossly flattering as to be nonsensical. We refer to the passage in *The Prince* (*caput* vii) in which the Borgia deeds in Romagna are praised, in fact extolled, as a striking example of political success and cunning almost unique in history. This was not true. Caesar's attempts at kingdom-building in Romagna fell very short of the most pessimistic expectations. His realm collapsed almost at once with the death of Alexander VI. As soon as the Spaniards were ousted from the court of Rome, Caesar's political power vanished. What Machiavelli described as a monument more lasting than bronze was but an instance, or a fragment, of the mundane prestige of Caesar's father.

The other nonlogical reference of Niccolò's to the Borgia may be found in his description of the manner in which Caesar dispatched Vitellozzo Vitelli, Pagolo Orsini, and Oliverotto da Fermo, whom he had invited to dinner for the purpose of having them murdered. This maneuver, which the secretary recommended to his Signoria as the epitome of sound and original political procedure, was not only hackneyed to the point of being *vieux jeu,* but unsound, pointless, and singularly unsuccessful. Caesar's bloodletting dinner party did not change his destiny nor blaze new trails in political behavior. One of the victims, we may note with Lord Morley,[5] was Oliverotto da Fermo, who had become Lord of Fermo exactly through such techniques. This Machiavelli blandly ignored, *et pour cause,* as it would have annihilated his myth and his hero with it.

To reconcile Machiavelli with his own writings is a thankless and useless enterprise, because the apostle of cold logic very often is not logical at all. Villari undertook moral accounting by putting side by side, like columns of a ledger, what Niccolò said of Caesar that was positive and what he uttered that was damning. The reason for this extremely uninspired attempt at understanding, or rather at whitewashing, the Florentine may be found in the foul reputation of the Spaniard and in the lavish praise Niccolò had heaped on him. By proving that together with praise Machiavelli had also heaped scorn, Villari hoped to show him as a moralist led astray now and then by superficial emotions. In this Villari behaved like other Machiavellian scholars of his times, Tomasini, or Ferrari, who strove to reconstruct Machiavelli *ad usum Delphini,* and, more precisely, as a Dauphin endowed with the specific moralistic qualities that prevailed in the latter decades of the nineteenth century.

Much more acute and to the point is the portrait of Caesar left by Gregorovius in his biography of Lucrezia Borgia. The Pope's son was a decadent, infantile person who found security only in the desperate pampering by which the Pope displayed his affection. Bishoprics, the cardinalate, kingdoms, dukedoms, and royal marriages were bestowed upon the handsome bastard like toys upon the child-favorite of an adoring father. These rich presents, with the emotional support they gave him, were Caesar's strength and life. He disappeared when their giver died.

Machiavelli waxed enthusiastic about the Borgia manner not in spite of, but because of, its foulness. Always near to the great, but never really close to them, his apologia of a great lord without friends made it possible for him to believe that he had reached a status and a station about which he dreamed and which had constantly escaped him. It was a desperate attempt at showing himself free of prejudice. His amazingly exaggerated praise of Caesar had the cheap merit of *épater le bourgeois.*[6] Machiavelli, who had admired Caesar at the summit of his—or rather his father's—glory, chanced to see him in Rome at the time of his father's death not merely as a fallen hero, but as a craven beggar. When, more than ten years later, he praised his greatness and his acumen, he performed a feat

[5] Morley's Romane Lecture on Machiavelli in *Miscellanies,* Fourth Series (London: Macmillan & Co., 1908), pp. 36-37.

[6] Letter to Francesco Guicciardini in Modena, dated May 18, 1521. ". . . Dissigli della malattia di Cesare e degli Stati che voleva comprare in Francia in modo che gli sbavigliava." ("I told him of Caesar's illness and of the States he wanted to buy in France in a way that left him open-mouthed.")

of stunted logic but of dazzling originality. The bourgeois to be *épaté*
was Machiavelli himself.

Caesar was the only great with whom Niccolò boasted friendship, and,
as the Borgia was universally despised, their imaginary friendship was
ipso facto more fetching. The Pope's son was very much part of the history of the times, and yet, since his father's death, was removed from it
so that he could not bear witness to the Florentine's fantastic imagination.
His sinister reputation was one more charm for Niccolò, who liked, in
fact loved, success. His judgment was not determined by the desire for
being amoral, detached, or experimental, but by the fact that, unable to
secure a successful career for himself, he invented a successful career for
Caesar. The obvious clash between his glowing approval and the pica-
yunish reality of Caesar's glory was one of those many parcels of reality
that Niccolò blithely ignored in order to build a system of flawless logic.

This letter, copied at the time of Caesar's exit from public life, can
be interpreted as follows: Niccolò derived deep if infantile pleasure from
seeing his handwriting coupled with Caesar's signature. The copied state
paper was concerned with an episode as sordid as it was petty. Yet it became the toy with which to play an all-important little private game that
was not more illogical nor more puerile nor more fatuous than the judgment that Niccolò gave of Caesar and his accomplishments.

The other theme suggested by this letter concerns the idea that Machiavelli had of himself. We may begin by saying that the Florentine,
known throughout his life as a most brilliant, exceptionally gifted person,
never held any position or performed any task, public or private, com-
mensurate with his intellect or his ambitions or his capacities. This may
have led him to have an unclear or twisted idea of his own self. It was
perhaps the most accepted principle of the times that personal worth was
demonstrated through public services. Ἀρχὴ ἄνδρα δείκνυσι was so accepted
a principle that Guicciardini concluded his *History* with it. It was Machiavelli's destiny never to be given such an opportunity. His merits and
demands were forever removed from that trial or ordeal that assumes
that "Magistratus virum ostentat"; Niccolò's wish was power, his lot was
frustration. The theorist of practical politics, the theorist who despised
theoreticians, was never more than a theoretician himself.

Bandello[7] writes how once under the walls of Milan the author of *The*

---

[7] Bandello, 1, Novella no. 40. In the dedication to John of the Black Bands he writes
that "messer Niccolò is one of the wittiest raconteurs (uno dei più belli e facondi dici-
tori) of your Tuscany." Bandello also relates that "messer Niccolò kept us under the
sun for more than two hours because he wanted to drill three thousand foot soldiers
according to the rules he had written, and he was unable even to keep them in rank."
Bandello cites the episode as an instance of the virtue of practice over theory. Niccolò
made amends by telling a story at the dinner table, a story dealing with "the trick employed by a woman in order to deceive her husband with sudden astuteness" (*ibid.*).

Art of War explained some principles of tactics to John of the Black Bands and proceeded to demonstrate them by giving orders to some of John's troops. Niccolò proved to be so inept a field commander that soldiers, onlookers, and staff would have melted under the broiling sun had not John taken a drum and with a few drumbeats reassembled his soldiers from the dusty confusion. Similarly, the extremely dramatic style of his minor works on military matters (e.g., *Discorso dell'Ordinare lo Stato di Firenze alle Armi; Discorso Sopra l'Ordinanza e Milizia Fiorentina; Consulto per l'Elezione del Capitano delle Fanterie e Ordinanza Fiorentina*) once brought into line with the order it strove to create, appears for what it is: a superb manner of presenting the dreams of a frustrated politico whose literary gifts were far more impressive than his grasp of reality.[8]

Such hopes and dreams of greatness through magistracy are even more evident in *The Prince*. The letter in which the opus is announced to Francesco Vettori from the exile in Sant' Andrea in Percussina (December 10, 1513) candidly presents it for what he meant it to be, an attempt at securing some worthy task from the Medici.[9] When Lorenzo,[10] the unhappy youth burdened with a name far too great for his meaningless person, was mentioned as a possible ruler of some town in the Po Valley, Suzzara or Guastalla, Machiavelli undertook at once to write an application for a position of trust with the ruler-to-be. One of the quirks of history is that such an application ended by being what is perhaps the most famous treatise on politics we know, yet the dedication to Lorenzo, particularly the explicit last paragraph and *caput* xxii in which he invited the Prince to choose a competent secretary, leave no doubts as to the purpose of the treatise. In fact, *caput* xxii, in which the virtues of

---

[8] On this point, cf. Joseph Kraft, "Truth and Poetry in Machiavelli," *The Journal of Modern History*, Vol. xxiii, No. 2 (June 1951), pp. 109 ff.

[9] Letter to Francesco Vettori, dated from Sant' Andrea in Percussina, December 10, 1513. ". . . (This book) should be well liked by a Prince and in particular by a Prince who has never ruled, because of this I am dedicating it to the magnificency of Giuliano. . . ." "I have spoken of this book with Filippo (Casavecchia), whether it was wise to give it (to Giuliano) or not, and in the former case whether it would be better to take it myself or to send it . . . for I do wish that the Medici give me something to do." *The Prince*, instead of being dedicated to Giuliano di Lorenzo il Magnifico, was dedicated to Lorenzo, Duke of Urbino. Machiavelli tarried and hesitated for a number of years. Giuliano died in 1516 and the Prince who had never ruled was by then Lorenzo.

[10] Lorenzo, for whom the dedication of *The Prince* was finally written, was the object of a rather cheap admiration by Niccolò. In a letter to Francesco Vettori in Rome dated from Florence during August 1513 (no day given), and published in Machiavelli's *Lettres* in the edition of the Società Nazionale per il Rinascimento del Libro (Florence, 1929, p. 85), Niccolò favorably compares the puny nephew to his Magnificent namesake. He also exhorts Vettori to relate his admiration to the Pope in an attempt to enter his graces. Giuliano de Medici had been elected Pope on March 11, 1513, and this letter to Vettori can be considered a personal message of congratulation and an obvious attempt at flattering the brightest of the Medici by praising the dullest.

the excellent secretary are listed, is a summary of what Machiavelli thought of Machiavelli. *The Prince,* is not, as Bertrand Russell stated, a handbook for gangsters, nor, as Mussolini wrote, the *vade mecum* of the statesman, but rather the desperate plea of a man who "unbeknownst to the great had to bear the indignities of a severe and constant misfortune." [11] Much that seems rational in the Florentine was born not from reason but from anger, impatience, and phantasy, from bitterness and yearning. The seemingly pointless exercise by which Machiavelli copied Caesar's circular letter and then signed it with a signature almost perfectly imitating Caesar's own appears to be a striking instance of his real inner life, of his phantasy at work, of his own forces having for once a free play. For a brief moment the secretary could believe that he was not the simple secretary of the Ten of Balia, but the minister and counselor of a ruler only he understood and only he could guide to power. It was simple for Niccolò to overlook Caesar's failure, as it was a device to overlook his own. And the Borgia's sinister reputation added poignancy to the frustrated diplomat's dreams.

Once we look at Machiavelli and his work—as so many others have done —not merely philologically or historically but with an effort at seeing what he really meant, we may also look in a novel way not only at his writings but at the science he created. The apparent logic or dispassionate experimentalism of his science covers anxieties, ambitions, and disappointments. His discourse must needs have the appearance of logic and of detachment because it hides conflict, phantasies, and resentment. His prose is still today, perhaps today more than ever before, appealing in its stunning beauty, in its startling simplicity, in its adamantine reasoning, in its impudent directness of judgment. It is the prose of a diplomat who, at the age of thirty-four, apparently had gone far enough with his phantasies to entertain himself with a bit of elegant penmanship which gave him the delusion of being what he dreamt himself to be and was not. There is madness in that method.

[11] *The Prince,* Dedication, last paragraph.

A Psychoanalytic Interpretation
of Woodrow Wilson

Bernard Brodie

In this volume the authors have produced the first completely satisfactory account of the strange relationship between the two figures mentioned in the title, and of their part in history. But in so doing they have accomplished more than that. The book is, quite appropriately, much more about Wilson than about House, and the authors have given us the first interpretation of the character of that already legendary president which impresses one as having depth, coherence, and consistency.

To say this is to announce that the authors have attempted a psychoanalytic study of the personality structure of Woodrow Wilson. For no other kind of approach can suffice to make his behavior quite believable, let alone explicable. It is impossible to discuss his motivation within a frame of reference that makes simply the normal allowances for the effects of personal ambition, interest, and vanity. Wilson was intensely neurotic—though the authors refrain from using this or like terms throughout the book—and to get into the dynamics of his actions inevitably requires recourse to concepts and insights that have developed out of the discoveries of Sigmund Freud.

Others, including such biographers of Wilson as Ray Stannard Baker and William Allen White, have called attention to the special necessity

"A Psychoanalytic Interpretation of Woodrow Wilson." A review of *Woodrow Wilson and Colonel House* by Alexander L. George and Juliette L. George [New York: The John Day Company, 1956, 362 pp.]. Copyright 1957 by Alexander L. George & Juliette L. George.

in the case of this driven man to discover and present his inner life. White, for example (as quoted by the present authors), wrote that one who followed the Wilson story felt ". . . like clamoring wildly . . . for someone to come and release the festering rage in our hero's undercon- sciousness, by a whacking blow, spiritual, or even physical, to give his soul relief and to restore wholesome circulation to his moral blood" (p. xvi). Those who knew Wilson personally testified after his death to the consuming inner conflict that forced him in effect to destroy those things to which he had himself given life, including what was to have been his greatest monument—the League of Nations. As Professor Thomas A. Bailey pointed out in *Woodrow Wilson and the Great Betrayal,* it was not Senator Lodge and his cohorts but Wilson who "with his own sickly hands . . . slew his own brain child." The present authors acknowledge Bailey's interpretation and overwhelmingly confirm it, save that they are obliged to qualify the implications of the term "brain child." The ideas that Wilson made his own and put into the Covenant did not originate with him.

Of the statements made by those who knew Wilson which the authors found among the Baker Papers in the Library of Congress, the one by Thomas F. Woodlock demands quoting:

"The nemesis that Woodrow Wilson vainly fought was within him- self, but it was as unchangeable, as inexorable as the Greek Fates. In the last few years of his life there was something Promethean about him. The eagle's beak and claws were in his vitals as he lay bound and help- less on his rock of sickness, but he was grimly enduring and coldly defiant to the last. In the lonely citadel of his soul, proud in the conviction that his cause was wholly just, utterly intolerant of criticism, utterly ruthless to opposition, he could not compromise with his daemon. Tragedy if it be not noble is not tragedy, and no one will deny to Woodrow Wilson the elements of nobility. Yet it must be said that the world suffers when Prometheus suffers, and that the very essence of statesmanship lies not in the grim endurance of foreordained defeat, but rather in the wisdom to know when to take occasion by the hand by yielding the shadow to gain the substance. To deny to Woodrow Wilson the quality of supreme statesmanship is only to say that he followed his daemon to the last. And his is a tragedy that Sophocles might well have imagined" (p. xv).

Thus, the insights that Dr. and Mrs. George bring to bear are not wholly revolutionary even in the field of Wilson biography. What they contribute most of all is a kind of equipment which no previous biog- rapher of Wilson or historian of the era has had—a firm, disciplined understanding of the basic discoveries of the last sixty-odd years about human behavior, plus utter scrupulousness in the application of the in- sights so derived to the facts which they have carefully marshaled. They are not themselves psychoanalysts, and they have a certain detachment from the conceptual tools which they have borrowed from analysis and an ability to use the ideas without the jargon (with what restraint is suggested in their "Research Note" at the end of the book, where they permit themselves to slip away from their otherwise invariably lucid English). They have also a diligence and competence in historical research which no professional analyst has yet demonstrated to this reviewer's knowledge—with the possible exception of Ernest Jones in his monumental biography of Freud.

One must acknowledge that to call a biography "Freudian" or "psychoanalytic" in its approach (the authors themselves shrewdly refrain from such boldness) is, even now, to damn it utterly in the minds of many scholars as well as laymen. Good biographies have indeed been written, and no doubt will continue to be written, even about complex personalities, by scholars who are innocent of contemporary knowledge about human behavior. And very bad ones have been written by persons who stretched too thin a smattering of such knowledge, or by those who knew plenty of psychology but were simply unwilling to do the amount of historical research which any good biography requires. Nevertheless, while it is merely regrettable when a biographer or historian handicaps himself unnecessarily by neglecting to cultivate useful tools which could be available to him, it is something else again when he rejects out of prejudice the work of others who are not so handicapped.

What we want to establish here, however, is less the general validity of psychoanalytic concepts, or their pertinence to biography, than the fact that the present authors have used them well. They themselves concede that the merit of their book lies in the degree to which they have succeeded in illuminating the *why* and *how* of Wilson's behavior, rather than in the marshaling of important new facts about his life. Not that they have been content to examine the life from secondary sources alone. Obviously, they could not depend on the compilations of those who did not know what to look for. They have in fact exhaustively examined the primary sources—especially the Wilson, Baker, Hitchcock, and Lansing papers at the Library of Congress, and the Edward M. House papers at the Yale University Library. Even an historian who rejected their basic theses would find much novel and valuable material in this book. He would even find himself with fewer aches and pains than he had expected from going over the course, because the book makes such good reading.

Still, the book interests us basically as an outstanding portrayal of how great enterprises can be turned awry for reasons other than the opposition of wicked or stupid men. How much evil could stem from the compulsive stubbornness of one man, whose claim to distinction among the statesmen of his time was his conspicuous and in a sense genuine morality, is the nearly incredible burden of this book.

The authors are inevitably on weaker ground when they try to explain the genesis of the Wilsonian neurosis than when they describe the man-

ner in which it expressed itself full-blown. Not that their explanation
is implausible. On the contrary, it is arresting and persuasive, and the
evidence to support it is weighty, though necessarily presumptive and incomplete. It is one thing to observe compulsive behavior and identify
it for what it is; it is quite another to find the original causes.[1] The
former is what a sensitive and appropriately educated person can discern
in his friends and acquaintances as well as in himself and, in some instances, in historical figures; the latter usually requires the expert therapist and the couch.

In any case, the authors find as the origin of the adult Wilson's inner
deformity the experience of the child and youth with a demanding and
yet mocking father. Dr. Joseph Ruggles Wilson, a Presbyterian minister
who was noted for his caustic wit, took an extraordinarily active role in
his son's education. He used ridicule freely as a sanction to force his son
to meet his own perfectionist standards, particularly with respect to the
use of language. The son's resentment and rage were almost entirely
repressed, as indicated by, among other things, the esteem and apparent
affection in which he held his father throughout his life. However, the
rage expressed itself early in an atrociously poor performance in his first
years at school. This failure, which the authors interpret as an unconscious *refusal* to learn, of course called for more of the father's characteristic intervention. All his life Wilson felt inferior to his father—significantly enough, in looks as well as in morals and accomplishment. All
his life he struggled against an inner feeling of inadequacy and worthless-
ness *which must ever be disproved.*

For lack of materials the authors have almost nothing to say about
Wilson's mother, save that she "was a rather plain, serious woman, extremely reserved, greatly devoted to her family." They quote also a statement by Wilson written many years later: ". . . I remember how I clung
to her (a laughed-at 'mama's boy') till I was a great big fellow" (p. 5).
We must conclude that she did little or nothing to save her son from the
serious loss of self-esteem which his father was inflicting on him.

The authors, moreover, attempt no conjectures about Wilson's early
sexuality, though one can make some few presumptions from the fact
that he was reared in and completely adhered to a strict Calvinist doctrine. "He prayed, on his knees, daily; read the Bible daily; said grace
before every meal; attended church regularly. These were the outer expressions of a faith which penetrated to his innermost being" (p. 5).
There is also a telltale remark that he made as a youth to a female relation (concerning the melancholia of an artist acquaintance): "Cousin
Mary, it is possible to control your thoughts, you know" (p. 11). We
know also that in later life he was especially dependent on women

---

[1] [This seems to support the view that documents pertaining to the childhood of
historical figures—always difficult to secure—are not necessarily of crucial importance
to a psychoanalytic interpretation of history. *B.M.*]

for the extraordinarily high dose of flattery which was his constant need, as evidenced, for example, in his long-continued correspondence with Mrs. Hulbert.

So far as his adult career is concerned, the evidence supporting an interpretation of compulsive and obsessive behavior is abundant and, in the aggregate, overwhelming. What was the pattern of this behavior? We find, first of all, an intense striving for political domination, which, according to the authors, "was for him a compensatory value, a means of restoring the self-esteem damaged in childhood" (p. 320). But the function of this striving had to be in some fashion concealed. "He could indulge his hidden desire to dominate only by 'purifying' his leadership, by committing it to political projects which articulated the highest moral and idealistic aspirations of the people. His desire for power was mitigated by a simultaneous need for approval, respect and, especially, for feeling virtuous" (*ibid.*). In order to accomplish his ends he hit upon the "highly constructive strategy . . . of committing his desire for domination and his ambition for great accomplishments only to reform projects which already enjoyed considerable support and were within reasonable possibility of achievement" (*ibid.*). Because of this strategy, "the vast energies unleashed by his personal involvement in politics were committed to political objectives both desirable and feasible" (*ibid.*).

One of the things which defeated him was the insatiableness of his ambition. Wilson once said of himself: ". . . I am so constituted that, for some reason or other, I never have a sense of triumph" (p. 320). In other words, he was "unable to derive normal gratification and pleasure from his achievements" (*ibid.*). Success could not satisfy him. "No sooner did Wilson put through one reform plan than he would discover another great work calling for his attention. He was soon pressing it upon legislators as something urgently and immediately to be accepted" (*ibid.*). Such behavior naturally engendered its own opposition, especially since credit for his worthy works was something which he found it extremely difficult to share with others. A suggested modification of his plans he tended to look upon both as criticism of himself personally, which was intolerable, and also as a move to share (i.e., take away from him) some of the glory of his accomplishment. He responded accordingly.

It is impressive how the cyclic pattern of Wilson's behavior was repeated in three executive posts he held during his lifetime, first as President of Princeton University, then as Governor of New Jersey, and finally as President of the United States. In each case he came into office on a wave of support and approbation as an energetic reformer, proceeded to accomplish many worthy reforms, beat people over the head in the process, began to inspire personal opposition, and thereupon became wholly oriented to that opposition rather than to the object for which he was presumably fighting. Arthur S. Link, another contemporary biographer of Wilson, has also compared the Princeton period with the White

House period, calling the former the microcosm of the latter and ascribing to both situations "the character and proportions of a Greek tragedy."

We have so far said little in this review about Col. Edward M. House, and it is not to be assumed that the authors are comparably niggardly. The title of their book is an honest one, despite the fact that they give considerably fewer pages to Colonel House than to his eminent partner, and also feel impelled to carry the narrative beyond the time when House ceased to have any influence on Wilson. For that period contained what is the tragic denouement of the entire narrative—the wholly needless fight with the Senate resulting in the rejection of the Paris treaty with its League Covenant.

One regrets that House's character is not as well illuminated as Wilson's, for in the absence of explanation it is comparably confounding. Here is a man, of extraordinary political insight and executive talent, who deliberately sought out and attached himself to an alter ego who could endure, as he could not, the hazards of tremendous celebrity and of supreme political status and authority. The explanation offered by our authors—that an illness suffered from a fall when he was twelve left him lacking in physical strength and that he did not own the looks for high leadership—is not altogether convincing.

After his first meeting with Wilson, while the latter was still Governor of New Jersey and only a subject for speculation as a presidential candidate, House wrote to his brother-in-law: "It is just such a chance as I have always wanted for never before have I found both the man and the opportunity" (p. 93). Could such an aspiration toward supreme and yet indirect power ever have been more deliberate? And that he should have succeeded in making his man president and then guiding him for the better part of two administrations, his man being a Wilson in temperament and character, argues a personal and political achievement of the first magnitude. History records many court favorites, but few of them assisted in creating the monarch from whom they derived their power, and few of them were as consistently an influence for good rather than evil.

House was eager to fit himself into a role which for most persons of anything like comparable ability would be impossibly demanding—demanding in terms of the required flow of flattery and of other forms of dissimulation. In view of the crippled personality of Wilson, and his incessant demands for reassurance concerning his own wisdom and goodness, it is difficult to comprehend the degree to which House succeeded in remaining for eight long years the intimate confidant *and* adviser to Wilson. One cannot suppress the feeling that House was also deformed inwardly, but in a happily complementary way. And when he made a move toward a more normal relationship and greater integrity of character, the break occurred. At the Paris Peace Conference he accepted for the first time an official status—as one of the five American commissioners (including the President)—and at that conference he began to push upon the President some unwelcome advice, concerning, significantly, the latter's relationship with the Senate.

As the authors point out, "Wilson's affection for House seems to have been rooted in House's extraordinary capacity for enhancing the President's self-esteem. House's willingness readily to accept Wilson's opinions no matter what his own were, and the fact that he enjoyed status only insofar as Wilson chose to bestow it, figured importantly in the President's ability to accept the Colonel as a close friend and adviser. By the time Wilson left Paris in mid-February, these twin foundations of the relationship were disturbed" (p. 242). And immediately upon Wilson's return, they collapsed entirely. Toward the end of the conference, Wilson was sitting as the lone American member in the Council of Four, and telling neither House nor anyone else what was going on. In passing we may observe also the miserable role played by Secretary of State Lansing, who, along with the other American commissioners, was "reduced to seeking information from the gossip of the staffs of other delegations" (p. 249).

The story of Wilson's conduct at the Peace Conference is fascinating and astounding, especially the revelation of his unwillingness to see issues reopened even when doing so promised to regain for him positions which he had previously relinquished at great pain and cost. Not having any sense for the requirements of the bargaining process, and being temperamentally unable even to capitalize on his own stubbornness, he comes out as an extraordinarily poor negotiator; and his insistence on going alone to the meetings of the "Big Four" must be classified as sheer recklessness. But the great, tragic climax of the book is the story of the battle with the Senate and the utterly needless defeat. It is not the story of a "little group of willful men," as the President categorized his opposition, but of one supremely willful man, himself. It was he who was the one great "irreconcilable."

A two-thirds majority of the Senate favoring ratification of the Treaty with its League Covenant was assured—since the public overwhelmingly favored such action—provided only that Wilson accepted the insertion of some exceedingly mild reservations in the instrument of ratification. These reservations for the most part made explicit certain understandings that would normally be considered to be implicit in the language of the covenant. Wilson early expressed a willingness to make those reservations the subject of a separate statement expressing the United States government's understanding of the treaty and the covenant. But he would not include this statement in the instrument of ratification. And on such a difference as this the whole treaty was permitted to founder!

Senator Lodge, who led the small group of senators that wanted entirely to reject American adherence to a league, based his strategy on a supposition which he expressed well in his own words: "Never under any set of circumstances in this world could he [Wilson] be induced to accept a treaty with Lodge reservations appended to it" (p. 279). He correctly intuited that Wilson would be more intent on punishing his Senate opposition for defiling his treaty than on getting that treaty through even in modified form.

Lodge's tactics were in the main to delay approval and wait for Wilson's stubbornness to drive the moderate-reservationists into his arms. But even at the end of his maneuvers, the most the Senate was holding out for was a group of mild reservations, which, however, they insisted on having attached to the instrument of ratification.

Wilson's assertion that this requirement would necessitate a complete renegotiation of the Treaty was patently false, and was exposed as hollow by a discreet letter to the London *Times* by Viscount Grey. Grey had previously come to Washington at the request of his government to persuade Wilson that he was exaggerating the importance of the reservation issue, but Wilson had let him cool his heels for four months without seeing him, using his illness as an excuse (although toward the end he was seeing other callers). In the meantime there had been the preposterous journey to bring the issue to "the people," who, inasmuch as no election was impending, could do nothing about it save write letters. Then there had been the collapse and the stroke. But Wilson was completely in possession of his faculties when he refrained from changing his standing instructions to Senator Hitchcock at the moment the ratification issue came up for a vote.

Earlier the French Ambassador had assured the President that the British and French governments would accept the reservations then being discussed in the Senate. "Mr. Ambassador," Wilson had declared, "I shall consent to nothing. The Senate must take its medicine" (p. 311). And when the treaty came up for the vote, with what were now called the Lodge reservations, Hitchcock insisted that the duty of the administration supporters was to vote "nay." Twenty-three of them did, and these, along with the "irreconcilables," were enough to bring the opposing vote to 35, with 49 in favor. The majority in favor of the treaty did not reach the necessary two-thirds. "Some years later, Hitchcock admitted that he had had 'all I could do' to hold enough Democrats in line to beat the Treaty" (p. 313). As the last name was called and it was clear the Treaty was dead, one of the "irreconcilables," Senator Brandegee, turned to Lodge and remarked: "We can always depend on Mr. Wilson. He never has failed us" (*ibid.*).

Whatever one may think of the intrinsic value of the League of Nations, the American rejection of the treaty with the League Covenant meant the nonparticipation of the United States in all the subsequent peace arrangements of Europe. In view of what occurred in the two decades following, it is hard to believe that nonparticipation was anything but deeply unfortunate. Perhaps the United States would have passed through a phase of intense isolationism anyway, but we know that the rejection of the League followed by the Republican victory at the polls was a tremendous stimulus to that mood. And this rejection could have been avoided if Wilson had followed the urging of, among others, his predecessor in office, William Howard Taft, or if he had not expunged from his councils the canny and modest-though-ambitious Col. Edward House.

This book is a good antidote to the irrepressible tendency of political scientists, as well as laymen, to think of high politics as something carried on by disembodied spirits, whose larger actions may vary in degree of shrewdness and foresight but are seldom affected by submerged and hidden passions. It is incidentally also sobering to Americans to observe that a man like Wilson, although exceptional even in the history of the American presidency, was nevertheless able to win two terms of office at a time of cataclysmic world events. Because he was the kind of man who inevitably wore out his friendships and the enthusiasm of his supporters, he could almost certainly never have risen to the top in a system like the British.

It remains to be noted that the authors of this excellent and beautifully written book pay a handsome tribute in their "Research Note" to the stimulus originally given them in this enterprise by Drs. Nathan Leites and Harold D. Lasswell. Their pioneering work in this field, especially the latter's, is well known to all political scientists, but this volume represents the fullest and best fruition of their influence that this reviewer has yet seen.

On the Character and
Married Life of Henry VIII

J. C. Flügel

It is doubtful whether the married life of any monarch in the world's history has aroused such interest and attained such notoriety as that of Henry VIII. In popular estimation the relations of King Henry to his wives probably outweigh in fascination all other features of a lengthy and momentous reign; while even to the professed historian the study of Henry's six marriages—closely connected as they are with events of great importance occurring at a particularly critical period in the cultural and political development of Europe—must also be of very considerable importance. No apology is needed, therefore, for attempting a further treatment of this theme—even in brief and summary fashion—if by so doing we can throw a few fresh rays of light upon the factors which were at work in producing the events recorded in this page of history.

A well-known historian, commenting on the long series of Henry's matrimonial experiences, has justly remarked that "a single misadventure of such a kind might have been explained by accident or by moral infirmity. For such a combination of disasters some common cause must have existed, which may be, or ought to be, discoverable." [1] It has seemed to the present writer that the common cause in question is to be found largely in certain constant features of Henry's mental life and character, the proper understanding of which concerns the psychologist as much as

"On the Character and Married Life of Henry VIII." Reprinted from *International Journal of Psycho-Analysis*, I, 1920, pp. 24-55. Copyright 1920 by the *International Journal of Psycho-Analysis*.

[1] J. A. Froude, *History of England*, II, p. 469.

the historian. It is in the hope of indicating the nature of some of the more important of these constant features that the present short essay has been written. The conclusions at which it arrives are tentative only, and are put forward with all the diffidence that is due to the circumstance that the writer is very well aware of the shortcomings of his historical knowledge and training. The historical materials bearing on the reign of Henry VIII are now very numerous, and would require years of patient study for their adequate assimilation: indeed, it is evident that their complete elucidation and evaluation at the hands of historians are as yet far from being accomplished. Much that is here suggested may therefore have to be revised, both as the result of expert historical criticism and of an increased understanding of the relevant facts. The application of psychological knowledge to the task of interpreting the events of history will, however, certainly constitute a very necessary piece of work for future scholarship, and as a small addition to the relatively few attempts that have been made in this direction, the following suggestions as to the nature of the psychological influences at work in the married life of Henry VIII may perhaps be of some interest both to psychologists and to historians.

It is unfortunate that, in spite of the many known facts which bear upon the adult life of Henry VIII, our knowledge of his early life is very slender. The researches of Freud and of the workers of his school have shown that a knowledge of the events of childhood and of youth is a very valuable aid to the interpretation of the mental characteristics of later years. In the case of Henry VIII, however, we have to be content with few facts, and those mostly connected with affairs of state but little calculated to throw light on questions of psychology.

Henry was born in June, 1491, and was the fourth of his parent's five children, the earlier children being Arthur (Henry's only brother), Margaret (afterwards Queen of Scotland), and Elizabeth (who died in infancy), while the single younger child was Mary (afterwards Queen of France and, later, Duchess of Suffolk). Henry's father (Henry VII) had ascended the throne of England as the result of his triumph over Richard III in the last battle of the War of the Roses, and by his able and successful rule of twenty-four years had definitely put an end to that bloody and disastrous struggle. He had claimed the throne by right of inheritance and conquest; but to add to the strength of his position he had married Elizabeth of York, eldest daughter of Edward IV, uniting thus the rival houses whose dissensions had devastated England for the preceding thirty years. There was, indeed, a difficulty in the match, inasmuch as Henry and Elizabeth were within the prohibited degrees of affinity (both being descended from Catherine, wife of Henry V), a papal dispensation being necessary before the marriage could legally be made. Henry, however—anxious, no doubt, for the additional security of title which the marriage would provide—did not wait to receive the dispensation, and the wedding was celebrated a few months after he ascended the throne—the dispensation, fortunately, arriving shortly afterwards.

Throughout the reign there were not wanting efforts of rival claimants to the throne to displace Henry from the position he had won, nor uprisings on the part of a people grown ill used to long periods of settled government. The long conflict between the rival roses did not give place suddenly to an era of assured internal peace, but, in dying, continued for many years to manifest itself in minor upheavals which formed a continual menace to the sovereignty of the first of the Tudors. Henry, it is true, successfully weathered every storm that threatened to engulf him, and was in the main upheld by the great majority of his subjects, who realized that his rule was the only alternative to a return of anarchy and civil war. Nevertheless, we cannot but suppose that the difficulties and dangers which surrounded his father's throne must have exercised a powerful influence over the younger Henry's mind. The envy with which, even in ordinary families, a son is apt to look upon the superior powers and privileges of a father is liable to be intensified when the father enjoys the exceptional influence and honor appertaining to a king. Under these circumstances any threat to the father's authority almost inevitably arouses in the son the idea of superseding the father.

In the present case such ideas were liable to be still further reinforced by the following facts: first, that the mother's claim to the throne (and therefore, of course, that of her children) was regarded by confirmed Yorkists as superior to that of the father; and, secondly, that the marriage of the parents was not a happy one, the behavior of the elder Henry being in general much wanting in warmth and affection toward his consort, in spite of the good looks, piety, and learning by which the latter is reported to have been distinguished.

The conditions were thus favorable (1) for the arousal in young Henry's mind of the hope and the desire to succeed to his father's place of authority (tendencies which may have been still further strengthened by the fact that he was invested at a tender age with various high offices—a device of his father's for concentrating as much power as possible in his own hands); (2) for the development of a powerful Oedipus complex—i. e., the desire to get rid of the father and possess the mother in his stead: the cold relations between mother and father and the beauty and goodness of the mother both constituting strong incentives to that desire.

The hostile feelings toward the father which may well have arisen under these circumstances were, however, in the case of young Prince Henry, fated to suffer to a large extent a process of displacement onto the person of his elder brother Arthur. To ambitious younger sons the privileges of primogeniture are always irksome; particularly so, it would seem, in the case of royal families, where the privileges in question are so exceptional in nature. In the present case young Henry's title to succeed his father was of course barred by the presence of Arthur—a prince who seems to have possessed qualities and abilities not inferior to those of his younger brother, and whose future reign was destined, in the hopes of many persons, to mark the opening of a new period of peace and prosperity, free from the unhappy dissensions of the immediate past.[2]

In 1501, when Henry was ten years old, Arthur, himself then only just fifteen, was married to Catherine of Aragon, daughter of Ferdinand of Aragon and Isabella of Castile. Henry himself was no mere spectator at the wedding ceremony, but led his sister-in-law and future wife to the altar. At her formal reception into England six weeks earlier, he had already played an equally important part. It is not improbable that these events induced in Henry some degree of jealousy toward his brother, thus adding a sexual element to the more purely personal envy which may well already have existed. To meet a comely girl and to hand her over with much ceremony to a brother—a brother who already appears to possess more than a fair share of the good things of life—is a procedure which is well calculated to arouse an emotion of this kind. Students of folklore and legend are familiar with the not infrequent type of story in which a situation of this sort is represented—the young hero being despatched to welcome, and escort to her new home, the bride destined for the prince or king—stories which usually end with the awakening of illicit love between the hero and the lady, whose hand is already promised to another. In the light of later events we may perhaps be permitted to suppose that Henry, in spite of his youth, did not altogether escape the temptations to which his legendary predecessors in the same office had succumbed, and that the sexual elements of the Oedipus complex (which, as we know, are present in every child, and which, as is abundantly clear to the psychoanalyst, find expression in the legends in question) received in this way an additional motive for the transference onto brother and sister-in-law respectively of the feelings originally directed onto father and mother.

Arthur and Catherine had but little time in which to enjoy their married life. For a few months they kept a merry court as Prince and Princess of Wales at Ludlow Castle, and then Arthur succumbed to an attack of the sweating sickness which was ravaging the Welsh borders, leaving Henry, therefore, as the legitimate successor to the throne.[3]

[2] This hope was indicated in the very choice of the name of the young Prince of Wales—a name which aroused no painful or exciting memories of the period of civil war, but which was associated with noble traditions of remoter British history.

[3] In later life Henry showed a very lively fear of the sweating sickness—a fear which has exposed him to a charge of cowardice at the hands of unfavorable historians. If, as seems to be the case, this fear was a somewhat isolated and unusual feature of his character, it would seem not unreasonable to suppose that its abnormal strength was due to the notion of a talion punishment—an idea often found in the unconscious levels of the mind: in other words, that Henry was afraid lest the same sickness which had unexpectedly swept away his rival (thus gratifying his desires of greatness) would in turn prove the means of his own undoing. [Cf. William L. Langer, "The Next Assignment," pp. 95-103, on the psychological effect of plagues. *B.M.*]

Immediately on the receipt of the tragic news, Catherine's parents—unwilling to abandon the diplomatic advantages offered by the marriage of their daughter to the English heir apparent—started negotiations for the marriage of the young widow to her still younger brother-in-law. A marriage of this kind was, of course, forbidden both by earthly law and heavenly injunction; but fortunately a dispensation from the Pope was capable of overcoming both these obstacles. Henry's father, too, was not unwilling for the match: but a dispute arose over Catherine's dowry, part only of which had been paid. Ferdinand not only refused to pay the balance, but even demanded the return of the part already paid, while Henry VII on his side required the whole of the dowry as originally contemplated.

While the dispute was still in progress, Henry VII became a widower and thereupon proposed, as a fresh solution of the problem, that he himself should marry Catherine. Whether this proposal was an earnest one or not, it was certainly calculated to stir the Oedipus complex in young Henry's mind, by bringing him into a situation of such a kind that he could scarcely but regard himself as in some sense a sexual rival of his father, while at the same time it was likely to reinforce the transference of the mother-regarding feelings onto Catherine.

Whatever its ultimate psychological effects may have been, the proposal was undoubtedly successful as an immediate diplomatic measure. Ferdinand and Isabella moderated their terms with regard to the dowry: the marriage of brother and sister-in-law appeared eminently respectable as compared with the more shocking union of father and daughter-in-law, and the marriage treaty between young Henry and Catherine was definitely settled, it being arranged that the wedding should be celebrated as soon as Henry should have attained his fourteenth year.

But the death of Isabella shortly afterwards induced Henry VII to repent of this arrangement. There were various claimants for the crown of Castile, and the whole political situation became for a time uncertain and obscure. The alliance with Ferdinand lost much of its attractiveness, a variety of fresh schemes for the marriage of young Henry were freely discussed, and on the eve of his fifteenth birthday he solemnly repudiated the marriage contract which he had previously signed.

Three years later, however, in spite of various projects, no further betrothal had been made. Meanwhile Henry VII had reached the end of his career, and on his deathbed seems to have reverted to his original plan as regards the younger Henry's marriage. The dying king exhorted his son to complete the long-projected and much-delayed union with his sister-in-law, gave at the same time sundry other pieces of advice, most of which Henry took well to heart. Indeed there can be but little doubt that a tendency to follow the wishes of his dead father—a "postponed obedience" of the kind with which psychoanalysts are familiar—formed a by no means unimportant element in Henry's character during the earlier years of his reign. Among his other deathbed wishes Henry VII expressed the desire that his son should defend the Church, make war upon the infidel, pay good heed to his faithful councilors and (perhaps also) that he should put out of the way Edmund de la Pole, Earl of Suffolk, the nearest White Rose claimant to the throne. The troubled state of European politics prevented young Henry from making war on an extensive scale upon the Turk,[4] but the other behests he truly carried out. Henry, throughout his early years (and indeed in some sense throughout his life) was much concerned to preserve the true religion and the institution of the Church; both by his deeds and by his written words he fought against all doctrines and tendencies which he regarded as heretical. So great, indeed, was his ardor in this direction that he won from the spiritual head of Christendom the title of Defender of the Faith—a title borne by his successors to this day. With regard to councilors, his dependence on their approval and advice (and especially on that of Wolsey) in the first half of his reign is notorious; while de la Pole, imprisoned from the first, was executed four years afterwards.

If in these matters Henry obeyed the dying wishes of his father, he was no less willing to follow the latter's instructions as regards marriage, especially perhaps, in this case, because these instructions coincided with the tendencies emanating from his own unconscious Oedipus complex, enabling him in this way to combine a conscious obedience to the behests of filial piety with a realization of unconscious desires connected with hostility and jealousy toward his father and brother. The marriage was indeed hurried forward with almost indecent haste, being celebrated in a little over a month after the elder Henry's death. A few days later the young couple were crowned king and queen with much splendor and ceremony in Westminster Abbey.

Henry having now succeeded to the throne in his eighteenth year, a variety of circumstances combined to make his position in some ways an exceptional one in the whole history of English monarchy. He was the only surviving son of his father, and it was generally recognized that in his person were bound up all hopes of freedom from internal discord. The Wars of the Roses were by now sufficiently distant to make the claims of other possible aspirants to the throne appear unsubstantial as compared with the firm *de facto* rights of the Tudor family, while at the same time the memory of those wars was still strong enough to make even a tyrannous exercise of royal power seem preferable to the alternative of civil war or anarchy. Added to these circumstances tending to make Henry's power as king more than usually absolute were other factors of a more personal nature. Henry possessed abilities and qualities unusual in degree and number and of such a kind as to make him as

---

[4] It should be noted, however, (1) that his very first military undertaking was of this kind (the expedition of 1511 to cooperate with his *father-in-law* Ferdinand against the Moors; (2) that Henry declared that "he cherished like an heirloom the ardour against the Infidel which he inherited from his father" (A. F. Pollard, *Henry VIII*, p. 54).

a prince intensely popular. All contemporary authorities agree in describing him as exceptionally handsome, tall, strong, skillful and talented in arts and letters, with a very special degree of aptitude for all the manly sports and exercises of his age. Englishmen of the sixteenth century had in their way as much affection for a true "sportsman" as those of the nineteenth and twentieth centuries, and Henry's popularity with many of his subjects was, as one historian suggests,[5] probably not less than that which would at the present time fall to the lot of a young monarch who was a hero of the athletic world, "the finest oar, the best bat, the crack marksman of his day." Henry, moreover, was very fond of all kinds of social festivity and merriment, delighting in sumptuous display and courtly ceremony—qualities which, though they eventually led to difficulties through the extravagance which they engendered, yet appeared at first a welcome contrast to the somewhat austere and parsimonious regime of his father.

This combination of happy circumstances may well have fostered in the young king an undue development of the positive "self-regarding" and self-seeking motives, the tendencies calculated to lead to such development being in his case greater even than are those to which most youthful ruler are exposed. Nevertheless, although fully conscious both of the prerogatives due to his circumstances and station and of his own personal abilities, he seldom (especially during the early part of his reign) became harsh, overbearing, tyrannous, or disrespectful of the advice or opinions of others. His self-reliance and self-will were happily tempered by a sound appreciation of the nature and extent of the forces—psychological and sociological—with which he had to deal, and by a certain piety and regard for persons or bodies carrying the weight of constitutional or traditional authority.

Psychoanalysts will be inclined to regard this last characteristic as a displacement of tendencies and feelings originally directed to the person of his father. We have already seen some evidence of this in connection with the carrying out of his father's deathbed wishes. Henry's reliance on his councilors—Warham, Wolsey, Cromwell, and others—his persistent desire to proceed in accordance with, rather than against, legal and constitutional authority, his anxiety to gain the approval of, and—later—to conciliate, the Pope, may all very probably be correctly regarded as further manifestations of this side of his character—a side which is of great importance for a true appreciation of his personality, and one which may easily be overlooked on a first casual view of his career.

These two sets of motives—the egoistic and the venerative we may perhaps, for the sake of brevity, be allowed to call them—through their conflicts, interactions and combinations probably played a very weighty role in determining Henry's conduct, and through this, of producing many of the outstanding features—political and domestic—of his reign. We shall

[5] Pollard, *op. cit.*, p. 41.

have occasion to refer to them more than once in our examination of the subsequent events of his life.

To return now to the history of Henry's married life: The early years with Catherine seem to have been gay and happy. Only very gradually did Henry become dissatisfied and superstitious as regards the union with his sister-in-law. No doubt a variety of causes contributed to the eventual rupture, which did not begin till 1527—eighteen years after the celebration of the marriage. Catherine, in spite of some excellent qualities, was tactless, obstinate, and narrow-minded, and had not that (real or apparent) pliability and subservience which Henry, in virtue of his egoistic tendencies, demanded in a consort. Worse than this, Catherine appears to have suffered from a father fixation of some strength, in virtue of which she was unable to transfer adequately her loyalty and affection from her parents and the land of her birth to her husband and the land of her adoption.[6] For many years she wrote to her father in the most pious and obedient terms, and regularly acted as his ambassador and the supporter of his interests—interests that often did not coincide with, and were sometimes in direct opposition to, those of her husband; while even in purely English affairs, she sometimes acted in a manner prejudicial to Henry's influence and desires.

The most important factor was however, beyond doubt, Catherine's inability to produce a male heir to the throne and the general unfruitfulness of the marriage, which from the point of view of issue was a long and almost unbroken series of disasters (due to miscarriages, premature and still births), the only surviving child being the Princess Mary, born in 1516. Henry's need of a legitimate son was a very real one. Without a recognized successor, the security of the throne and the kingdom was in danger, as there could be no doubt that in such a case there would arise at Henry's death many claimants for the supreme power. Henry, moreover, was peculiarly sensitive on this point. There can be little doubt that, like many others, he saw in his heirs a continuation of his own life and power —an immortalization of himself, without which his egoistic impulses could find no complete satisfaction.

Furthermore, this failure in the fertility of his marriage aroused superstitious fears connected with Henry's Oedipus complex. The idea of sterility as a punishment for incest is one that is deeply rooted in the human mind,[7] and in the case of a union such as that of Henry and Catherine, there was scriptural authority for the infliction of a penalty of this description.[8] The scruples of conscience which were originally urged as a reason

[6] It must be said, however, in Catherine's defense that the circumstances of Arthur's early death and of the none too flattering or considerate treatment that she received in England during the period of her young widowhood were certainly calculated to produce a regression of feeling in favor of her own family and home.

[7] See, for instance, Sir J. G. Frazer, *Totemism and Exogamy*, vol. IV, pp. 106 ff.

[8] "If a man shall take his brother's wife, it is an unclean thing. He hath uncovered his brother's nakedness. They shall be childless." Leviticus XX, 21.

for the delay in the marriage may have been a mere diplomatic move on the part of Henry VII, but in the case of the younger Henry, in view of his genuine respect for religion and of the nature of the unconscious feelings he entertained toward his brother, they may well have had some real psychological foundation. Quieted for a time as the result of his father's deathbed wishes and Henry's own inclinations, these scruples gradually rose again when the course of events seemed to be bringing the divine prophecy very near to fulfillment; and beyond all reasonable doubt, they constituted a genuine and all-important factor in Henry's desire for a divorce from Catherine. Brewer, as the result of a prolonged study of contemporary documents, tells us that Henry's doubts and fears upon this subject rose slowly in his mind as the result of more or less unconscious processes.

> The exact date at which Henry began to entertain these scruples and their precise shape at the first, can never be determined with accuracy; for the most sufficient of all reasons: they were not known to the king himself. They sprung up unconsciously from a combination of causes, and took definite form and colour in his breast by insensible degrees. They must have brooded in his mind some time before he would acknowledge them to himself, still less confess them to others.[9]

Such gradual growth of feelings of this kind is totally opposed to the popular view that Henry's desire to divorce Catherine was merely an outcome of his sensual longing for Anne Boleyn, and indicates the operation of more deep-lying mental processes, such as those we have suggested, i.e., the arousal of fears resting on the repression of incestuous desires—desires in all probability originally connected with his parents (Oedipus complex), but, through the force of circumstances, transferred to his brother and sister-in-law.

This is not to say, of course, that Henry's attachment for Anne did not also play an important part in his desire to be rid of Catherine. Probably nothing else but a genuine passion for Anne would have kept him constant and inflexible during the long and difficult period of the divorce. Catherine was six years older than Henry, and the mental and physical strain attendant on her long and unsuccessful series of attempts at child-bearing had no doubt considerably diminished her attractiveness. Before his infatuation with Anne Boleyn, Henry had enjoyed the favors of two mistresses: Elizabeth Blount, by whom he had, so far as we know, his only illegitimate child—a boy, whom, with the failure of male heirs, he afterwards thought seriously of raising to the position of successor to the throne; and Mary Boleyn, sister of Anne Boleyn.

---

[9] *Op. cit.*, vol. II, p. 162. [This must refer to John Sherren Brewer's book, *The Reign of Henry VIII from His Accession to the Death of Wolsey*, ed. by James Gairdner, 2 vols. (London, 1884); Flügel is in error in thinking that he has already cited it. *B.M.*]

We know comparatively little of these affairs, and the very existence of the second liaison has been sometimes doubted.[10]

By psychoanalysts, accustomed as they are to attach importance to apparently inessential details of this kind, it may not be considered unworthy of notice that the Christian names of the two ladies in question are the same as those held by important members of Henry's own family —his mother and younger sister respectively. The suspicion thus raised that the name may have been of some importance in determining Henry's choice in these two cases is strengthened by three further facts, which may be briefly mentioned here: (1) Henry's two daughters were also called by the same two names, viz., Mary and Elizabeth respectively; (2) his only other female favorite whom we know by name, was Margaret Shelton, the Christian name being here identical with Henry's elder sister (afterwards wife of James V of Scotland); (3) Mary Boleyn's mother was Lady *Elizabeth* Boleyn, and there existed a curious rumor that Henry had indulged in improper relations with the mother, as well as with the daughter.[11]

It is true that Henry is reported to have himself denied the truth of this; but even if (as is very possibly the case) the rumor itself is exaggerated, it may well have been founded on some genuine attraction which Henry may have felt for the Lady Elizabeth. If this is so, in the light of psychoanalytic knowledge, it would appear not overbold to suggest that the mother and daughter, Elizabeth and Mary Blount, were, to Henry's unconscious mind, substitutes for Elizabeth and Mary Tudor—his mother and his sister respectively. This would at once constitute additional evidence in favor of the existence in Henry of incest tendencies and family fixations and fit in with certain important features of Henry's relationship to Anne Boleyn, which are as follows.

One of the most inconsistent facts about the divorce of Catherine and subsequent marriage with Anne is that, although the incestuous relationship between Henry and Catherine was made the sole and all-important ground for claiming the divorce, the immediately succeeding second marriage involved the consummation of a relationship extremely similar to that which was supposed to invalidate the first. Catherine was Henry's sister in virtue of her previous marriage with his brother Arthur; Anne was his sister in virtue of his own (illicit) relationship to her sister Mary. He was therefore only giving up one sister in order to take on another; and the very same (papal) powers that had to be invoked to grant the dissolution of the first marriage on the ground of incest had to be approached with a view to granting a dispensation because of the incestuous nature of the second union. Viewed in the light of sound diplomacy or of reasonable moral sense, the inconsistency involved in this procedure is

[10] Though the proofs of its existence seem quite adequate. See Paul Friedmann, *Anne Boleyn*, vol. II, Appendix B.

[11] Brewer, *Letters and Papers*, IV, CCCXXIX, footnote; also *Reign of Henry VIII*, vol. II, p. 170; Friedmann, *op. cit.*, vol. II, p. 326.

absurdly evident. It cannot, in fact, be accounted for on either of these
planes of thought. Such inconsistency, however, is quite a characteristic
feature of conduct determined—partly or wholly—by unconscious complexes, and as such, probably, it has to be regarded and explained.

It is not necessary here to enter into the long and tedious history of the
proceedings for divorce, which extended over a period of six years, from
1527 to 1533. These proceedings derive their great historical importance
from the fact that they were the occasion of the breach with Rome (the
breach that opened the way to the Reformation in England). Their importance for the development of Henry's mind and character is due to a
similar reason. The main original difficulty in the granting of the divorce
(apart from the very strong popular feeling in England in favor of
Catherine) was due to the following facts: first, it involved the annulling
of the previous papal dispensation—a procedure which might seem liable
to bring future papal dispensations (and indeed the papal power generally) into disrepute; secondly and chiefly, the Pope was at that time in
the power of Charles V, who, both for political and family reasons—he
was, of course, Catherine's nephew—was opposed to the divorce.

The Pope being thus, by the force of circumstances, brought into opposition with Henry's policy and unable to grant the divorce, as he had
done recently in the case of other highly placed persons (notably in the
case of Louis XII before he married Henry's sister Mary, in that of Bran-
don, Duke of Suffolk, previous to his marriage to the same sister after
Louis's death, and in that of Henry's other sister Margaret—cases which
were certainly in Henry's mind as precedents), obstacles of one kind or another were continually placed in the way of Henry's desire. The consequent
long delay in the realization of his wishes brought up in Henry's mind a
conflict between the two aspects of his character to which we have previously referred—the egoistic and venerative aspects—with results of
great importance, both for his future married life and his career in general. In virtue, probably, of the feelings of love and respect which he held
toward his father, Henry was in his early years most anxious to win and
retain the approval of the Pope.[12] He had ever been willing to defend the
Pope and the Church in word and deed, both against armed force and
spiritual heresy; in fact, "his championship of the Holy See had been the
most unselfish part of Henry's policy";[13] and there was no doubt that he
was most anxious to obtain the quasi-paternal sanction of the divorce and
remarriage which a papal edict would afford.

But as time passed, and the inability to obtain the fulfillment of his
desires with the Pope's consent and approval became more and more apparent, Henry's egoistic motives began to gain the mastery and to over-

[12] The Pope of course, as his very title signifies, is one of the most regular and normal
father substitutes.
[13] Pollard, *op. cit.*, p. 107.

whelm the venerative tendencies, which had hitherto formed such an important element in his character. So far, indeed, did the former motives eventually prevail that Henry ultimately brought himself not only to arrange for the divorce to be carried out at home without the Pope's authority, to defy at once the Pope, the Emperor, and his own people, and to brave the terrors of the papal excommunication, but even to set himself in the Pope's place by becoming the head of the Church in England and to assume a power, temporal and spiritual, which has never perhaps been equaled by any other British sovereign. This splendid triumph of self-assertion, in the face of severe obstacles,[14] can only have been achieved by a very complete victory of the egoistic over the venerative tendencies. That such a victory took place is indicated by Henry's contempt of the power which he had formerly exalted, as when he said that "if the Pope issued ten thousand excommunications, he would not care a straw for them," that "he would show the Princes how small was really the power of the Pope" and "that when the Pope had done what he liked on his side, he (Henry) would do what he liked here." In such an attitude of defiance psychoanalysts will immediately recognize a displacement of the desire to overthrow the rule of the father and usurp his authority—a desire based on the primitive Oedipus complex.

From the time of his split with Rome, Henry's character underwent a marked transformation. He became vastly more despotic, determined to rule as well as to reign; more intolerant of any kind of limitation of his power, and dependent on his own decisions in all matters, great and small, instead of submitting to the advice of councilors, as he had hitherto so largely done.

The most significant and important step in this last direction was of course that which brought about the fall of Wolsey. It is fairly certain that, in the day of his power, Wolsey too was regarded by Henry with feelings originally connected with his father-venerative tendencies. These feelings may have flowed more freely and more consistently onto Wolsey's person because, as Friedmann well suggests,[15] Wolsey, as an ecclesiastic, was not brought into such direct competition with Henry's claims to manly qualities as layman would have been. The fields of war, sport, and sex were, for instance, excluded, and the sphere of politics, in which Wolsey so excelled, was one in which Henry only gradually began to take a lively interest. However, when this interest reached a certain degree

[14] Cp. the words of Pollard, *op. cit.*, p. 306. "It was the King and the King alone, who kept England on the course which he had mapped out. Pope and Emperor were defied; Europe was shocked; Francis himself disapproved of the breach with the Church; Ireland was in revolt; Scotland, as ever, was hostile; legislation had been thrust down the throats of a recalcitrant Church, and, we are asked to believe, of a no less unwilling House of Commons, while the people at large were seething with indignation at the insults heaped upon the injured Queen and her daughter."

[15] *Op. cit.*, vol. I, p. 34.

of intensity, as it did under the stimulus of the proceedings for divorce, Henry became intolerant of Wolsey's guidance, with the inevitable result of Wolsey's fall.[16]

After Wolsey's fall none other attained his unique position, even Cromwell, in the height of his power, occupying a far inferior place. As regards religion too, Henry moved on a consistent road to power. In creating himself head of the Church, he not only took unto himself the paternal authority of the Pope, but became to some extent a sharer of the divine power of which the Pope had been the earthly representative. As Luther declared, "Junker Henry meant to be God, and to do as pleased himself." [17]

This identification of himself with God—the *Gottmenschkomplex,* as Ernest Jones has called it[18]—found further expression in his breaking up of the monasteries, his prohibitions against the worship of saints and images, the consistent exclusion of clerics from the higher posts of state which they had hitherto occupied, and the endeavors to define the orthodox faith and produce—by force if necessary—a general uniformity of religious belief within his dominions; all measures tending to prevent the possibility of opposition or rivalry to his quasi-omnipotent power in the religious sphere.

Throughout all this magnificent triumph of the egoistic tendencies, Henry steered his course with a level head. His success in the face of circumstances which would have been the undoing of most other monarchs was due partly to the unique conditions of his time, which, as we have seen, made possible and even agreeable a degree of despotism which at the other periods would have been resented; partly, to the exceeding strength of will and self-reliance that Henry developed after the overthrow of the father-regarding venerative attitude, in the course of his struggle with the Pope; partly too, to his firm grasp of reality in the field of politics. Few men have been able to reconcile, as he did, an intense egotism and an enormous lust for power with an undistorted vision of

---

[16] Though other important influences were also, of course, at work, notably (1) Wolsey's connection with the Church; (2) the well-founded suspicion that Wolsey was not too favorably disposed to the projected marriage with Anne Boleyn, Wolsey thus becoming an obstacle to the consummation of Henry's sexual desires, and in this way bringing upon himself the hostile elements of Henry's Oedipus complex.

In his later dealings with Wolsey and with Warham, Archbishop of Canterbury, Henry would seem sometimes to have had in mind a comparison between his own relations to the Cardinal and the Archbishop and those of his predecessor, Henry II, to Thomas à Becket (e. g., Pollard, *op. cit.,* p. 271). It is noteworthy in this connection that, whereas during the early part of his career Henry was in the habit of showing his respect for the murdered archbishop by making a yearly offering at his shrine, in 1538 he added to his offenses against the Church by despoiling the same shrine and burning the saintly bones, and is even said to have held a mock trial of the saint, who was condemned as a *traitor.*

[17] *Letters and Papers,* XVI, 106.

[18] "Der Gottmenschkomplex," *Zeitschrift für ärztliche Psychoanalyse,* I, p. 313.

forces and events; and in the unique degree to which he achieved his combination is probably to be sought the secret of his political success.

The divorce of Catherine, which had provided the occasion for this gradual but momentous change in Henry's character, was after many delays and vicissitudes eventually hurried forward to a rapid conclusion by the fact of Anne having become pregnant and the consequent necessity of legalizing her relationship to Henry, if her child (supposing it should be a son) was to become the recognized heir to the throne. In spite of Henry's long infatuation for Anne, he had not succeeded in making her his mistress till toward the end of 1532. Warned, perhaps, by the somewhat fickle nature of Henry's affection for his previous mistresses, Anne determined to avoid the consummation of her intimacy with the king, and kept her resolution until the success of the divorce seemed certain.

Subsequent events amply demonstrated the wisdom of her conduct. She was married to Henry in January, 1533, and in the following May Henry was already beginning to grow tired of her. Though steadfast in his affections for years in the face of difficulties, as soon as all obstacles were removed and he had full and unquestioned possession of her whom he had so long desired, Henry's love began to cool and he became conscious of defects in Anne of which he had previously been unobservant. Here we see clearly for the first time the manifestation of what seems to have been a very important trait of Henry's sexual life—viz., that there was usually some impediment in the way of the free expression of his love toward the women of his choice. In Anne's case the impediment lay doubtless to some extent in her refusal to give herself up fully to her royal lover, until she became certain that she would be his consort rather than his mistress. But there were deeper underlying factors connected with the very circumstance of the love having been previously illicit—a circumstance which gave it an attraction that a legalized union failed to possess.

In an illuminating paper on the varieties of the love life Freud [19] has shown that the need for an obstacle to be present as a condition for the arousal of love can be traced back to the operation of the Oedipus complex. In the earliest love of a boy to his mother such an obstacle is constituted by the incestuous nature of the relationship, which, because of this nature, is a forbidden one. Furthermore, the mother, as the object of the boy's love, is already bound by ties of law and affection to a third person, the father. In a number of cases where the psychosexual development has not been carried far enough to ensure adequate freedom from the infantile fixation on the parents, the continued existence of the Oedipus complex manifests itself in the choice of a love object between whom and the lover there is an impediment of the kind that existed in the original incestuous love; i.e., either the love itself is unlawful or the loved object is already bound elsewhere, or else (as often happens) both

[19] "Beiträge zur Psychologie des Liebeslebens," *Jahrbuch für psychoanalytische und psychopathologische Forschungen*, II, 1910, p. 389.

conditions are present. Now there can be little doubt that Henry was a person whose Oedipus complex found expression in such a way. On this hypothesis it becomes possible to explain two very constant features of his love life; his fickleness (which tended to make him unable to love a woman, once his possession of her was assured) and the desire for some obstacle between him and the object of his choice. We shall come across sufficient examples of these, as we study the further course of his checkered conjugal career.

The facts connected with the fall of Anne Boleyn show more clearly than any other event not only the existence of a desire for an impediment of this kind, but the foundation of this desire in an incestuous fixation. At the same time they give the key to a true understanding of the central conflict involved in Henry's sexual life—that "common cause" of Henry's matrimonial difficulties, which, as Froude says, "ought to be discoverable." Henry, as we saw, soon tired of Anne after his marriage with her. The fact that her child, born in 1533, was a daughter (the future Queen Elizabeth), instead of the long-desired male heir, only served still further to alienate Henry's affections. During the three years of his married life with Anne, Henry consoled himself, first with some lady whose name does not seem to have come down to us, then with Margaret Shelton, and finally with Jane Seymour, his future wife, who appears to have aroused his genuine love. The thought of putting Anne aside seems to have been present for some considerable period before it was put into execution, matters being delayed for a time by the fact that a repudiation of Anne might have necessitated a return to Catherine.

Catherine's death in January 1536 (hurried on, as some think, by means of poison) removed this difficulty, and Anne's miscarriage (probably her second) in the same month served to revive the scruples with regard to incest that Henry had already experienced in relation to his first marriage. These scruples, which on their first arousal had grown slowly and by insensible degrees, now quickly regained their mastery over Henry's mind. The union with his second sister-representative (Anne) was now as repellent to him, on account of its incestuous flavor, as had been that with his first sister-representative (Catherine). Anne was accused of having been unfaithful to her husband, quite a number of persons being charged as her accomplices, and of having been repeatedly guilty of incest with her brother, Lord Rochford. She was further accused of having conspired with her lovers to bring about the death of the King and of having, through her treasonable behavior, so injured his health as to put his life in danger. All the more important male prisoners concerned in these charges were found guilty of high treason and were put to death, Anne herself following them to the scaffold a few days later.

At the same time her marriage with Henry was declared invalid, probably on one or more of the following grounds:[20] (1) the existence of an

---

[20] See Pollard, *op. cit.*, p. 344.

alleged precontract with the Earl of Northumberland; (2) the affinity between Anne and Henry arising from the latter's relations with Mary Boleyn. The very day after Anne's death, Henry was married to Jane Seymour.

Historians are pretty generally agreed that (although Anne was far from being incapable of loose living or even of more serious offenses) there was as a matter of fact little or no truth in any of the long series of grave charges brought against her. In particular there seems to be no satisfactory evidence at all in favor of the charges of incest and of treason. We are therefore free to regard these accusations as for the most part reflections of Henry's own mental state, for although Cromwell and others were responsible for the details of the matter, "Henry was regularly informed of every step taken against Anne and her associates and interfered a good deal with the proceedings," and "his wishes probably influenced the form in which the indictments were drawn up" [21] His interest in the proceedings and their psychological significance for him is further shown by the fact that he composed a tragedy on the subject, which he showed to the Bishop of Carlisle at a gay supper very shortly after Anne's execution.[22]

In accusing Anne of incest with her brother, Henry produced with reference to his brother-in-law a repetition of the situation which had formerly existed as between himself and his own brother in the case of Catherine. In both cases he was (in reality or in imagination) brought into competition with his brother over the person of his sister. The circumstances under which he had first been brought, as it were, into rivalry with his brother Arthur (calculated, as these were, to arouse in a slightly altered form the original Oedipus complex)[23] had, it would appear, made so firm an impression on his psychosexual tendencies and dispositions, that he continued to desire a repetition of the situation under which his sexual impulses had first been aroused.

But the feelings called forth by his relations to Arthur and Catherine were ambivalent in character, as is almost invariably the case with those connected with the Oedipus complex and its displacements. On the one hand there was the desire to kill his brother (father substitute) and marry his sister (mother substitute), while at the same time there was also present a horror of these things. At the time of Catherine's divorce, it was of course the horror that was uppermost in Henry's conscious mind; but at the same time the attractiveness of incest manifested itself in the choice of a fresh sister substitute in the person of Anne; giving rise to that strange

---

[21] Friedmann, *op. cit.*, vol. II, p. 268.

[22] Friedmann, *op. cit.*, vol. II, p. 267.

[23] It must not be forgotten that the facts of his parents being within the forbidden degrees of affinity and of their requiring a papal dispensation, just as he himself did later on, were doubtless known to Henry and thus probably constituted a strong associative link between his parents' marriage and his own union with Catherine; another link being formed probably by his father's proposal to marry Catherine after Arthur's death.

contradiction in Henry's behavior of which we have already spoken. After a time (shortened, it would appear, by Anne's miscarriages, which aroused Henry's previous superstitions) the negative attitude to incest was transferred in turn to his relations with Anne. In the hatred of Anne which was thus occasioned Henry *projected* onto her his own incestuous desires; i.e., she was accused of incestuous relations with her brother, whereas the real fact was that Henry himself desired incestuous relations with his sister. In this way Henry was able to enjoy by proxy the fulfillment of his own repressed desires, while at the same time giving expression to his horror and disgust at the relationship concerned.

By the same means, too, he was able to provide an outlet for the jealousy, fear, and hatred he felt toward his brother. Just as Henry himself had, through the accident of Arthur's death, inherited the throne in place of his brother, so now he seems to have feared that his own place in turn would be usurped by a brother. Hence the charge of treason, for which there seems to be even less evidence than for the supposed sexual offenses, and which therefore, to the psychoanalyst, reveals clearly enough the circumstance that, although Henry was not in fact guilty of Arthur's death, he nevertheless felt guilty on the subject, since the death constituted a realization of his own repressed desires.[24]

By a process familiar to the student of unconscious mental life, the brother role seems to have been filled in Henry's phantasy by more than one person at this time. The sexual aspects of the part were of course taken principally (but not entirely) by Anne's brother, Rochford, but the accusations of treason were directed more especially against one Henry Noreys, who was supposed to have arranged to marry Anne after Henry's death. Noreys appears to have been the only one of the accused whom Henry honored with a personal interview on the subject of his misdemeanors and whom he privately urged to confession.[25] Now it is suggestive that shortly before this incident Noreys had acquired a quasi-personal relationship to Henry by becoming betrothed to Margaret Shelton, who had quite recently been Henry's favorite and probably his mistress. In view of the fact that much emphasis was laid on Anne's becoming a sister of Henry's in virtue of his relations to Mary Boleyn, it would seem not unlikely that, by a similar process of thought, Noreys might be regarded as Henry's brother in virtue of his betrothal to Margaret. If any such process did take place in Henry's mind, the reason for the special charges against Noreys and the special attention paid to him by Henry is to a great extent explained.[26]

[24] Here again the brother enmity was probably only a displacement of the earlier father enmity, for, as we have seen above, Henry had in some respects special grounds for imagining himself in his father's place.

[25] Friedmann, *op. cit.*, vol. II, p. 251.

[26] It is just possible too that, as perhaps in other cases, the name *Henry* may have been of some importance, referring of course to the Oedipus complex in its original (parent-regarding) form.

In order to prevent the recurrence of such schemes as had been attributed to Anne and Noreys, Henry had resort to legislation. By a clause in the Act of Succession (an act passed primarily to declare Anne's daughter Elizabeth a bastard and to settle the crown on Henry's prospective issue by Jane) it was made high treason for anyone to marry a king's daughter, sister, or aunt without royal permission—a measure by which Henry would appear to have made an endeavor to do away for ever with the fear of sexual rivals in his own family.

We have seen how, during the divorce of Catherine, while the negative (horror) aspect of the incest complex was in the ascendant toward Catherine herself, the positive (love) aspects were at the same time active in respect of Anne, so that, while Henry was getting rid of an incestuous relation with one sister, he was actually engaged in starting a fresh relation of the same kind with another sister. A very similar state of affairs seems to have arisen just before the fall of Anne. Undeterred by the result of his two preceding incestuous adventures, Henry was again contemplating marriage with a woman who was within the forbidden degrees of blood relationship. Jane Seymour "was descended on her mother's side from Edward III, and Cranmer had to dispense with a canonical bar to the marriage arising from her consanguinity to the King in the third and fourth degrees." [27] Although the actual relationship between Henry and Jane was thus relatively remote, it is probable that Henry's fancy saw in Jane a relative of a nearer kind; for, shortly before their marriage, he was in the habit of meeting her in the rooms of her *brother*, Sir Edward Seymour, whom he thus made as it were, a participant in the affair[28]—in this way endeavoring once more to re-establish the original brother-sister triangle.[29]

The circumstances connected with the fall of Anne Boleyn thus afford very clear evidence of two leading tendencies in Henry's psychosexual life—both of them being conditioned by the facts of Henry's early love experiences, and through them by the still earlier Oedipus complex. These tendencies are (1) the desire for (and hatred of) a sexual rival; (2) the attraction toward (and at the same time the horror of) an incestuous relationship.

The same period gives us the first unmistakable indications of a third tendency (one intimately connected with the other two) which was henceforward to be of great importance—viz., Henry's insistence on chastity in his consort. We have already seen that his passion for Anne Boleyn seemed to be maintained in its original strength over a considerable number of years, to some extent at least because she refused to allow Henry the

---

[27] Pollard, *op. cit.*, p. 346.

[28] And who, it appears, had moved into these rooms (to which Henry had access by a secret passage) expressly for this purpose, the rooms having been previously occupied by Cromwell.

[29] Friedmann, *op. cit.*, vol. II, p. 222.

intimate privileges of her person. The same means were employed with
equal effect by her successor Jane Seymour in the early days of her intimacy with Henry. So great was her assumption of virtue that she even
refused presents from the king, because of their possible implication—a
course which called forth much approval and admiration from Henry
himself. While she thus made great show of chastity to Henry, there is
reason to believe that she was not always as careful of her honor as she
professed to be. Indeed, some of Henry's contemporaries seem to have
taken the view that Henry was more or less willfully shutting his eyes to
certain (probably well-known) facts in Jane's past history, facts of which
he might afterwards become well aware, should it suit his purpose. Thus
Chapuys, the ambassador of Charles V and a friend of Jane's, says in a
letter written in May 1536: "She (Jane) is a little over twenty-five. You
may imagine whether, being an Englishwoman, and having been so long
at court, she would not hold it a sin to be still a maid. At which the king
will perhaps be rather pleased . . . for he may marry her on condition
that she is a virgin, and when he wants a divorce he will find plenty of
witnesses to the contrary." [30]

In the light both of psychological knowledge and of later events (particularly those connected with Catherine Howard), it is probable that the
inconsistency here involved was not altogether willful or deliberate. It is
more likely that we have to do with the manifestations of a conflict in
Henry's mind—a conflict similar to those connected with the desire for
a sexual rival and for an incestuous relationship, and leading, as in their
case, to an inconsistent, fluctuating, and ambivalent attitude. In fact,
there would appear to have existed two opposing motives, in virtue of the
first of which Henry desired the most scrupulous chastity on the part of
his wives, while at the same time, in virtue of the second, he secretly (and
probably unconsciously) delighted in a partner who had already enjoyed
sexual experience with other men, or who was actually unfaithful after
marriage.

The explanation of this attitude is to be found, as before, in the facts
connected with the Oedipus complex.[31] To the young boy the idea of sexual relations between the parents is apt to be a very disagreeable one.
Jealousy of the father, the necessity of dissociating the parents from sexual
thoughts (in order to surmount the stage of incestuous fixation) and a
number of other potent factors, into which it is unnecessary to enter here,
frequently give rise to the phantasy that no sexual relations exist or have
existed between the parents—a phantasy that finds its supreme expression
in the notion of the virgin mother and the virgin birth which plays such a
prominent part in religion, myth and legend. Now since, in later life, the
wife is often unconsciously identified with the mother, it is not surprising
that the ideas concerning chastity, originally aroused in connection with

[30] Quoted in Friedmann, *op. cit.*, vol. II, p. 200.
[31] Cp. Freud, *op. cit.*

the latter, should be displaced onto the former: hence, in large measure, the attraction which virginity exercises over many men.

On the other hand, the boy may soon discover or suspect the occurrence of sexual relations between his parents; and the having of such relations (in the past or in the present) may come to be regarded as an essential characteristic of the mother; and therefore any substitute for her in later life may be expected to exhibit the same characteristic, so that, insofar as the wife represents a mother surrogate, only women who have already enjoyed sexual experience are eligible for the position: hence, to some extent, the fascination of widows.[32]

Now it would seem probable that in Henry's unconscious mind both these (mutually incompatible) notions of the mother had found a place, and that in the conflict between them we have the key to the inconsistency of his conduct in this respect.[33]

Having now arrived at a definite conception of the nature of the chief unconscious mental factors which were operative in Henry's married life, we may content ourselves with a rapid examination of their influence on the remaining part of his career. His union with Jane Seymour was not destined to be of long duration. Jane died in October 1537, one year and four months after her marriage, and a few days after she had given birth to a son (afterwards Edward VI). Henry seems to have had throughout some genuine attachment to her, and she and Catherine Parr share the honor of being the only two of Henry's six wives who completed their conjugal career without a rupture. Possibly the brevity of this career in Jane's case may have prevented the occurrence of an alienation of Henry's affections such as Chapuys had anticipated (in the letter quoted above). Furthermore, the fact that she had presented him with the long-wished-for male heir probably added considerably to the warmth of Henry's feelings toward her. At any rate Henry seems to have cherished her memory for some considerable time, and at his own death, ten years after Jane's, accorded her the signal honor of being laid to rest in her tomb at Windsor.

During the period between Jane's death and Henry's eventual mar-

---

[32] By a further peculiar mental process, the mother will not infrequently come to be regarded as a prostitute, or at least as one who is very free with her favors. (Cp. Freud, *op cit*.) Such an extension of the phantasy may very well have taken place in Henry's case, and would help to account for the *numerous* accusations of infidelity in the case of Anne Boleyn (only one of the accused men subsequently pleaded guilty and even the fact of his guilt has been doubted) and for the overlooking for so long a time of the rather openly promiscuous life led by Catherine Howard both before and after marriage. Cp. below, p. 146.

[33] To the existence of these notions in Henry's mind was probably due much of the importance that was attached (during the divorce proceedings against Catherine of Aragon) to the question as to whether Catherine's marriage with Arthur had or had not been consummated. Catherine herself stated at a comparatively late stage of the proceedings that there had been no consummation, and in so doing she may have hoped to touch Henry at a point on which she knew him to be sensitive.

riage with Anne of Cleves, his fourth wife, in 1539, various projects of marriage were discussed, none of which were destined to come to fruition, but in which the workings of Henry's unconscious tendencies can still to some extent be traced. The most important of these projects was connected with Mary, Duchess of Longueville, better known as Mary of Guise. Mary was *already affianced to Henry's nephew*, James V of Scotland, (the desire for a rival and the tendency to incest—cp. too the name in this connection—both therefore being manifested in this case); but Henry insisted that the importance of his own proposal ought to outweigh that of the previous arrangement. Francis I refused, however, to offend his ally James by acceding to Henry's demand, and proposed as a substitute Mary of Bourbon, daughter of the Duke of Vendôme. Henry, however, rejected her forthwith, on hearing that her hand had already been refused by James (absence of attraction where there is no rivalry); the two younger sisters of Mary of Guise were then suggested, together with a number of other ladies at the French court; and Henry, growing impatient and irritated, demanded that a selection of the handsomest available beauties should be sent to Calais for his personal inspection and eventual choice. Francis, however, rebelled against this scheme for "trotting out the young ladies like hackneys," and the whole idea of a French marriage was thereupon abandoned.

Meanwhile negotiations of a similar kind had been started in the Netherlands. The lady here selected was Christina, daughter of the deposed king of Denmark. Christina had been married at a very early age to the Duke of Milan and after a brief married life was now a widow of sixteen—circumstances that recall vividly those of Catherine of Aragon after Arthur's death. For political reasons, however, the match was not concluded and Henry was still without a wife.

Francis I and Charles V were at this time united in friendship, and their alliance made Henry look for support elsewhere, as a means of counterbalancing their power. The Protestant princes of Germany suggested themselves for this purpose. Religious difficulties for some time barred the way, but in the person of the Duke of Cleves Henry encountered one whose policy was a compromise between Protestantism and Romanism rather similar to that which he himself adopted.[34] A match between Henry and Anne, the daughter of the Duke, was arranged, largely through Cromwell's influence, though an obstacle was present in the fact that Anne had been already promised to the son of the Duke of Lorraine. Though this fact may, here as elsewhere, have been an attraction to Henry, he seems on the whole to have behaved with remarkable passivity as regards the marriage. But a short time before, he had said with reference to his contemplated French marriage, "I trust to no one but myself. The thing touches me too near. I wish to see them and know

---

[34] Cp. Pollard, *op. cit.*, p. 383.

them some time before deciding." Now, however, he agreed to accept Anne on no better assurances than Cromwell's praises of her beauty and Holbein's none too flattering portrait. Perhaps he was willing to put an end at any cost to the worries of wife-hunting; perhaps, too, he was genuinely alarmed at the threatening political situation, for the Pope, the Emperor, and the Kings of France and Scotland were all arrayed against him and an invasion of England seemed not unlikely. Whatever the reason, he was very pliable in Cromwell's hands, and even after he had seen and disapproved of Anne (whose appearance was homely, whose accomplishments were small when judged by the standard of the English and French courts, and who could speak no language but her own), he nevertheless consented to proceed with the marriage, distasteful as it was to him.

It was destined, however, to be the shortest of all his matrimonial ventures. In a few months the political situation had changed. Henry no longer needed the Protestant alliance, and lost no time in freeing himself from the *mariage de convenance* which had been entered into with that end in view. In the summer of 1540 Cromwell, who had engineered the match and the alliance, was arrested and beheaded; while at the same time Henry's marriage with Anne was declared null and void, Henry pleading that he had not been a free agent in the matter, that Anne had never been released from her contract with the son of the Duke of Lorraine, that he (Henry) had only gone through the ceremony on the assumption that a release would be forthcoming and that consequently, actuated by a conscientious scruple, he had refrained from consummating the marriage.

Superficial as these reasons may well seem (for there is no doubt that Henry really wished to dissolve the match because Anne was unattractive to him—of which fact, indeed, he made no secret—and because the alliance for which the marriage stood was no longer necessary), it will be observed that they nevertheless bear unmistakable traces of Henry's unconscious tendencies, showing that these tendencies were active in this case also.[35]

Anne of Cleves being thus put out of the way, Henry immediately entered into a fifth marriage, with a lady to whose charms he had already fallen a victim—Catherine Howard, a niece of the Duke of Norfolk. For about a year and a half Henry lived with his new bride more happily perhaps than with any other of his consorts. He congratulated himself that "after sundry troubles of mind which had happened to him by marriage" he had at last found a blissful solution of his matrimonial difficulties; and in his chapel he returned solemn thanks to Heaven for the felicity which

---

[35] Henry had previously complained to Cromwell that he suspected Anne (groundlessly, so far as we know) of being "no true maid"—thus showing the operation of the chastity complex as well as that connected with the presence of a rival.

his conjugal state afforded him, directing his confessor, the Bishop of Lincoln, to compose a special form of prayer for that purpose.

This spell of happiness, however, was built on a delusion. Catherine Howard had lived anything but a chaste life before her marriage, though the king seems to have closed his eyes to the fact, as he had probably done before on a similar occasion. Even after her marriage, Catherine continued to receive her former lovers, particularly one Culpepper, to whom she had been previously affianced. Reports of the Queen's misconduct reached the ears of Cranmer, who with much trepidation brought the facts to Henry's knowledge. The latter at first refused to believe the charges, but on the evidence becoming too strong to be resisted, was overwhelmed with surprise, grief, shame, and anger, wept bitterly in public, and generally manifested such emotion that "it was thought he had gone mad." He at first contemplated granting Catherine a pardon, but on further proofs of quite recent misdemeanors coming to light, she was executed, together with her lovers and all those who had been her accomplices in one way or another.

We have here another very clear example of the working of Henry's unconscious complexes. Bearing in mind the great importance which he was wont to attach to virginity and chastity, together with the marked dissoluteness of Catherine's life and the comparatively little care she took to conceal it, it would seem that Henry was guilty of an almost pathological blindness in remaining ignorant of the true circumstances for so long. That there was indeed some definite repression at work is indicated, too, by his inability or unwillingness to believe the facts when they were first brought to his notice, and by his very great emotion on finally realizing the truth.

The mental forces here at work are of course those with which we are already familiar. On the one hand, Henry, as we have seen, desired a woman who had other lovers besides himself, while on the other hand he ardently desired her exclusive possession and her chastity. The conflict between these incompatible longings produced a temporary dissociation. For a time Henry was able to enjoy Catherine as if her dissoluteness and her infidelity did not exist—his enjoyment being, indeed, probably heightened by the very fact of her loose living, though the knowledge of this loose living was excluded from his conscious mind. When this knowledge did at length enter consciousness, he was overcome by his feelings, in much the same way as the bringing to light of unconscious factors in the course of psychoanalysis will often give rise to an emotional crisis.[36]

[36] The emotion itself was probably complex both in nature and origin. From the accounts we have of his conduct, we may surmise that there were present, among other constituents, (1) grief, at the breakdown of his delusion—his happy life with Catherine being brought to a sudden and disastrous end; (2) shame, both because he dimly realized that in the past his enjoyment had been largely due to gratification of forbidden desires (connected with the Oedipus complex) and because he had been made to look foolish before others; (3) anger, directed both against Catherine and her accomplices for having deceived him and against himself for having allowed himself to be deceived.

As he had done after the fall of Anne Boleyn, so now also, Henry resorted to legislative measures to prevent a recurrence of the disaster that had befallen him. On the previous occasion it had been made high treason to marry any woman nearly related to the king without the king's consent. The present enactments were primarily directed against female, rather than against male, offenders (following perhaps a development of Henry's mind, in virtue of which the chastity motif had been for some time increasing in importance), and it was declared treason for any woman to marry the king if her previous life had not been strictly virtuous.

The new measure seems to have aroused considerable interest and amusement both in court and country, for the long series of Henry's matrimonial misadventures had now assumed to his contemporaries much the same laughable and yet tragic aspect which they still possess for us. In view of the strictness of the qualifications now required for the post of Queen, Chapuys suggested that "few, if any, ladies now at court will henceforth aspire to such an honour," [37] while Henry's subjects, with a true appreciation both of his psychological needs and of the course of action to which these needs would impel him, jokingly remarked that only a widow would be able to meet the king's demands, as no reputed maid would ever be persuaded to incur the penalty of the statute.[38]

So indeed it actually turned out. In the early summer of 1543 Henry married Catherine Parr, his sixth and last wife. Although only 31 years of age, Catherine was then in her second widowhood—her second husband, Lord Latimer, having died at the end of 1542. In thus espousing one the fact of whose widowhood was especially striking, Henry was adopting the best compromise between his own conflicting tendencies and emotions. Catherine was chaste (her moral character was beyond reproach) and yet she had undoubtedly enjoyed previous sexual experience—a circumstance which, as we have seen, was necessary for the gratification of Henry's unconscious desires. At the same time another circumstance connected with Catherine Parr enabled Henry to satisfy to a large extent his other complexes. After the death of her second husband, Catherine's hand was sought by Sir Thomas Seymour, *Henry's brother-in-law* (younger brother of Jane Seymour) to whom she appears to have been sincerely attached (and whom she eventually married after Henry's death—thus being, as Pollard says, "almost as much married as Henry himself"). Henry, however, overruled the engagement—in much the same way as he had attempted to do in the case of Mary of Guise—and compelled Catherine to abandon her lover in favor of himself.

The circumstances of Henry's last marriage thus strongly recall those connected with his first. The name of his bride was the same in both

---

[37] *Letters and Papers*, XVII, 124.

[38] And certainly, as we are now in a position to see, no sagacious woman would have done so; for however pure her past life might in reality have been, Henry would probably sooner or later have been impelled by his unconscious complexes to rake up some accusation of unchastity against her.

cases,[39] and in both cases he took the place which would otherwise have been filled by a brother. We thus see how the unconscious jealousy of Arthur (a jealousy which was itself probably only a displacement of that originally directed against his father) operated to the end of Henry's matrimonial career and acted as the determining factor in the choice of a wife more than forty years after Arthur's death. At the same time Catherine Howard's betrothal to Seymour in one sense constituted her a sister to Henry, so that the desire for an incestuous union was also satisfied.

A marriage entered into, as this one was, as the result of a satisfactory compromise between the opposing forces of Henry's mind (all Henry's primitive unconscious desires rooted in the Oedipus complex finding gratification, but none of them too blatantly) gave promise of greater permanency and stability than had been exhibited by most of his previous ventures in matrimony: nor was this promise belied by the course of subsequent events. On one occasion, it is true, Catherine was in danger through having come into conflict with Henry's egoistic tendencies (which had become less and less restrained as he grew older), but her tact enabled her to surmount all difficulties arising from this source, and the marriage seems to have remained a happy one until Henry's death three and a half years later, in January 1547.

We have now traced the operation of certain unconscious motives throughout the whole of Henry's sexual life. For the sake of clearness we have distinguished three principal such motives: (1) the desire for opposition and the presence of a sexual rival, (2) a desire for incest, (3) a desire for chastity in his sexual partner. All these motives are closely interconnected, and they are all dependent on, and derived from, the primitive Oedipus complex; each motive, moreover, is present both in a positive and in a negative form. That which Henry was impelled to do by the operation of his unconscious desires he was equally impelled to oppose, by the operation of (an often equally unconscious) resistance to these desires. Regarded as the outcome of the interaction of these various conflicting forces, the abnormal features of Henry's married life can, it would appear, very largely be explained.

The importance of studies such as that upon which we have been here engaged, apart from such value as they may have for the elucidation of historical problems, lies in the confirmation which they afford of results obtained by the process of psychoanalysis carried on with living individuals. These results are often so opposed to what we are accustomed to regard both as common sense and common decency, that their acceptance is a matter of very considerable difficulty in the case of all persons who have not themselves extensively employed the psychoanalytic method. Even by psychoanalysts themselves additional evidence for the validity of their conclusions from a fresh field of inquiry must always be most wel-

[39] The name may of course very well have been significant in the case of Catherine Howard also.

come. As such a source of additional evidence, the data of history would seem in some respects to be peculiarly acceptable. Although these data must always be inferior in scope and detail to evidence obtained from living persons, they present the following two great advantages: first, that the full data are open to investigation and verification by others, whereas in most psychoanalytic investigations the complete material on which conclusions are based are available only to the analyst himself; and secondly, that in the case of persons long since dead there can be no question of the influence either of direct suggestion or of the more subtle effects of psychoanalytic training and tradition. The actions and sayings of historical personages can have no possible reference to Freud's theories, whereas the patient in the physician's consulting room is, it may be said, necessarily to some extent affected by the atmosphere of belief in psychoanalytic doctrine in which he finds himself.

Thus it would appear that the application of the psychoanalytic findings to historical material [40] should furnish in general a most necessary and desirable test of the validity of the psychoanalytic method itself. If the psychic mechanisms revealed by the process of psychoanalysis upon the living subject are to be regarded as fundamental features of the human mind, and not as mere artifacts or pathological conditions occurring only in neurotic persons, they should be discoverable as factors operating in the lives of men and women of the past, wherever the available data bearing on these lives are adequate in quantity and quality. A certain number of studies directed to this end have already been made, and by their demonstration of the fact that the behavior of individuals long since dead can be satisfactorily accounted for on psychoanalytic theories (and perhaps in no other way), have afforded very valuable corroboration of the utility and validity of the psychoanalytic method. In the present paper we have endeavored, it is hoped not altogether fruitlessly, to bring to light some further evidence pointing to the same conclusion.

[40] As of course to all records of human life and labor which have come about independently of the work of psychoanalysts themselves—such as myths, legends, customs, literary and artistic productions, etc.

Personal Identity
and Political Ideology

Lucian W. Pye

I

Much of political science may be thought of as an attempt to understand the connections between individual and group behavior.[1] While such a statement may not provide the most satisfactory beginning for a definition of the discipline, it does accentuate the concern of political science with both the nature of the individual and the nature of society. Political theorists have traditionally been interested in the state and the statesman, the law and the lawmaker, the community and the citizen, and historical forces and individual choices. All political theories are premised on either explicit or implicit assumptions about the nature of man and of society; hence the political scientist must be to some extent both a psychologist and a sociologist.

These were the qualities of the traditional political scientists. The most important forerunners of the discipline were also the leading authorities on questions about human nature and the structure of society. Thus Aristotle, Machiavelli, Hobbes, Locke, and Rousseau were concerned not just with the traits and arts of political leaders but with the basic nature of man; and in Plato we have some remarkable anticipations of modern

"Personal Identity and Political Ideology." Reprinted from *Political Decision Makers*, edited by Dwaine Marvick. Copyright 1962 by The Free Press of Glencoe.

[1] [Although Pye is talking here of political science, much of what he says can apply to history, especially political history; in any case, this first part supplies a useful setting for his treatment of Erikson's book and for that reason has been retained. *B.M.*]

psychology. Similarly, traditional political theorists were concerned with more than just the polity: their interest usually covered the entire web of human associations. They were extraordinarily successful in building their systematic political theories out of the most advanced psychological and sociological knowledge available to them, producing syntheses that related the character of man and society to normative standards and judgments about the design of public institutions. For example, one strand of this Western tradition of political science can be summed up readily under the rubric of reason, an essentially psychological concept. The universe was conceived of as rational, and man as having the rational power to understand it: given the right sort of institutions, men would act rationally according to their enlightened self-interest, and the result would be a happy and harmonious social order.[2] Other systems were erected on the premise that man's essential nature is brutal, selfish and inherently evil. Clearly, the traditional political theorist did not shrink from psychological considerations. On the contrary, he often permitted them to color all aspects of his theories.

The contemporary political scientist wishing to follow in the tradition is confronted with an infinitely more difficult task. The first problem is the extraordinary rate of growth of specialized knowledge about psychological and sociological matters. Many political scientists have come to feel that it is hopeless to attempt to incorporate these intellectual developments into systematic political theories. Finding it impossible to follow the practices of the earlier political theorists, they have decided instead to examine systematically, and with reverence, the works of these earlier thinkers. Furthermore, a second and more fundamental problem is posed in our new understanding of the basic nature of man. In his insight into the full dimensions of man's inner nature, Freud made it embarrassingly clear that previous theories of political relationships were generally premised on impoverished and inadequate notions of human nature. The concept of the rational man has had to be altered. At the same time, Freud held out the promise of a deeper understanding of political phenomena—a promise that has not been fully realized.

It is one thing to suggest that all political theories depend upon some psychological view of man, and quite another matter to relate the insights of psychoanalysis to political analysis. In spite of the enthusiasm of those who are ready to try to enrich political science with Freud's psychoanalytic contributions, it must be acknowledged that the results are often awkward, and at times even grotesque. How can the political scientist significantly benefit from the contributions of those psychologists who have altered our image of man?

In performing the path-breaking task of applying psychoanalytical con-

---

[2] For an excellent outline of the psychological premises of classical political theory and of the problems posed by modern psychology see Thomas I. Cook, "Democratic Psychology and Democratic World Order," *World Politics*, I (July, 1949), 553-64.

cepts to political analysis, Harold D. Lasswell focused on the relationship between private motivations and public acts. He suggested that the dynamics of political action were to be found in the configuration of the individual personality and not just in the grand issues of history. Lasswell suggested a formula for expressing the developmental aspects of political man: $p]d]r=P$, in which "p" stands for private motives; "d" is displacement onto a public object; "r" is rationalization in terms of public interest; "P" is the political man; and "]" symbolizes "transformed into." [3] Political man is characterized as being moved by private motives, which are displaced on public objects and rationalized as being in the national interest. By employing the assumption about the nature of man that dominated psychoanalytical thinking during the 1930's, Lasswell was led to believe that release of tension is fundamental to all political behavior and the key to human action in general. We find him writing that: "Nations, classes, tribes, and churches have been treated as collective symbols in the name of which the individual may indulge his elementary urges for supreme power, for omniscience, for amorality, for security."[4] Again, he stated that: "Indeed one of the principal functions of symbols of remote objects, like nations and classes, is to serve as targets for the relief of many of the tensions which might discharge disastrously in face-to-face relationships." [5]

Lasswell's efforts to trace the connections between private motivations and public acts were an attempt to deal systematically with the kinds of problems that political biographers have long sought to untangle: the relationship between the child and the man, between personal peculiarities and political preferences, between private frustrations and public ambitions. Lasswell's critics have charged that he exaggerated the importance of private and irrational considerations because he so undervalued the significance of political issues and rational choice. On the other hand, his critics have generally failed to appreciate that, despite the special attention he gave to psychological matters, he steadfastly maintained a remarkably rigid distinction between the psychological and the political, between the pattern of personality development and the logic of institutional change, between private motivations and public policy.

Thus, in advancing the view that the social process consists of people pursuing *values*, through *institutions*, by means of available *resources*, Lasswell implied that the individual and his value preferences are one thing, and social institutions another.[6] Some institutions may be more

[3] Harold D. Lasswell, *Psychopathology and Politics* (Chicago: University of Chicago Press, 1930), pp. 74-76.

[4] Harold D. Lasswell, *World Politics and Personal Insecurity* (New York: Whittlesey House, 1930), p. 39.

[5] *Ibid.*, p. 73; quoted in Helen Merrell Lynd, *On Shame and the Search for Identity* (New York: Harcourt, Brace and Co., 1958), pp. 97-98.

[6] Harold D. Lasswell, *Power and Personality* (New York: W. W. Norton & Co., 1948), pp. 16-17.

appropriate than others for maximizing particular values, but, in the final analysis, institutions are based on functions that involve more than individual preferences. Similarly, Lasswell pointed to the likelihood of certain personality types being more successful in particular political roles. However, he rigidly held that the basic character of any political role is determined by its functions in the political process and not by the personality. By posing the problem in these terms, Lasswell avoided the error, frequently made by psychologists, of seeing the *homo politicus* as a distinct personality type characterized by an inordinate craving for power. He defined instead a variety of political roles and political personality types.[7] In particular, Lasswell identified personality types with the political roles of the administrator, the agitator, and the theorist.[8]

Lasswell's method of bringing psychoanalytical considerations to bear on political analysis opened the way for a tremendous growth in studies of factors traditionally considered to be "nonpolitical." (Indeed, some critics have held that "political behavior" studies are nothing more than studies of the nonpolitical—i.e., the social and personal aspects of group behavior.) For example, Lasswell's formulation of the relationship between personality and politics encouraged studies of the social backgrounds of political elites, the symbols of political identifications, and the informal factors influencing decisions.[9] The same assumptions about the relationships between personality and politics are usually present in the studies of voting behavior.[10] Implicit in most such studies is the notion that personality and "informal" considerations are largely "irrational" with respect to the logic of public institutions.

There have been numerous attempts to bridge the gap that Lasswell has left between the private and the public, between the dimension of personality and the sphere of politics. In general, these attempts may be divided into two categories. First, there are those efforts to find direct correlations between specific personality types and political behavior. These are attempts to see the political from the perspective of psychological insights, and they generally concentrated on the dynamics of personality formation during childhood.[11] The second category consists of

[7] *Ibid.*, chaps. ii-iv.

[8] Harold D. Lasswell, *Psychopathology and Politics*, pp. 53-55.

[9] The most outstanding examples would be the Hoover Institute Studies in the RADIR project that were authored by Daniel Lerner, Ithiel deSola Pool, Robert North, and others.

[10] Harold F. Gosnell, *Grass Roots Politics: National Voting Behavior of Typical States* (Washington: American Council on Public Affairs, 1942); Paul F. Lazarsfeld, Bernard Berelson, and Hazel Gaudet, *The People's Choice* (New York: Columbia University Press, 1948); Bernard R. Berelson, Paul F. Lazarsfeld, and William N. McPhee, *Voting* (Chicago: University of Chicago Press, 1954); and Angus Campbell, Gerald Gurin, Warren E. Miller, *The Voter Decides* (Evanston, Ill.: Row, Peterson and Co., 1954).

[11] Among the best statements of the methodology of this form of psychocultural analysis are: Nathan Leites, "Psycho-Cultural Hypotheses about Political Acts," *World Politics*, I (October, 1948), 102-19; Abram Kardiner, *The Psychological Frontiers of*

those attempts to fill the gap between the psychological and the political with other social processes. Instead of moving directly from personality formation to political action, the psychological factor is related to all the other factors that might influence political behavior. The "psychological" dimension thus includes cognitive processes. In the main, this approach has centered on various aspects of the political socialization process.

Most studies in the first category are made by cultural anthropologists and others involved in work on personality and culture. In defining culture as the pattern of basic values reflected in all phases of life, the anthropologist has assumed a close and direct relationship between personality and political behavior. This approach has largely taken the form of national character studies; the names of Ralph Linton, Margaret Mead, Ruth Benedict, and Geoffrey Gorer come readily to mind. Historians have, of course, long employed unspecified notions concerning the characteristics of different nations and peoples.[12] Psychoanalytically oriented students of national character have been much more explicit; consequently, it has been easy for their critics to take exception to particular details.[13]

Within the category of attempts to relate directly personality and politics are those seeking to establish a connection between specific personality configurations and susceptibility to particular political ideological orientations. The outstanding example of this form of study is, of course, *The Authoritarian Personality*.[14] This monumental study, originally conceived as a search for the possible psychological sources of anti-Semitism, became an attempt to demonstrate congruence between personality type and political ideology. Despite its impressive reception in the social sciences, most students of political behavior have found it difficult to accept its suggestion of a direct correlation between authoritarian personality types and membership in authoritarian political movements.[15]

Society (New York: Columbia University Press, 1945); Margaret Mead, "The Study of National Character," in Daniel Lerner and Harold D. Lasswell (eds.), *The Policy Sciences: Recent Developments in Scope and Method* (Stanford: Stanford University Press, 1951).

[12] The advantages for historians of the newer insights of psychoanalysis are well stated by William L. Langer in his presidential address to the American Historical Association, "The Next Assignment," *The American Historical Review*, LXIII (January, 1958), 283-304.

[13] David Potter, a historian, has written an excellent and sympathetic critique of much of the work on national character. See his *People of Plenty* (Chicago: University of Chicago Press, 1954).

[14] T. W. Adorno, E. Frenkel-Brunswik, D. J. Levinson, R. N. Sanford, in collaboration with Betty Aron, Maria H. Levinson, and W. Morrow, *The Authoritarian Personality* (New York: Harper & Brothers, 1950); sponsored by the American Jewish Committe, "Social Studies Series," publication No. 3.

[15] Herbert McClosky has continued to search for correlations between political conservatism and a set personality type. See "Conservatism and Personality," *American Political Science Review*, LII (March, 1958), 27-45.

A common characteristic of such studies is that the methodological treatment of psychological matters has been considerably more sophisticated than the political analysis. Subtlety in psychological insights has not necessarily yielded significant knowledge about the political realm. Advances stemming from public-opinion research have further encouraged the study of social processes that intervene between personality formation and political behavior. These studies, which we have put in the second category, tend to be more influenced by orientations common to social psychology than by psychoanalysis. The shift has also been away from a central interest in childhood development and toward an appreciation of the immediate total social context within which action occurs.

For example, Gabriel Almond, in his study of the appeals of communism in four European countries, found it necessary to trace the total process of personality development from early determinants to the later cognitive developments.[16] By working in terms of political socialization, Almond developed the concept of "political culture." The process of political involvement is seen as similar to, but distinct from, the process by which an individual becomes a member of his culture. Out of the early childhood experiences, and later influenced by the way in which he is introduced to the political world, the individual finally assumes a specific political role.[17] Subjective psychological factors can be treated at all stages in the analysis. At the same time, objective factors relating to the social and political setting can be given their full weight. Other attempts to narrow the gap between personality and politics are to be found in the works of M. Brewster Smith, Jerome Bruner, and Robert W. White;[18] Herbert Hyman;[19] Daniel Katz and Charles McClintock; Irving Sarnoff;[20] and Harold R. Isaacs.[21] The rate of advances in political psychology is impressively demonstrated by the recent books of Robert E. Lane[22]

[16] Gabriel Almond, *The Appeals of Communism* (Princeton: Princeton University Press, 1959).

[17] Gabriel Almond, "Comparative Political Systems," *Journal of Politics,* XVIII (August, 1956), pp. 391-409; "Theoretical Introduction," in G. Almond and J. Coleman (eds.), *The Politics of Underdeveloped Areas* (Princeton: Princeton University Press, 1960).

[18] M. Brewster Smith, Jerome Bruner, and Robert W. White, *Opinions and Personality* (New York: John Wiley & Sons, Inc., 1956).

[19] Herbert Hyman, *Political Socialization* (Glencoe, Ill.: The Free Press, 1959).

[20] Irving Sarnoff and Daniel Katz, "The Motivational Bases of Attitude Change," *Journal of Abnormal and Social Psychology,* XLIX (January, 1954), 115-24; Daniel Katz, Charles McClintock, and Irving Sarnoff, "The Measurement of Ego Defense as Related to Attitude Change," *Journal of Personality,* XXV (June, 1957), 465-74; Daniel Katz, Irving Sarnoff, and Charles McClintock, "Ego-Defense and Attitude Change," *Human Relations,* IX (January, 1956), 27-45.

[21] Harold R. Isaacs, *Scratches on Our Minds: American Images of China and India* (New York: John Day Co., 1958).

[22] Robert E. Lane, *Political Life: Why People Get Involved in Politics* (Glencoe, Ill.: The Free Press, 1959).

and Seymour Martin Lipset[23] which systematically build upon the best of current research in the field.

There are two principal reasons why these various authors have been able to add the psychological dimensions to their studies without grossly oversimplifying basic political considerations. First, they have balanced their analysis of the shaping of the unconscious with explicit treatment of ego functioning in the total development of the personality. Second, they have related personality factors to the social context of action and, wherever possible, to specific sociological variables. The link between "personality" and political behavior is established by recognizing that personality development depends upon the individual's perceptions of social reality, his emotionally conditioned responses to his environment, and his learned modes of evaluating reality. This approach has led some scholars to a rigorous search for relationships between attitudes, opinions, and "basic orientations," on the one hand, and social or demographic distinctions on the other. Others—like Erich Fromm[24] and David Riesman[25]—have related more broadly defined personality or character types to the main social or economic configurations of an historical period. A highly original and complex analysis has been Daniel Lerner's treatment of the connections between basic aspects of personality and the dynamics of social change in transitional societies.[26]

The use of this image of personality, largely derived from social psychology, has been extremely rewarding when combined with survey techniques. It focuses attention on the relationship between "personality type," basic social and political attitudes, and the distribution of each according to demographic and socio-economic categories.[27] But there is some concern among those who have worked with survey techniques that studies built largely upon a psychology of the cognitive processes will give too "flat" a picture, lacking in the nuances that depend upon the functions of the unconscious. In order to avoid this problem, it may become increasingly necessary to supplement social survey studies with "interviews in depth." These approaches all represent significant advances in the use of psychological theory for political analysis. It would seem, however, that political scientists have yet to arrive at satisfactory methods of realizing the full potentialities of psychoanalytical theory. Every now and then there is the rare work—such as that of Nathan Leites[28]—which

[23] Seymour Martin Lipset, *Political Man: The Social Bases of Politics* (New York: Doubleday & Co., 1960).

[24] *Escape from Freedom* (New York: Rinehart & Company, Inc., 1941).

[25] *The Lonely Crowd* (New Haven: Yale University Press, 1950).

[26] Daniel Lerner, *The Passing of Traditional Society* (Glencoe, Ill.: The Free Press, 1958).

[27] An outstanding example of such a study is Alex Inkeles and Raymond A. Bauer, *The Soviet Citizen* (Cambridge: Harvard University Press, 1959).

[28] *A Study of Bolshevism* (Glencoe, Ill.: The Free Press, 1953). For two excellent commentaries on Leites' methods and his analytical assumptions, see Daniel Bell, "Ten Theories in Search of Reality," *World Politics*, X (April, 1958), 327-65; and Clyde Kluckhohn, "Politics, History and Psychology," *World Politics*, VIII (October, 1955), 112-23.

taps this potential and demonstrates what may be accomplished if the new image of man is truly incorporated in a political analysis. Thus, although political science has been greatly enriched by the insights of modern psychology, we are still seeking new ways of bridging the gap between the dynamics of individual behavior and the forces of history.

II

It is from such a background of experience as we have just outlined that the political scientist looks for guidance to Erik H. Erikson's *Young Man Luther: A Study in Psychoanalysis and History*.[29] In what ways can the clinical analyst, who has made great contributions to ego psychology and cultural anthropology, assist the student of history?

Erikson is concerned in this volume with the problem of the great man in history, who creates the ideologies in which people find their beliefs. He is concerned with clarifying how the lone individual, in seeking to find himself and give meaning to his own character, can give shape and form to a period of history. More precisely, Erikson is interested in the relationship between the identity crisis in the personality development of the reformer and the ideology he creates. Erikson reduces the gap between the public and the private spheres, between the psychological and the political, by stressing the links between personal identity and public ideology.

It has not been fashionable for political scientists to grapple with the problem of the great man who tries to change the course of history. Modern political science grew up during a time when the notion of "science" was largely one of a quest for uniformities. This assumption encouraged political analysis oriented toward sociology and economics. Even when the pendulum began to swing back to a greater emphasis upon the individual—and, hence, upon psychological considerations—attention still centered largely on aggregates and not on the unique person. The search has been mainly for relationships between social and economic factors and personality types. Recent interest in the study of decision making and of elite roles has centered primarily upon the webs of relationships through which individual decision makers have to fight their way, and not upon the function of the leader's personality. One exception to this tendency is Alexander and Juliette George's provocative analysis of Woodrow Wilson's personality. . . .[30]

III

In turning to the content of Erikson's analysis, we must begin with his key concept of the identity crisis. This is the crisis of late adolescence, when the young person, after having synthesized and resynthesized the experiences and reactions of each of the earlier stages of childhood, must

[29] (New York: W. W. Norton & Co., 1958).
[30] Alexander L. George and Juliette L. George, *Woodrow Wilson and Colonel House* (New York: John Day Co., 1956).

move out of childhood and assume a place in the adult world.[31] Erikson finds significance in all the typical characteristics of this stage of life: the periods of moodiness and sentimentality; the restless spirit but lethargic body; the sense of ambition and the desire to explore and know all possibilities, but also the endless moping and hanging around; and the unexpected vacillations between excessive worldliness and unbelievable naïveté—between trying to be more adult than adults, and then being more childish than children. Above all, it is the crisis of uncertainty when the youth must commit himself—usually after many fitful starts—to a definition of himself that he and others will recognize. Erikson says:

> I have called the major crisis of adolescence the *identity crisis;* it occurs in that period of the life cycle when each youth must forge for himself some central perspective and direction, some working unity, out of the effective remnants of his childhood and the hopes of his anticipated adulthood; he must detect some meaningful resemblance between what he has come to see in himself and what his sharpened awareness tells him others judge and expect him to be [p. 14].

Erikson has emphasized elsewhere that the term "identity" expresses a "mutual relationship in that it connotes both a persistent sameness within oneself (self-sameness) and a persistent sharing of some kind of essential character with others." [32] Thus, *identity formation*

> arises from the selective repudiation and mutual assimilation of childhood identifications, and their absorption in a new configuration, which, in turn, is dependent on the process by which a *society* (often through subsocieties) *identifies the young individual,* recognizing him as somebody who had to become the way he is, and who, being the way he is, is taken for granted. The community, often not without some initial mistrust, gives such recognition with a (more or less institutionalized) display of surprise and pleasure in making the acquaintance of a newly emerging individual. For the community, in turn, feels recognized by the individual who cares to ask for recognition; it can, by the same token, feel deeply—and vengefully—rejected by the individual who does not seem to care.[33]

[31] Erikson has developed his theories of ego identity in numerous writings: *Childhood and Society* (New York: W. W. Norton & Co., 1950); "Ego Development and Historical Change," in *The Psychoanalytical Study of the Child* (New York: International University Press, 1946), Vol. II; "Growth and Crises in the 'Healthy Personality' " (For Fact-Finding Committee, Midcentury White House Conference; New York: Josiah Macy Jr. Foundation, 1950), and in Kluckhohn and Murray (eds.), *Personality in Nature, Culture and Society* (New York, Alfred A. Knopf, 1953); "On the Sense of Inner Identity," in *Health and Human Relations* (Report on the International Conference in Hiddesen, Germany, 1951; New York: The Blakiston Co., 1953); "The Problem of Ego Identity," *Journal of The American Psychoanalytic Association,* IV (January, 1956), 56-121.

[32] Erik Erikson, "The Problem of Ego Identity," *Journal of the American Psychoanalytical Association,* IV (January, 1956), 57.

[33] *Ibid.,* pp. 68-69.

It becomes immediately apparent that Erikson's concept of ego identity provides a far more complex and multifaceted model of the human personality than is customarily used in political analysis. His concept covers not only the individual's constitutional givens and his idiosyncratic libidinal needs, but also the nature of his cognitive processes and the historically specific quantities of information that he has stored in his memory. The concept goes beyond this. It implies that there are systematic relationships among not just these dimensions of the personality, but among the particular mental or physical faculty favored and best developed by the individual, his effective psychological defense mechanism, his successful sublimations, and even the degree of consistency with which circumstance has required him to assume particular roles.

The political scientist is not one to pass judgments on the technical aspects of Erikson's concept of ego identity.[34] In order to appreciate, however, the ways in which Erikson relates the great ideological reformer to his times and to history, it is necessary to understand the outlines of Erikson's theories about the development of the individual. Erikson assumes that the way in which the major problems of each stage in the development of the individual are met will be reflected in the evolving configuration of that individual's identity; in the case of the great man, this means that his peculiar pattern of development will be reflected in his political ideology. Erikson thus implies that there is a minimum but fundamental structure to any ideology, which is related to elemental aspects of personality development. Therefore, in reviewing Erikson's theories about the development of the individual, we shall focus on those aspects that are most relevant in contributing to the tone and the spirit of ideologies.

It is only in the last chapter of Erikson's book on Luther that he sets forth his theory of the various stages of personality development. Indeed, those readers who have not previously been exposed to his views on the subject may find that they can get more out of his analysis of Luther if they read this chapter as an introduction. For our purpose of summarizing the stages of development and suggesting their relationship to the identity crisis, we may rely upon a diagram Erikson has devised.[35] It should be noted, however, that a diagram often suggests well-defined and rigorous relationships without actually articulating their precise nature. This is an important warning, and, as Erikson has remarked, such a

---

[34] The political scientist with curiosity about ego psychology may want to read, in addition to Erikson's writings: Anna Freud, *The Ego and the Mechanisms of Defense* (New York: Basic Books, 1952); H. Hartmann, "Ego Psychology and the Problem of Adaptation," in D. Rapaport (ed.), *Organization and Pathology of Thought* (New York: Columbia University Press, 1951), chap. xiv; H. Hartman, "Comments on the Psychoanalytic Theory of the Ego," in *The Psychoanalytic Study of the Child* (New York: International Universities Press, 1950), V, 74-96.

[35] Erikson, "The Problem of Ego Identity," p. 75.

STAGES OF DEVELOPMENT AND THE IDENTITY CRISIS

	1	2	3	4	5	6	7	8
I INFANCY	Trust vs. Mistrust							
II EARLY CHILDHOOD		Autonomy vs. Shame, Doubt			Bipolarity vs. Autism			
III PLAY AGE			Initiative vs. Guilt		Play Identification vs. (Oedipal) Phantasy-Identities			
IV SCHOOL AGE				Industry vs. Inferiority	Work Identification vs. Identity Foreclosure			
V ADOLESCENCE	Time Perspective vs. Time Diffusion	Self-Certainty vs. Identity Consciousness	Role-Experimentation vs. Negative Identity	Anticipation of Achievement vs. Work-Paralysis	Identity vs. Identity Diffusion	Sexual Identity vs. Bisexual Diffusion	Leadership Polarization vs. Authority Diffusion	Ideological Polarization vs. Diffusion of Ideals
VI YOUNG ADULT					Solidarity vs. Social Isolation	Intimacy vs. Isolation		
VII ADULTHOOD							Generativity vs. Self-Absorption	
VIII MATURE AGE								Integrity vs. Disgust, Despair

diagram "can be recommended to the serious attention only of those who can take it *and* leave it." [36]

The diagram is so constructed that the diagonal line of squares reading from the upper left-hand corner to the lower right present the major crises in personality development for each of the stages of growth, which are listed in the left-hand margin from top to bottom. The basic pattern of personality development, from infancy to early childhood and on through to adolescence and the mature age, is outlined along this diagonal. Each crisis is of a dialectical nature. In the diagram, what would generally be considered as the more successful outcome of each crisis is stated first.

The diagram also shows the relationship of the other stages to the critical stage of the identity crisis. Vertical column 5 states the ways in which the identity crisis is foreshadowed during each of the earlier crises. In each of these earlier ages, there is some aspect of the identity crisis. Horizontal row V outlines the principal implications of the way in which the other crises may be resolved. Thus, horizontal row V should be matched up with the diagonal line of squares, while vertical column 5 should be related to the age categories.

If we begin with the beginning, we have the crisis of *basic trust* during infancy, which corresponds in large measure with Freud's oral stage. Out of this first social relationship between the mothering adult and the mothered child, the individual gains that first and most fundamental of all psychosocial traits—that original "optimism," that assumption that "somebody is there," the treasure of "basic trust." Or, denied the necessary security, he comes to a profound sense of mistrust which will color his entire existence. He will miss something others can take for granted most of the time, and, according to Erikson, only psychiatrists, priests, and born philosophers can appreciate how sorely he will miss it (p. 118). The question of identity at this age takes the paradoxical form of the "positive" development being the lack of differentiation or a sense of "unipolarity," while the "negative" development would be a premature sense of self-differentiation. Erikson's concept of a sense of unipolarity goes beyond the more traditional Freudian concept of narcissistic omnipotence, which is customarily associated with this age. The infant not only feels that he can command his world, but, more fundamentally, he feels that the world is for him and he can be for the world. If, on the other hand, the infant feels that in his first relationship he is unrelated to the other, that the world can ignore him and he can have no control over it, then the consequence will be a sense of isolation, of premature self-differentiation, of basic mistrust.

Shifting next to the subsequent consequences for identity formation of the basic trust crisis (1, V), the main issue is that of the relationship of the individual to time. With trust comes a sense of time perspective, an optimism about the future, a feeling that good things will come with waiting, that stress will soon be relieved with pleasure. On the other hand, a failure of the ego function to maintain this perspective is related to an early inability to develop satisfactory expectations about need tensions and their satisfactions. Time diffusion is a basic mistrusting of time: every delay appears as deceit; every need to wait becomes an experience of impatience; every hope, a signal of danger; every potential provider, a probable traitor.

Going beyond the level of individual identity to that of ideological formulations, the crisis of basic trust is related to the role of faith. With a perspective on time and a powerful sense of trust, Utopias become possible, planning and programing give hope and meaning, and loyalty is in itself rewarding. When the efficacy of faith must be denied, planning and policy must lose all meaning, and deceit is seen in all actions. Presumably, a political ideology might meet the needs of some who have not had the full measure of basic trust. But according to Erikson: "Of all the ideological systems, however, only religion restores the earliest sense of appeal to a Provider, a Providence. In the Judeo-Christian tradition, no prayer indicates this more clearly than 'The Lord make His Face to shine upon you and be gracious unto you. The Lord lift up His countenance upon you and give you peace' " (p. 118). What was to Freud the oral stage has become with Erikson that which also makes the "face" so important in human affairs: "face-to-face relationships," "face the facts," "face the future," "face up to life," "let's face it."

The next age of early childhood, comparable to Freud's anal stage, brings the crisis of autonomy as against shame and doubt. From this stage comes that element in the sense of autonomy "which can and does mean independence, but does and can also mean defiance, stubbornness, self-insistence" (p. 122). What is basic faith in the earlier age becomes human will, "in its variations of will power and willfulness" (p. 225). And what is basic mistrust in the oral stage becomes shame and doubt in the second stage. In Erikson's view, shame is different from, and quite as important as, guilt. Shame is "the loss of social innocence, the blushing awareness that one can 'lose face,' have 'too much cheek,' and suffer the wish to be invisible, to sink into the ground. Defiance obviously, is shame's dialectical opposite: and it makes sense that the wilful exposure of the behind came to mean a defiant gesture of shamelessness . . ." (p. 122). With respect to the later identity crises, the issue of autonomy versus shame will be resolved either in favor of a sense of self-certainty, a sense of autonomy with will and purpose, or with a crushing sense of self-consciousness and a defiant need to claim a self.

It is impossible to summarize accurately Erikson's extremely subtle interpretation of young Luther's experiences during these first two crises of his life. It must be recognized that we are doing Erikson an injustice when we reduce his analysis to the following bare statements: First, Luther obtained an extraordinary reservoir of basic faith from his mother, and thus always had a deep understanding of the dynamics of faith. However:

> Martin was driven early out of the trust stage, out from under his mother's skirts by a jealously ambitious father who tried to make him precociously independent from women, and sober and reliable in his work. Hans succeeded but not without storing in the boy violent doubts of the father's justification and sincerity; a lifelong shame over the persisting gap between his own precocious conscience and his actual inner state; and a deep nostalgia for a situation of infantile trust. His theological solution—spiritual return to a faith which is there before all doubt, combined with a political submission to those who by necessity must wield the sword of secular law—seems to fit perfectly his personal need for compromise [pp. 255-56].

These are the origins, as Erikson sees it, of that combination of faith and wrath; of the belief that behind a God that shames and a God that is demanding, there is still the possibility of mutual recognition, of the face-to-face meeting of personal salvation. As Erikson puts it: "It would be much too easy (although some stalwart opponents of all interpretation would consider even this easiest and most obvious explanation far-fetched) that Hans' son was seeking in religion what he would not find in Hans" (p. 115).

We have gone into detail with these first two stages, in order to give some feeling of Erikson's mode of analysis. We must treat the other stages in more summary fashion.

The third crisis, that of initiative versus guilt, covers more than the Freudian concept of the Oedipus complex. Erikson reflects his personal values and, above all, his ability to be hardheaded yet sympathetic, without being precious and sentimental, when he writes of the Oedipus complex. For example, he says:

> . . . we . . . most certainly . . . would ascribe to Luther an Oedipus complex, and not a trivial one at that. We would not wish to see any boy—much less an imaginative and forceful one—face the struggles of his youth and manhood without having experienced as a child the love and the hate which are encompassed in this complex: love for the maternal person who awakens his senses and his sensuality with her ministrations, and deep and angry rivalry with the male possessor of this maternal person. We would also wish him with their help to succeed, in his boyhood, in turning resolutely away from the protection of women to assume the fearless initiative of men [p. 73].

Clearly, Erikson does not minimize the Oedipus complex; yet it is not a dominant theme in his total analysis. The influence of the initiative versus guilt crisis on the subsequent identity crisis depends upon whether the individual resolves his Oedipus complex by turning outside of the family to seek his future development, thus envisioning the possibility of experimenting with other roles. The alternative would be a sense of *negative identity*, that is, a need to become what one has been warned not to become, which is something one can only do with a divided heart. Since there seems to be a need to protect one's wholeheartedness, those who have a sense of negative identity cannot even be steadfast rebels.

Erikson's analysis moves without interruption from this stage into the crisis of industry and inferiority. In this fourth stage, the individual's "budding will to phantasy, play, games and early work" are all related to the occupational and technological ideals that the child perceives in his environment. What for Freud was the phallic stage becomes with Erikson a period of systematic learning and of collaboration with others:

> The resolution of this stage decides much of the ratio between a sense of industry or work completion, and a sense of tool-inferiority, and prepares a man for the essential ingredients of the ethos as well as the rationale of his technology. . . . In Martin's case, the tool was literacy, Latin literacy, and . . . he was molded by it . . . and later he remolded, with the help of printing, his nation's literary habits. With a vengeance he could claim to have taught German even to his enemies [pp. 258-59].

A major dimension of personality formation in Erikson's view is learning a craft or a skill and developing proficiency in manipulating particular tools, instruments, or symbols.

Next comes the identity crisis, the principal one in Erikson's analysis, in terms of which his book on Luther is written. The last three crises—those of intimacy versus isolation, generality versus self-absorption, and integrity versus despair—are fairly self-evident and need no further elaboration here. We need only note that, in Erikson's view:

> The integrity crisis, last in the lives of ordinary men, is a lifelong and chronic crisis in a *homo religiosus*. He is always older, or in early years suddenly becomes older, than his playmates or even his parents and teachers, and focuses in a precocious way on what it takes others a life-time to gain a mere inkling of: the question of how to escape corruption in living and how in death to give meaning to life [p. 261].

IV

It has been considerably easier to set forth Erikson's views on the "metabolism of generations" than it will be to state his theory about the dynamics of the great man in history. In this volume Erikson is still experimenting with his theory, and he is extremely reluctant to use any direct propositional statements. We can only outline what seems to be the direction of his explorations.

The story of the great man, ideologically speaking, is the story of an individual striving to find his own identity. By following the peculiar logic of that struggle, he gives, without necessarily intending to, a sense of identity and meaning to a people at a particular juncture of history. The individual pattern of development may be extremely complicated, but Erikson suggests that there are certain uniformities. In particular, he makes comparative references to the lives of Freud, Darwin, G. B. Shaw, and Hitler.

The beginning point—indeed, the central theme—of the development of the great man is his need to settle a personal account on a large scale and in a grand context. This involves far more than the idea that public life provides the opportunity for reducing psychic tensions. In Erikson's view, the great man must have some score to settle with others and the score must be of such grand proportion that it is appropriate to seek a public arena. The problem must be far more than just the sting of the Oedipus complex. Erikson elsewhere has commented: "Whoever has suffered under and identified with a stern father, must become a stern father himself, or else find an entirely different means of moral strength, an equal measure of strength. Young Martin Luther's religious crisis is a transcendent example of the heights and depths of this problem." [37]

This magnitude of the personal problem and the compelling need to resolve it seems to produce a deep sense of ambivalence: a feeling of sinfulness on the one hand, and a feeling of being chosen on the other. The great man may come to seek greatness, to believe in his own destiny, and yet he can be consumed with a fear of failure, a precocious fear that may arise at a very early age. Indeed, Erikson suggests that such men often fail as children, in that they are people with lost childhoods—people who place excessive demands upon themselves from a very early age. In their lives, the identity crisis is likely to involve a conflict between a sense of allness and a feeling of nothingness. The fear of failure becomes a dread of nonexistence, and the individual vacillates between a sense of nothingness and a sense of being everything. Erikson is convincing when discussing the thin line that separates the feelings of omnipotence and of insignificance.

A key element in the identity crisis—but something which may last through life—is the "moratorium." Erikson attaches considerable significance to the need of all individuals for a period of moratorium: a withdrawal from full involvement, a time of loneliness and uncertainty, a time during which psychic growth may catch up with physical development. Most societies have institutionalized, in varying degrees, this moratorium, in the sense that they withhold responsibility from young people who are physically as developed as adults. During the moratorium, the young person generally develops some skill or technique that will either

[37] Erik Erikson, "The First Psychoanalyst," *Yale Review,* Autumn, 1956, p. 50.

subsequently become central to his identity or give him the necessary sense of discipline so that he will be able to employ more effectively some other faculty or skill. Luther's moratorium was spent in the monastery; Freud's "monastery" was his medical and scientific training; G. B. Shaw spent his moratorium in a business house; Darwin spent his in medical training and two years aboard the *Beagle*;[38] for Winston Churchill, it was the Indian army. Erikson suggests that the common pattern of the ideological innovator is one of coming upon his life work without prior planning or design. Disciplined training is in one area, and creative innovation in another.

To achieve his sense of identity and break out of his moratorium, the great man must rely upon some dominant faculty, some special gift. In Erikson's reading of history, there is also likely to be at this juncture some technological innovation that can peculiarly complement the special qualities of the great man, becoming the bridge that links him to his times. In the case of Luther, it was his understanding of the Word and Gutenberg's invention of the printing press. Erikson has some subtle things to say about playing with words and about the importance people will attach to isolated words and characters, to doctrines and pronouncements, to the Word and to the Good Book. Even more important is Erikson's appreciation of the compulsions that lie behind the need of the great ideological innovators to talk, to manipulate words. Above all else, such people do not need simply to talk: they need to *talk back*. It is not at the level of the content of their words, but at a much deeper level, that they really mean what they say. This is the need to settle their score; this is the real "Meaning of Meaning It."

Once the reformer has found his identity and commands a medium through which he can act without conflict, the stage is set for a great moment in history. This is the moment of consummation, when both the reformer's search and the period's search for identities are mutually realized. Erikson suggests that this moment of success affects the ego of the leader and the ego of those reached by, and receptive to, his word. All who are involved know that they "mean it," and a historical force of great power is produced.

For the people, a long-needed shift in outlook has occurred; they will never be the same again. For the leader, this can only be a moment of balance, and then the inner conflict must be resumed. While Luther was "in the cloister all three factors—his sense of identity, his potential for intimacy, and the discovery of his generative powers—were stubbornly engaged in the life-or-death struggle for that sense of total justification which both the father and The Father had denied him, and without which a *homo religiosus* has no identity at all" (p. 149). Once he did find

---

[38] [Actually, Pye is wrong here; as Darwin himself says, it was "nearly five years." *B.M.*]

the main executive of his identity, the Word, he was caught up again in the conflict between a sense of nothingness and an urge for fame.

This conflict can result in the collapse of the innovator and even in his becoming in time the very thing he fought. However, this is only part of the problem. The leader may also realize that he really did not intend to do what he did on the grand scale; he may come to recognize that it was only a private score he had to settle.

> The crisis of an ideological leader naturally emerges when he must recognize what his rebellion—which began with the application of a more or less disciplined phantasy to the political world in the widest sense—has done to the imagination, the sense of reality, and the conscience of the masses. The fact is that all walks of life, revolutionized but essentially leaderless, exploited Luther's reformation in all directions at once. They refused to let him, and a few people like him, settle down in parsonages as the representatives of the praying orientation in life, and otherwise accept the estate and occupation in which, as he claimed, God had placed them. The princes became more absolute, the middle-class more mercantile, the lower classes more mystical and revolutionary; and the universal reign of faith envisaged in Luther's early teachings turned into an intolerant and cruel Bible-quoting bigotry such as history had never seen. As Tawney put it, "the rage of Luther . . . was sharpened by embarrassment at what seemed to him a hideous parody of truths which were both sacred and his own" [p. 242].

The final result is that the ideological leader produces consequences that are quite the opposite of those he intended.

> Consider for a brief moment certain great names of our time, who pride themselves on a dominant identity enhanced by scientific truth. Darwin, Einstein, and Freud—omitting Marx, who was a conscious and deliberate ideological craftsman—would certainly deny that they had any intention of influencing, say, the editorials, or the vocabulary, or the scrupulosity of our time in the ways in which they undoubtedly did and do. They could, in fact, refute the bulk of the concepts popularly ascribed to them, or vaguely and anonymously derived from them, as utterly foreign to their original ideas, their methodology, and their personal philosophy and conduct. Darwin did not intend to debase man to an animal; Einstein did not preach relativism; Freud was neither a philosophical pansexualist nor a moral egotist. Freud pointed squarely to the psychohistorical problem involved when he said that the world apparently could not forgive him for having revised the image of man by demonstrating the dependence of man's will on unconscious motivation, just as Darwin had not been forgiven for demonstrating man's relationship to the animal world, or Copernicus for showing that our earth is off-center [pp. 177-78].

In summary, the great man, in seeking to settle his own inner problem, strikes out against his environment. He is both destructive and constructive; indeed, without a capacity for destruction he cannot be truly constructive. It is through leveling blows against the existing system that the great man first wins his audience. His public must also feel some uncertainty over the times, some loss of identity. Then comes the role of charisma, the basis of a new mode of communication, and the beginnings of a new sense of identity for both the leader and the followers. The particular faculty and the particular technology provide the foundations for institutionalizing the relationship of charisma and for giving structure to the new sense of identity. Then come the extremist reactions: first the leader overdoes it, and then the followers overdo it.

V

What is Erikson's purpose in this book? What special value does the study have for political scientists? In making his point that the consequences of ideological leaders are often the opposite of their intended purposes, Erikson presents a penetrating comparison of Luther and Freud. There is considerable significance in each of the points he makes about Luther, who came at the end of the age of absolute faith, and Freud, who came at the end of the age of reason. I was particularly struck by the following:

> Both men endeavored to increase the margin of man's inner freedom by introspective means applied to the very center of his conflicts; and this to the end of increased individuality, sanity, and service to men. Luther, at the beginning of ruthless mercantilism in Church and commerce, counterpoised praying man to the philosophy and practice of meritorious works. Subsequently, his justification by faith was absorbed into the patterns of mercantilism, and eventually turned into a justification of commercialism by faith. Freud, at the beginning of unrestricted industrialization, offered another method of introspection, psychoanalysis. With it, he obviously warned against the mechanical socialization of men into effective but neurotic robots. It is equally obvious that his work is about to be used in furtherance of that which he warned against: the glorification of "adjustment." Thus both Doctor Luther and Doctor Freud, called great by their respective ages, have been and are apt to be resisted not only by their enemies, but also by friends who subscribe to their ideas but lack what Kierkegaard called a certain strenuousness of mental and moral effort [p. 252].

Here and there throughout the book Erikson criticizes the popularizers of Freudian analysis. At the surface level, he is particularly critical of their soft-headed and sentimental qualities and of their lack of appreciation for the high costs and the self-discipline that must go into any form of human excellence. Erikson repeatedly reminds us of a point that some popularizers of psychoanalysis ignore: Freud did not merely seek to help the individual adjust to his environment; he also demanded that the individual make the "environment" adapt to him. The difference is extremely important for political analysis. A peculiar set of biases, largely favoring static analysis and equilibrium concepts, is likely to predominate if it is assumed that the individual must either adjust to, and be molded by, "society" or revolt against society. A radically different outlook comes from picturing the individual as not only adapting to others, but in turn changing and controlling his surroundings. With such an orientation, initiative, creativity, and the basic dynamics for the system do not come from anything as abstract as "society," but rather from particular individuals. All people are to some extent creative, for all people must shape their worlds in finding their identities.

At a deeper level, Erikson's concern over what he considers to be the popular misinterpretations of Freud involves another problem, which is left largely unarticulated but which colors much of the analysis. This is the problem of the proper relationship of the disciple to his ideological father. How can one find one's own identity while remaining true to one's leader and mentor? This, of course, is the dynamic element behind all controversies about who is perpetuating the true faith and who is deviating from it. This has been the problem of those who took their inspiration from Luther and of those who took theirs from Freud. Erikson is known as a Freudian; yet he has quite possibly done more original and innovational work than any of the neo-Freudians. (Freud only used the term "identity" once, and with a rather different meaning from that of Erikson's.) A clue to Erikson's method in becoming both the complete follower and the creative innovator is to be found in the following words, which he once used to sum up his appraisal of Freud:

> Freud, before he went into medicine, wanted to become a lawyer and politician, a lawmaker, a *Gesetzgeber*. When, in 1938, he was exiled from his country, he carried under his arm a manuscript on Moses, the supreme lawgiver of the people whose unique fate and whose unique gifts he had accepted as his own. With grim pride he had chosen the role of one who opens perspectives on fertile fields to be cultivated by others. As we look back to the beginnings of his work, and forward to its implications, we may well venture to say: Freud, the physician, in finding a method of healing himself in the very practice of emotional cure has given a new, a psychological rationale for man's laws. He has made the decisive step toward a true interpenetration of the psychological with the technological and the political in the human order.[39]

Erikson thus claims that Freud was centrally concerned with the larger order of human relationships, and that such historical studies as this one of Luther should belong at the heart of the intellectual revolution sparked by Freud. The insights of psychoanalysis should not be treated as marginal ideas that may add novelty to otherwise completed studies. Erikson would

[39] Erikson, "The First Psychoanalyst," p. 62.

hold that these insights must be placed at the center of political analysis and become an integrated part of research. Erikson, however, is quick to recognize that this will be a difficult development because there is such widespread misconception about what Freud's contribution really was. This is why Erikson is so critical of the superficial popularizers of psychoanalysis. He also acknowledges that psychoanalysis has

> . . . developed a kind of *originology* . . . a habit of thinking which reduces every human situation to an analogy with an earlier one, and most of all to that earliest, simplest, and most infantile precursor which is assumed to be its "origin." Psychoanalysis has tended to subordinate the later stages of life to those of childhood. It has lifted to the rank of a cosmology the undeniable fact that man's adulthood contains a persistent childishness: that vistas of the future always reflect the mirage of a missed past, that apparent progression can harbor partial regression, and firm accomplishment, hidden childish fulfillment. . . . We must grudgingly admit that even as we were trying to devise, with scientific determinism, a therapy for the few, we were led to promote an ethical disease among the many [pp. 18-19].

Erikson's answer to this problem is that Freud's great contribution was not certain formulas about personality development, but a *technique of observation*. Throughout his book, Erikson says that if we are to understand, analyze, and appreciate those who shape history, we must really look at them and observe them as full individuals. Our ability to see others clearly depends, however, upon our readiness to take a hard introspective view of ourselves. This, of course, is where the argument becomes delicate and even sticky. Erikson, however, does not imply that only those who have, under the guidance of others, taken such a long introspective view are capable of sensitive and complete political analysis. Rather, he is warning us that we should be especially careful whenever we feel that we are being especially "honest," "objective," or "open-minded." We must recognize that some of our claims to being "objective" may be prompted by a desire to protect ourselves from an honest look at reality. We must be prepared, as Erikson says, "to relinquish the security of seemingly more objective methods." [40] There are times, of course, when the problem for the individual social scientist must become even more complex. In the words of Erikson:

> An adult studying a child, an anthropologist studying a tribe, or a sociologist studying a riot sooner or later will be confronted with data of decisive importance for the welfare of those whom he is studying, while the strings of his own motivation will be touched, sometimes above and sometimes well below the threshold of awareness. He will not be able, for long, to escape the necessary conflict between his emotional participation in the observed events and the methodological rigor required to advance his field

[40] Erikson, "The First Psychoanalyst," p. 60.

and human welfare. Thus, his studies will demand, in the long run, that he develop the ability to include in his observational field his human obligations, his methodological responsibilities, and his own motivations. In doing so, he will, in his own way, repeat that step in scientific conscience which Freud dared to make.[41]

Erikson's basic criticism of the popularizers of psychoanalytical concepts is that they have given to the social scientist a set of phrases that have become mechanical and wooden formulas, shielding those who use them from the painful tasks of introspection and of honestly viewing reality. It is not surprising that intelligent, sensitive, and knowing people have found dubious value in studies which seek to make a direct connection between the nursery and world affairs, between crib and cabinet.

The primary contribution of Erikson's work for the political scientist is the reminder that Freud's main contribution was a technique of observation, and that observation is the key to the study of human relationships as it is the key to all sciences.

What about the particular theories and concepts that Erikson has developed? He has created a model of personality development which can be of great interest to the political scientist. It is, however, so complicated and subtle that it can probably only be used to full effect by its creator. With this in mind, Erikson's contribution is primarily one of making us more sensitive to a wide range of emotional nuances and of subjective relationships in human development and behavior.

Erikson's concept of identity can have a more specific impact on political research. It becomes an exciting and illuminating concept when applied, for example, to the problem of political development in the emergent countries. These are societies whose peoples, in spite of their slogans of nationalism, lack a sense of identity. When old forms and customs lose their binding, their sustaining, and their reassuring powers, the people must restlessly search for new personal identities and for a new sense of collective identity. The arena is prepared for the ideological reformer—in Erikson's terms, the great man of history. In this setting, it is all too easy for the shallow charismatic leader to appear for a moment as a prophet. Those who are facile with words may have great appeal, for the people need the word to find a new way. It is a time in which words are fundamentally more important than actions. It is also a time in which words become cheap and action becomes impossible. The setting is right for the politically anxious to try out—possibly with enthusiasm, but certainly without true commitment—all manner of ideological forms. Before the nation can develop, leaders must emerge who have found integrity in their own quests for identity, and who can therefore speak in terms that will bring meaning to other people's search for identity. The need is for that set of shared orientations which force a people steadfastly to face

[41] *Ibid.*

reality, and which make it impossible for them to turn from reality. This is the meaning Erikson gives to ideology.

Erikson's concept of identity thus suggests that the problem of consensus in transitional societies runs deeper than mere agreement over political forms and over the appropriate ends and means of political action; it involves the creation of an inner coherence of values, theories, and actions for the entire polity. The implication is that in underdeveloped countries there is a vicious circle at the subjective level, which is more crucial to the problem of national development than the more manifest vicious circle of poverty, ill-health, and illiteracy. Those who hope that national identity can come from modernization cannot escape the pressing psychological fact that modernity, in the mind of these people, has always been the monopoly of those who were their former masters. If they hated their colonial rulers, then they cannot expect to find their identities by following the same path. If they did not hate their former rulers, there might still be the problem of preferring dependency to autonomy, which would confuse the quest for identity. National identity cannot be built upon doing less well what one's former master excelled at. Similar psychological roadblocks appear when identity is sought among the recorded but forgotten remnants of a distant history, for such a search becomes, psychologically, a constant reminder of national impotence in recent history. These are only some of the subjective problems that impede the solution of the more objective problems in the underdeveloped countries, and that cannot be resolved until a sense of national identity is achieved.

The readily apparent utility of Erickson's concept of identity to the problems of the underdeveloped countries suggests that it must have a much broader value. Specifically, his concept can give focus to all forms of study concerned with the development of the political actor. By stressing the individual's need to find coherence in his self-image, Erikson suggests that we should see the process of political socialization, not as a series of random experiences, but as a trend in development in which there is always a central theme, an element of unity. There is an inner logic or coherence in the way in which people come to their political orientations. Our search should thus be for more than connections between isolated attitudes and opinions on the one hand, and particular demographic characteristics on the other; it should be for the more complete pattern, the total configuration, the full style of political actors.

By demonstrating that the gap between the private and the political can be effectively bridged by the relationship between personal identity and political ideology, Erikson helps the political scientist with more than the problem of the psychological aspects of behavior. He also offers an approach for studying ideologies themselves. For some time, political scientists have known that the logic of ideologies is not encompassed by mere reason. However, there has remained the problem of a systematic method for treating the nonrational components. Erikson, in suggesting that political ideologies express the total character of the human personality, has provided us with an analytical framework to understand the inner structure of ideologies. Psychoanalytical theory can be a guide for comprehending more than just individual patterns of behavior. Nathan Leites has shown how extremely rewarding it can be to examine an ideology—or in his phrase, an operational code—according to the insights of psychoanalysis. Leites chose to leave his theory implicit; Erikson has stated his theory in more detail. Both have worked at the creative stage in the development of a promising approach; the next stage will have to be one of increased precision in stating propositions and increased rigor in empirical testing.

Erikson is able to challenge and stimulate the thinking of political scientists because he combines so effectively in himself the qualities of both the scientist and the artist. Like a great artist, he evokes in others an urge to imitate him. Also like a great artist, he makes us sensitive to the wonders of what we had taken to be mere commonplaces. In referring to his own youth, Erikson once noted, "I was an artist then, which is a European euphemism for a young man with some talent, but nowhere to go." [42] In going far since then, Erikson has not lost the genius of the true artist.

[42] *Ibid.*, p. 40.

A Review of *Young Man Luther:*
A Study in Psychoanalysis
and History

Donald B. Meyer

Young Man Luther is about Luther as a young man, from about 1507 to about 1512, five years in his late twenties, long after infancy and childhood, well before fame, power, and self-consciousness as a public figure. Erikson offers piercing glances back to boyhood and infancy, and he also looks ahead, to the Reformer, the theologian, the teacher. But the focus is upon the young man, and thus Erikson falls between traditional Freudian emphasis upon the early years—the earlier the better—and the interest of traditional history in the years of public influence.

Erikson finds that in this period, from his entrance into the monastery to the time he gave his first lectures on the Psalms, Luther underwent the decisive crisis of his life.This was his crisis of "identity." It began with his decision to be a monk; by every means he knew Luther tried to become what, so far as he knew, he wanted to be; and he failed. The triumphant conclusion to his crisis was a consequence of a breakthrough to a higher stage of self-integration, a fuller recognition of the grounds of selfhood generally. Luther discovered why he had failed; he had made a mistake about himself, and he knew how such mistakes could be made. It was this act of understanding—Luther's "revelation in the tower"—that unleashed Luther the man. Protestantism was born.

"A Review of *Young Man Luther: A Study in Psychoanalysis and History* [by Erik H. Erikson. New York: W. W. Norton & Co., Inc., 1958, 288 pp.]. Reprinted from *History and Theory*, I, No. 3 (1961), 291-297. Copyright 1958 by George H. Nadel.

The book is phenomenally fascinating. Of course all books about Luther have the advantage of being about Luther, a phenomenally fascinating man. But it is easy to throw away much of this advantage by mistreating the sources. The fascination depends upon suppressing none of them, adding none, and refraining from confusing the historian's job with that of the judge or diagnostician. I think it well to stress the virtues of Erikson's performance in these respects, quite apart from issues about psychoanalytic history. He knows about the treatment of sources and shows it by a critical review of the Luther scholarship. I offer only the most obviously pertinent instances.

First: every Luther scholar "knows" that Luther, who had one of the great gifts for language in history, often used frank, blunt, raw vocabulary. What is one to do when a religious leader refers so persistently to the anus? One can edit the embarrassing words away; one can deem them unimportant; one can pass over them quickly as unfortunate evidence that, after all, Luther was not perfect; one can observe that, after all, everyone talked that way in the sixteenth century. The first—the sin of sins—is clearly unacceptable; but so are the others. Who says these words are unimportant? Whoever does say so must present his principles for selection as distinctly in this instance as he would in dealing with Luther's most edifying theology. Who says they are unfortunate? What are the historian's credentials for such flinching? And by what principle of selection may one dissolve Luther into his "age" at one point, when the reason for writing about him is to define him?

Second: every Luther scholar "knows" that Luther had a turbulent emotional life. It is known that he himself associated episodes of this turbulence with his religious feelings and his primal religious insights. What is one to make of these episodes if one is interested in the universal meaning and validity of his religion? Perhaps they were not "merely" psychological; perhaps they were "religious," perhaps they contained a spiritual element, revealing the activity of God. But what sort of evidence, if any, have historians learned to trust as signs of "spiritual" factors and divine activity in distinction from "merely" psychological manifestations?

This sort of adding on and dissolving away of evidence has usually been the work of Luther's friends, his Lutheran, Protestant, religious biographers. In contrast, there has been the attitude of his judges and diagnosticians. These have insisted upon the facts, and the facts, they say, show Luther as coarse and as emotionally warped. Catholic biographers have located, at the very center of the whole Luther, a moral flaw: this "explains" everything. All of Luther is traced back and reduced to one thing. Psychiatrists have been content with a diagnostic pigeonhole: he was sick, and what he did was what his sort of sickness does. Erikson is capable of recognizing moral flaws and he is capable of recognizing sickness, but he is also aware that to invoke either flaws or sickness as "explanation" is to petrify a man. Given that flaw or that sickness, the rest of his life is merely a kind of deduction. This is to turn a man into an object for natural science, not for history.

Erikson, in short, has advanced Luther scholarship on the most elementary of tests: he does not mistreat the sources. But has he turned up any "fresh" data? Has he gone to untapped sources? It is, to put the matter bluntly, a register of the theoretical bankruptcy of history to note just how frequently this question is used as a measure of professional competence. Biography of a man like Luther shows why: new Luther sources will always be welcome, but there is plenty of room for progress for anyone who knows how to use the basic, available sources. Erikson's book is based, not on fresh data, but upon data refreshened, rescued from suppression, from invention, and from reduction.

In studying the mature Luther, Luther the Reformer, can we assume that Luther knew what he meant in speaking and acting as he did? Can we assume that, if he did know, he chose to make it clear? Can we assume that we can tell what he meant, even supposing that he knew and tried to make it clear? One of the reasons why Erikson's book about Luther as a young man should have great appeal for historians is that he shows that Luther's crisis pivoted exactly on this problem of knowing what is meant. Certainly, in their pursuit of explanations, historians routinely explore what a man got from his education, his culture, and, in an old-fashioned sense, from his mother's side and his father's side. These debts may very well be unrecognized; a faulty education may prevent a man from realizing what he owes his culture; and he may therefore not know why he means what he means, or even what he means, because he is ignorant. But this has nothing to do with Luther's problem. Luther was concerned with "sincerity." As Erikson formulates that concern: what is "The Meaning of 'Meaning It' "? How can a man know he means what he says he means, what he thinks he means, what his actions appear to indicate he means? To put it somewhat ludicrously but usefully: how can a man leave documents for historians which they can believe? In 1507 Luther thought he meant to be a monk; but he found later he had been mistaken. Luther was preoccupied with the unconscious, not with ignorance. His historical significance is rooted exactly in his sensitivity to the evidence that he himself had prevented himself from truly meaning what he thought he meant. Luther was, in effect, one of the great psychoanalysts in history.

There are many fruitful ways to study Luther besides Erikson's; Erikson explicitly intends his method not to monopolize Luther but to make those other ways still more fruitful. Possibly the most valuable in the last fifty years has been the restudy of Luther's theology by Swedish scholars. But one compelling result of this theological study is that it points time and again at one question: how did the "meaning" intended by this theology come to be meant? The Swedish motif-research makes it plain that Luther's theology cannot begin to be exhausted in study of various logical problems coming to a head in medieval thought, or in consideration of its political, social, economic roots and ramifications. In every facet of the Swedish findings a drastically existential consciousness is indicated at work, and it is this consciousness which then becomes the central phenomenon for historical explanation. How did it come to be?

It is here that psychoanalysis makes its decisive offer to history. Freud's concept of the unconscious, his concepts of the id, ego, and superego, and his emphasis upon sexuality doubtless are the most famous features of his psychology. But these do not comprehend his importance to historians. Psychoanalysis is the most radically historical psychology: this is its basic challenge to all other psychologies, and it is only in terms of this challenge that historians can finally evaluate its usefulness to them. In liberating themselves from grossly nonhistorical principles of explanation—gods and demons, dialectical materialisms and idealisms, etc.—historians have come to see their task as that of understanding the interactions between the human agents of history with their environment. But this has not safeguarded them from neglecting their main task: to incorporate those human agents themselves fully into history. Freud made the most radical effort to explain the existence of these agents—"mind," "spirit," "soul," "instincts," the "individual," the "self," "human nature" itself—in exclusively historical terms. The alternative to a historical psychology must be at some point simply to postulate the existence of something standard, normal, and even normative that "behaves" in history, and to do this, simply to postulate it, is to surrender the historical method.

Probably the most alluring such postulation today is to be found in sociological history, with its freedom not only from theological and metaphysical assumptions but also, supposedly, its freedom from the fallacy of analogies drawn from the natural sciences as well: all shall be explained in terms of man. Here, the explanatory context of all events is a social system. Structural and functional sociology is in itself timeless and nonhistorical; it becomes history, supposedly, with the study of responses to disturbances in the system. These responses constitute the events which historians try to understand, and they find the terms of their understanding given them in the social system. The postulated psychology in this may be "nothing more" than that of a pure plasticity, a "human nature" capable of all the known varieties of social systems and more, capable of an infinity of "social characters" (in which case it becomes tempting to conclude that the words "human nature" have no operational meaning at all and comprise a needless concept carried over from prescientific habits of thought). The question for historians should be clear: suppose such plasticity does in fact describe a reality, how did *it* come to be? So far, no answer has been forthcoming from the nonhistorical sciences of biology, physiology neurology, biochemistry; and short of one it is a question for history. History must comprehend its essential subject matter, human nature, in historical terms.

Previous efforts to "apply" psychoanalytic concepts to history have come to grief. These have been of two sorts. One is to seize upon direct evidence—commonly sparse—about the nature of infant experience, and then, using clinical concepts, to leap directly into explanations of the largest public, cultural, institutional life. But there are more steps in any logic that leads from, say, swaddling to the Politburo than this sort of explanation dreams of. The second method is to infer the deepest meanings of the self from the most visible, accessible public life. The classic instance here, for our purposes, would be Erich Fromm's *Escape from Freedom*, in which this neo-Freudian author infers the dominant characterological contents of those who believed Reformation doctrines from the intellectual contents of those doctrines. This is neither history nor any evidence for Freudian (or neo-Freudian) concepts: if one knows what evidence to use before inferring its Freudian origins, one does not need Freud. Neither method is historical, only analogical, saying only that this seems to resemble that, therefore that explains this. In rejecting Freud's biological foundations, Fromm has said, in effect, not so much that Freud was mistaken as that Luther was mistaken. Unfortunately this leaves Fromm—and any Luther scholar—with a problem. Whatever Luther intended, he was trying to express something, to mean something, and he used anal language to do so. Perhaps he did not, despite all his heroic efforts, finally "know" what that meaning really was, and perhaps, therefore, historians will be guided to translating his language. But they can on no account whatever suppress and ignore it; that remains, except on the crudest propagandistic concept of the historian's task, the sin of sins.

But if Erikson is better than Fromm on Luther, what does that signify? We can be sure Erikson did not choose Luther to write about at random. He knew beforehand how marvelously Luther might serve to display psychoanalytic method at work. But most men—and certainly most of the historically conspicuous men—do not leave sources replete with anal or any other kind of overt body imagery. Psychoanalytic history cannot be validated until it proves its usefulness in dealing with sources containing none of the elements overtly and classically amenable to interpretation in Freudian clinical terms. If it is going to have any relevance to constitutional history, for instance, it can hardly expect to find anal vocabulary hidden in decisions of the supreme court. The bearing of Erikson's book here is, I think, clear, though mostly implicit. It can be opened up by a simple question: is biography history? Can a biography justify Erikson's subtitle, "A Study in Psychoanalysis and History"?

It might well be argued that this catches up the entire affair, and the point ought to be made flatly: psychoanalytic history is biography-centered history. It hardly follows from this, however, that psychoanalysis, even though it might be thoroughly adequate for the study of individuals, has no relevance to those social entities—institutions, states, classes, styles, cultures, groups, parties, churches, ideologies—which historians are anxious to illuminate. It follows rather that psychoanalytic biography constitutes a perspective, or a focus, from which history can organize all its narratives, no matter how vast a range of social data these may comprehend. What do given institutions, states, styles, churches, etc., mean for the selves involved with them? Specialized study of any of these—of the evolution of constitutional forms, of philosophical logic, of economic tools and organizations—can never be impugned: we need all such specialized knowledge we can get. These cease to be integral specialties, however, at the slightest inference, explicit or implicit, from the forms or the logic or the tools to their human meaning. At the point of such inference biography is required. Nor is the requirement for biography satisfied in the use of types, or models of social character: these have their use strictly in illumination of the structure of a social system, and it remains to establish the human meaning of that structure itself. Erikson devotes considerable attention to Luther as an organizing perspective for the study of sixteenth-century economics, religion, styles of social character, styles of family life, and, most particularly, "ideology," comprehending in this worn term the use by the ego of various publicly available verbal patterns for its own meaningful ends. He analyzes in existential detail the meaning of institutions—such as monasteries, in one of which Luther lived out his crisis. One sees how to move out from Luther into the Reformation and into society generally.

Some of the confusion and doubt clustering at this point can fairly be assigned to faulty pioneering in psychoanalytic history itself. Efforts to transport vocabulary, to locate a social unconscious, a collective ego, a community superego, to equate social events with processes discovered by clinicians in individual dynamics, are no good; these are analogies as dubious as analogies drawn from Newton and Darwin. Just as in moving out from the hard core of pathological data used by Freud, psychoanalysis has generated the vocabulary of ego psychology, so in moving out from the hard core of biography it will have to generate a vocabulary for discussing institutions, empires, ideologies, etc., retaining its integrity exactly as this vocabulary continues, as Erikson's does, to ground itself in biography, in the individual, in consciousness.

To say that psychoanalytic history is biography-centered history is to imply the largest challenge of psychoanalytic method. Schemes of historical interpretation have commonly been contrasted according to which among a multitude of "factors" is selected for emphasis as the primary, basic, fundamental cause of events. God? The Logos? The World Spirit? The economic system? Human reason? Human passions? Internal contradictions in the social order? Social character? Environment? Impatient with the palpably speculative quality of many of these, positivistic historians have insisted upon limiting explanation to factors which, presumably, it does not take philosophy and certainly not religion to discern. Many modern historians avail themselves—self-consciously or dumbly—of "multicausal" explanations, "letting the evidence speak" in each case. Psychoanalytic history contrasts with all such schemes in that "causation" is not its preoccupation at all. It is not in the arena competing with Marxist history or liberal history, cyclical theories or unilinear theories, sociological theories or, in fact, psychological theories where these assign some special causal priority to "psychological factors." It is most compatible with the "commonsense" multicausal method, with its neo-Rankean devotion to the unique event, but its aim is different.

Though Erikson makes nothing of it, it is perhaps no accident that in Luther, so marvelously suited to showing off psychoanalytic method, he is dealing with the restorer of Augustinian perspectives in theology. Augustine attacked classical history, essentially because it could never finally grasp its true subject matter, human consciousness. It failed in this primarily because of its preoccupation with categories of causation, even when these included various powers of man himself. The ultimate reason why men should have inhibited themselves in this way was one which deeply interested Luther, one which Freud was to echo, and one which can be discerned in Augustine. This sort of history revealed a sickness; it was the sickness of selves incapable—due to a mixture of fear and pride —of recognizing selfhood. Instead, men reached out to identify themselves with various forces which disguised selfhood. This effort produces history which oscillates perpetually between one scheme of determinism and another, and between schemes of determinism and indeterminism, each of which is as regularly discredited as partisan myth.

Erikson's biography of Luther illustrates the connection between a self-consciously historical, existential psychology and the historian's sense that his subject is in truth something that is in every case unique. In recognizing that his problem was to know what he meant, Luther was also recognizing himself as unique, since his identity problem could not even be adequately posed, let alone solved, in general terms, whether those of philosophy or biology, sociology or theology. The only adequate terms were those of his own existence, his own experience—including that which he expressed in terms of his body. As a psychology capable of doing justice to Luther, psychoanalysis points toward what Luther—and Augustine—discovered about all men: the equivalence of selfhood with the capacity for meaning, the capacity for acting (not just behaving), and the capacity to exist as an individual, as unique and as free. History is the study of the embodiments of these identities.

On the Nature of Psycho-Historical Evidence: In Search of Gandhi

Erik H. Erikson

I

About a decade ago, when I first participated in a *Dædalus* discussion, I represented one wing of the clinical arts and sciences in a symposium on Evidence and Inference.[1] I offered some observations of a "markedly personal nature," and this not only from predilection but because the only methodological certainty that I could claim for my specialty, the psychotherapeutic encounter, was "disciplined subjectivity." Of all the other fields represented in that symposium, I felt closest (so I cautiously suggested) to the historian: for he, like the clinician, must serve the curious process by which selected portions of the past impose themselves on our renewed awareness and claim continued actuality in our contemporary commitments. We clinicians, of course, work under a Hippocratic contract with our clients; and the way they submit their past to our interpretation is a special form of historicizing, dominated by their sense of fragmentation and isolation and by our method of restoring to them, through the encounter with us, a semblance of wholeness, immediacy, and mutuality. But as we, in our jargon, "take a history" with the promise of correcting it, we enter another's life, we "make history." Thus, both clinician and patient (and in psychoanalysis, at any rate, every clinician undergoes voluntary patienthood for didactic purposes) acquire

"On the Nature of Psycho-Historical Evidence: In Search of Gandhi." Reprinted by permission from *Daedalus,* Journal of the American Academy of Arts and Sciences, Boston, Massachusetts, Vol. 97, No. 3.

[1] Erik H. Erikson, "The Nature of Clinical Evidence," *Evidence and Inference* (Boston, 1958); revised and enlarged in *Insight and Responsibility* (New York, 1964).

more than an inkling of what Collingwood claims history is—namely, "the life of mind" which "both lives in historical process and knows itself as so living."

Since that symposium, the former caution in the approach to each other of clinician and historian has given way to quite active efforts to find common ground. These have been confined for the most part to the joint study of the traditional affinity of case history and life history. But here the clinician is inexorably drawn into super-personal history "itself," since he, too, must learn to conceive of, say, a "great" man's crises and achievements as communal events characteristic of a given historical period. On the other hand, some historians probably begin to suspect that they, too, are practitioners of a restorative art which transforms the fragmentation of the past and the peculiarities of those who make history into such wholeness of meaning as mankind seeks. This, in fact, may become only too clear in our time when the historian finds himself involved in ongoing history by an accelerated interplay of communication between the interpreters and the makers of history: Here, a new kind of Hippocratic Oath may become necessary. And as for him who would cure mankind from history itself—he certainly takes on the therapeutic job of jobs.

It is not my purpose, however, to blur the division between therapist and historian. Rather, I would like to try to delineate an in-between field which some of us have come to call the psycho-historical approach. Such a hyphenated name usually designates an area in which nobody as yet is methodologically quite at home, but which someday will be settled and incorporated without a trace of border disputes and double names. The necessity to delineate it, however, becomes urgent when forward workers rush in with claims which endanger systematic exploration. Thus, today, psychoanalytic theory is sometimes applied to historical events with little clarification of the criteria for such a transfer. Such bravado can lead to brilliant insights, but also to renewed doubt in the specific fittedness and general applicability of psychological interpretation. I will, therefore, attempt to discuss here, in a manner both, "markedly personal" and didactic, what parallels I have found between my clinical experience and the study of a circumscribed historical event.

Since the symposium on Evidence and Inference, my study *Young Man Luther* has also appeared;[2] and nothing could have better symbolized the methodological embarrassment on the part even of friendly critics than the stereotyped way in which editors, both in this country and in England, captioned the reviews of my book with the phrase, "Luther on the Couch." Now clinicians are, in fact, rather sparing in the use of the couch except in a systematic psychoanalysis; yet, "on the couch" has assumed some such popular connotation as "on the carpet." And it so

[2] Erik H. Erikson, *Young Man Luther* (New York, 1958).

happens that Luther all his life was a flamboyant free associator and in his youth certainly often talked as if he *were* "on the couch." His urbane superior von Staupitz, could we inform him of the new uses of this adaptable furniture, would gladly testify to that. He recognized in the young monk's raving insistence that his repentance had not yet convinced God a "confession compulsion" altogether out of proportion to what the father confessor was ready to receive or to absolve; wherefore he told young Luther that *he* was resisting *God,* not God him. And with the recognition of an unfunctional resistance operative within the very act of "free" self-revelation, the confessor of old was on good clinical grounds.

The recognition of an inner resistance to some memories is, in fact, the technical basis for the whole theory of defense in psychoanalysis. As such, it is one of the five conceptions which Freud in one little-known dogmatic sentence calls "the principal constituents of . . . psychoanalysis."[3] To begin on didactic home ground, I will briefly discuss these fundamental assumptions, which have remained fundamental to all modifications of psychoanalysis and to its application in other fields. A "resisting" patient, then, may find something in himself obstructing him in his very determination to communicate what "comes to his mind": Too much may come too fast, or too little too tortuously, if at all. For such *resistance,* Freud blamed the mechanism of *repression* and the fact of an *unconscious,* for what once has been repressed can reassert its right to awareness and resolution only in indirect ways: in the symbolic disguise of dreams and fantasies, or in symptoms of commission (meaning acts alien to the actor himself), or in symptoms of omission (inhibitions, avoidances).

On the basis of his Victorian data, Freud found "behind" repression and resistance primarily what he called the *aetiological significance of sexual life*—that is, the pathogenic power of repressed sexual impulses. But, of course, he included a wide assortment of impulses and affects in the definition of "sexual"; and he considered systematic attention to the *importance of infantile experiences* an intrinsic part of his method and his theory. The last two conceptions led to what has been called the Freudian revolution, although Freud has no more reason than have the fathers of other kinds of revolutions to acknowledge the "liberation" named after him.

But there is one more term, mentioned by Freud in the same study and called "neither more nor less than the mainspring of the joint work of psychoanalysis": *transference*—and for a good historical example of father transference, we again need look no further than Luther's relation to Herrn von Staupitz and the Pope. How he made this, too, historical

[3] Sigmund Freud, "An Autobiographical Study," *The Complete Works of Sigmund Freud,* Vol. 20 (London, 1959), p. 40.

in a grand manner is, for the moment, another matter. Transference is a universal tendency active wherever human beings enter a relationship to others in such a way that the other *also* "stands for" persons as perceived in the pre-adult past. He thus serves the re-enactment of infantile and juvenile wishes and fears, hopes and apprehensions; and this always with a bewildering *ambivalence*—that is, a ratio of loving and hateful tendencies which under certain conditions change radically. This plays a singularly important role in the clinical encounter and not only in the dependent patient's behavior toward the clinician. It is also part of what the clinician must observe in himself: He, too, can transfer on different patients a variety of unconscious strivings which come from *his* infantile past. This we call *counter-transference*.

All these seeming difficulties, however, are the very tools of the psychoanalyst. To a determined believer in free will, they may all sound like weaknesses, if not dishonesties, while together they are really an intrinsic "property" of the clinical situation. Relived and resolved in each case, they are a necessary part of the evidence; and their elucidation is the only way to a cure. But are they also applicable to some aspects of historical research? Here the difficulties of a hyphenated approach become only too obvious, for in the absence of historical training I can only describe the way in which my clinical tools either hindered or proved handy in an attempt to reconstruct a historical event. Yet, it would seem that even the best trained historical mind could not "live in the historical process" without underscoring and erasing, professing and denying, even loving and hating and without trying to know himself as so living and so knowing. I may hope, then, that the predicaments to be described will remind the reader of his own experiences or of those recorded in the other contributions to this symposium. As for historical data proper, I can only try to introduce a psychological dimension into what would seem to be well-established rules of evidence.

II

Three times in the early-sixties I visited the city of Ahmedabad in the Indian State of Gujarat. The first time I went on the invitation of some enlightened citizens in order to give a seminar on the human life cycle and to compare our modern conception of the stages of life with those of the Hindu tradition. My wife and I occupied a small house on the estate of an industrialist—the city being one of the oldest textile centers of the world. Nearby was the mill owner's marble mansion, always open for rest and work to men of the mind; in its very shadow was the simple house of his sister, a saintly woman called the Mother of Labor, in whose living room hung a portrait of Tolstoy inscribed for Gandhi. It came back to me only gradually (for I had known it when I was young) that this was the city in which Gandhi had lived for more than a decade and a half and that it was this mill owner and his sister (both now in their seventies) to whom Gandhi pays high and repeated tribute in his autobiography. They had been Gandhi's opponent and ally, respectively, in the dramatic event by which labor unionism was founded in India: the Ahmedabad textile strike of 1918.

At the age of forty-five Gandhi had returned to India "for good" in 1914, after having spent his student years in England and the years of his early manhood in South Africa. He had founded a settlement near Ahmedabad, the principal city of the province in which he had been born and had found a liberal benefactor in the man whom we shall simply refer to as "the mill owner" (as, in general, I will endeavor not to name in this paper individuals merely used for "demonstration"). Once settled, Gandhi had immediately begun to travel extensively to become familiar with the life of the masses and to find circumscribed grievances suited to his approach: the nonviolent technique which he had developed in South Africa and had called *Satyagraha*—that is, a method of recognizing and mobilizing the forces of truth and peace in the oppressor as well as in the oppressed. In 1917 he had found an opportunity to move in on the system of indigo growing in faraway Bihar in defense of the rights of the peasants there. And now, in 1918, he accepted at the mill owner's request the mediatorship in a wage dispute in the principal industry at home, in Ahmedabad. He had studied the situation carefully and had decided to accept the leadership of ten thousand workers, a decision which brought him into public, as well as personal, conflict with the mill owner and aligned him on the side of the mill owner's sister, who had been deeply involved in "social work" in the widest sense. In the weeks of this strike Gandhi developed, in deed and in words, his full technique, including even a brief fast. The whole matter ended in a compromise which nevertheless secured to the workers, in the long run, what they had asked for.

This story, then, seemed to harbor fascinating private, as well as public, issues. And it seemed significant that Gandhi would have chosen in the cataclysmic years 1917 and 1918 opportunities to demonstrate his kind of revolution in grievances involving first peasants and then workers and that he would do so on a local and even personal scale—visualize, in contrast, the global activities of other charismatic leaders in the concluding years of World War I. At the time, in fact, the mill strike was hardly noted: "We cannot see what Mr. M. K. Gandhi can win, but we can well see that he might lose everything," wrote the leading newspaper in the area. And in his autobiography, written a decade later, the Mahatma makes relatively light of the whole event—a diffidence which he transmitted to his biographers. Yet, the very next year he would lead the first nationwide civil disobedience and become forever India's Mahatma.

Enter the psycho-historian: Having learned to esteem the mill owner and his family and having become convinced of the historical and biographic significance of the strike as well as of the "resistance" against it, I determined to study both.

First, then, a word on the record of the event as written by Gandhi himself about a decade after the strike. In a previous publication,[4] I have pointed to the general difficulties encountered in using Gandhi's autobiography for either historical or psychoanalytic purposes—not to speak of a combination of both. Maybe more so in translation than in Gandhi's native Gujarati in which it was written, the autobiography often impresses the reader as monotonous and moralistic to the point of priggishness, or, at any rate, as devoid of any indication of Gandhi's presence described by witnesses as energetic and energizing, challenging and teasing. And, indeed, the autobiography originally was not a book at all. It was written over a number of years in the form of "columns" for a biweekly primarily addressed to youth: Each column, like our traditional homilies, had to have a moral. Furthermore, these columns were written when the Mahatmaship of India, gained in the years after the strike, seemed already forfeited both by political fortune and by approaching old age: Gandhi had been jailed and set free only to face again a politically divided India. Temporarily as we now know, but at the time often with depressing finality, he had turned from rebel to reformer. A Hindu reformer approaching sixty must face fully what the autobiography's foreword clearly states: "What I want to achieve . . . is self-realization, to see God face to face, to attain *Moksha.*" And *Moksha* in the Hindu life cycle means final renunciation and withdrawal. The autobiography is a testament, then, even though we now know that Gandhi's leadership had just begun.

One is almost embarrassed to point out what seems so obvious—namely, that in perusing a man's memoirs for the purpose of reconstructing past moments and reinterpreting pervasive motivational trends, one must first ask oneself at what age and under what general circumstances the memoirs were written, what their intended purpose was, and what form they assumed. Surely all this would have to be known before one can proceed to judge the less conscious motivations, which may have led the autobiographer to emphasize selectively some experiences and omit other equally decisive ones; to profess and reveal flamboyantly some deed or misdeed and to disguise or deny equally obvious commitments; to argue and to try to prove what seems to purify or confirm his historical role and to correct what might spoil the kind of immortality he has chosen for himself. Confession-like remembrances often seem to be the most naïvely

[4] Erik H. Erikson, "Gandhi's Autobiography: The Leader as a Child," *The American Scholar* (Autumn, 1966).

revealing and yet are also the most complex form of autobiography, for they attempt to prove the author's purity by the very advertisement of his impurities and, therefore, confound his honesty both as a sinner and a braggart.

As pointed out, past events make their often abrupt and surprising appearance in the psychoanalytic hour only as part of an observational situation which includes systematic attention to the reasons why they may come to mind just then: Factuality aside, what is their actuality in the developing relation of professional observer and self-observing client? It is, therefore, hard to understand how observers trained in clinical observation can accept an event reported in an autobiography—such as, say, Gandhi's account of his father's death—both as a factual event and as a naïve confession without asking why the item came to mind in *its* autonomous setting, the autobiography; and why, indeed, a particular form of autobiography was being practiced or newly created at that moment in history. Gandhi himself states that he knew an autobiography to be a rather un-Indian phenomenon, which makes his own an all the more elemental creation comparable to the confessions of St. Augustine and Abelard or to Rousseau's and Kierkegaard's autobiographic works.

To put this diagrammatically and didactically, a psycho-historical reviewer would have to fathom—in one intuitive configuration of thought if he can and with the help of a diagram if he must—the *complementarity* of at least four conditioners under which a record emerges.

A. *Functions of the Record*

	I Moment	II Sequence
1. INDIVIDUAL	in the recorder's stage of life and general condition	in the recorder's life history
2. COMMUNITY	in the state of the recorder's community	in the history of the recorder's community

Under I-1, then, we would focus as if with a magnifying glass on one segment of the recorder's life as a period with a circumscribed quality. Gandhi's autobiography served the acute function of demonstrating an aging reformer's capacity to apply what he called truth to the balance sheet of his own failures and successes, in order to gain the wisdom of renunciation for himself and to promote a new level of political and spiritual awareness in his nation. But we would also have to consider the special inner conflicts and overt mood swings which aggravated these, his often withrawn and "silent" years. Under I-2, we would consider all the acute circumstances in Indian history which would make Gandhi feel that he would find an echo for his message in those segments of India's awakening youth who could read—or be read to. Under II-1, we would remember that confession seems to have been a passion for him throughout life and that his marked concern over *Moksha* began in a precocious conscience development in childhood (which, in fact, he shared with other *homines religiosi*). In II-2, however, we would have to account for the fact that Gandhi's record, both in content and style, went far beyond the traditional forms of self-revelation in India and bridged such confessionalism as St. Augustine's or Tolstoy's awareness as Christians, as well as Rousseau's passionate and Freud's systematized insight into the power of infantile and juvenile experience. From the psychohistorical viewpoint, then, the question is not, or not only, whether a man like Gandhi inadvertently proves some of Freud's points (such as the power of the emotions subsumed under the term Oedipus Complex), but why such items which we now recognize as universal were re-enacted in different media of representation (*including* Freud's dream analyses) by particular types of men in given periods of history—and why, indeed, their time was ready for them and their medium: for only such complementarity makes a confession momentous and its historical analysis meaningful.

Our diagrammatic boxes, then, suggest the *relativity* governing any historical item—that is, the "concomitant variability" of passing moment and long-range trend, of individual life cycle and communal development.

III

Let me now turn to the autobiography's rendition of the strike of 1918 —the Event as I will call it from here on. There is besides Gandhi's retrospective reflections only one full account of it, a pamphlet of less than a hundred pages by the man who was then Gandhi's secretary.[5] Gandhi's own approach to the matter is even more casual and episodic and is, in fact, broken up by the insertion of a seemingly quite unrelated story.[6] This is the sequence: In a chapter (or installment) called "In Touch with Labor," Gandhi reports on the "delicate situation" in Ahmedabad where a sister "had to battle against her own brother." His friendly relations with both "made fighting with them the more difficult." But he considered the case of the mill hands strong, and he therefore "had to advise the laborers to go on strike." There follows a summary, less than one page long, of nearly twenty days of a strike during which he set in motion all the principles and techniques of his militant and nonviolent *Satyagraha*— on a local scale, to be sure, but with lasting consequences for Ahmedabad,

[5] Mahadav Desai, *A Righteous Struggle* (Ahmedabad).
[6] M. K. Gandhi, *An Autobiography* (Ahmedabad, 1927), Part 5, Chapters 20-22.

India, and beyond. Then the story of the strike is interrupted by a chapter called "A Peep into the Ashram." Here the reader is entertained with a description of the multitude of snakes which infested the land by the river to which Gandhi, at the time of the strike, had just moved his settlement. Gandhi recounts how he and his Ashramites in South Africa, as well as in India, had always avoided killing snakes and that in twenty-five years of such practice "no loss of life [had been] occasioned by snake bite."[7] Only then, in a further chapter, does Gandhi conclude the strike story by reporting its climax—namely, his first fast in a public issue, in spite of which (or, as we shall see, because of which) the whole strike ended with what looked like a kind of hasty compromise. What was at stake then, and what was still at stake at the writing of the autobiography, was the purity of the nonviolent method: The mill owner could (and did) consider Gandhi's fast an unfairly coercive way of making the employers give in, whereas Gandhi did (and always would) consider a fast only justified as a means of persuading weakening supporters to hold out.

The technical question that arises here is whether the chapter which interrupts the account of the strike could be shown to signify an inner resistance against the whole story, comparable to what we observe and utilize in clinical work. Again and again, one finds, for example, that a child undergoing psychotherapy will suffer what I have called "play disruption"—that is, he will interrupt his play in some anxious manner, sometimes without being able to resume it. And often the very manner of disruption or the way in which play is resumed will suggest to the experienced observer what dangerous thought had occurred to the child and had ruined his playfulness. Or an adult in psychoanalysis will embark on a seemingly easy progression of free associations only to find suddenly that he has forgotten what he was about to say next or to interrupt his own trend of thought with what appears to be a senseless image or sentence "from nowhere." A little scrutiny can soon reveal that what had thus been lost or had intruded was, in fact, an important key to the underlying meaning of the whole sequence of thoughts—a key which more often than not reveals a repressed or suppressed sense of hate against a beloved person. I will later report on Gandhi's sudden awareness of such a disruption in another part of the autobiography.

What, then, could the nonkilling of snakes have to do with the Ahmedabad strike and with Gandhi's relation to the mill owner? Mere thematic play would suggest Gandhiites bent on nonviolence in the first column meet mill owners; in the second, poisonous snakes; and in the third, mill

[7] An old Indian friend recounted to me an event taken almost for granted in those early days—namely, how young Vinoba Bhave (the man who in all these years has come and remained closest to Gandhi in spirit, style, and stature) sat by the *Ashram* grounds and a big and poisonous snake crawled under his shawl. He kept lovingly still, and another Ashramite quietly folded up the garment and took it to the riverbank.

owners again. Do snakes, then, "stand for" mill owners? This could suggest to a clinician a breakthrough of Gandhi's anger against the mill owners—an anger which he had expressly forbidden himself, as well as the striking and starving workmen. If one can win over poisonous snakes by love and nonviolence, the hidden thought might be, then maybe one can reach the hearts of industrialists too. Or the suggestion might be more damaging—namely, that it would be more profitable to be kind to poisonous snakes than to industrialists—and here we remember that another Man of Peace, also using an analogy from the bestiary, once mused that big lazy camels might squeeze through where a rich man could not or would not. Was Gandhi's suppressed rage apt to be "displaced" in such a flagrant way? This would have to be seen.

There is, however, an explanation closer to historical fact and to the propagandistic purpose of the autobiography. He and the mill owner had been involved in a public scandal. Briefly, the mill owner had noted hordes of ferocious looking dogs around his factory on the outskirts of the city and had ascertained that the municipal police, knowing how Hindus feel about killing animals, where in the habit of releasing captured stray dogs outside the city limits. Since hydrophobia had reached major proportions in the area, the mill owner had requested the police to kill these dogs, and some obliging officer, for reasons of his own, had arranged for the carcasses to be carted away through the crowded city streets. Such is the stuff that riots are made of in India. But Gandhi did not hesitate to speak up for the mill owner, saying he himself would kill a deranged man if he found him massacring other people. He wrote in *Young India:*

The lower animals are our brethren. I include among them the lion and the tiger. We do not know how to live with these carnivorous beasts and poisonous reptiles because of our ignorance. When man learns better, he will learn to befriend even these. Today he does not even know how to befriend a man of a different religion or from a different country.[8]

In this prophetic statement we see the reptiles "associated" with carnivorous beasts; and from here it is only one step to the interpretation that Gandhi, before telling the story of how he had made concessions to the mill owner at the end of the strike, had to tell himself and his readers that his basic principles had not suffered on that other and better known occasion when he took the mill owner's side.

Was Gandhi "conscious" of such pleading with the reader? Probably, for the whole trend of thought fits well into the professed aim of his self-revelations: to sketch his "experiments with truth." But factual explanation (and here is the psycho-historical point) should not do away with the

---

[8] L. Fischer, *The Life of Mahatma Gandhi* (New York, 1950), p. 238.

underlying and pervasive emotional actuality. For my story, the assumption of an ambivalence toward the mill owner is inescapable. In historical fact it is an example of a mutual and manly acceptance of the Hindu *dharma*—that is, of the assignment to each man of a place within the world order which he must fulfill in order to have a higher chance in another life. If, as Gandhi would put it, "fasting is my business," then making money was that of the mill owner; and Gandhi could not have fulfilled his role of saintly politician [or, as he put it, "a politician who tried to be a saint") had he not had the financial support of wealthy men. This, the Marxists might say, corrupted him, while the Hindu point of view would merely call for a clean division of roles within a common search for a higher truth. The Freudian point of view, however, would suggest that such a situation might cause an unconscious "transference" of unresolved conflicts of childhood to the present.

Young Gandhi had, in varying ways, forsaken his caste and his father when he left to become an English barrister; and he had forsaken his older brother who had wanted him to join him in legal work when he had become a reformer. Such deviations from one's ancestral *dharma* are a grave problem in the lives of many creative Indians. At any rate, when he returned and settled down in Ahmedabad—the city in which both his native language and the mercantile spirit of his ancestors had reached a high level of cultivation—and when he again deviated grievously by taking a family of Untouchables into his *Ashram,* the mill owner alone had continued to support him. The mill owner, thus, had become a true brother; and anyone familiar with Gandhi's life will know how desperate at times was the "Great Soul's" never requited and never fully admitted search for somebody who would sanction, guide, and, yes, mother *him.* This is a complex matter, and it will be enough to indicate here that without the assumption of such a transference of the prime actor in my story to the principal witnesses, a brother and sister, I could not have made sense of the meaning of the Event in Gandhi's life—and of his wish to "play it down."

IV

Nobody likes to be found out, not even one who has made ruthless confession a part of his profession. Any autobiographer, therefore, at least between the lines, spars with his reader and potential judge. Does the autobiographic recorder then develop a kind of transference on the potential reviewer of his record? Gandhi did, as we shall see.

But before reporting this, let me ask another question: Does not the professional reader and reviewer, who makes it his business to reveal what others do or may *not* know about themselves, also feel some uncomfortable tension in relation to them? Yes, I think that he does and that he should know that he does. There are, of course, some who would claim that, after all, they are voyeurs merely in *majorem gloriam* of history or humanity and are not otherwise "involved" with their subjects. But such denial often results only in an interpretive brashness or a superior attitude toward the self-recorder who seems to reveal himself so inadvertently or to hide his "real" motivation so clumsily. A patient offers his motivation for full inspection only under the protection of a contract and a method; and the method is not complete unless the "doctor" knows how to gauge his own hidden feelings. If it can be assumed that the reviewer of self-revelations or of self-revealing acts and statements offered in nonclinical contexts also develops some form of irrational countertransference, that, too, must be turned to methodological advantage not only for the sake of his work, but also for that of his friends and his family.

I hope to have aroused just enough discomfort in the professional reader to make him share the sting I felt when in the course of my study I came once again across the following passage midway through Gandhi's autobiography: "If some busybody were to cross-examine me on the chapters which I have now written, he could probably shed more light on them, and if it were a hostile critic's cross-examination, he might even flatter himself for having shown up the hollowness of many of my pretensions."[9] Here, then, we seem to have a real analogue to what I described above as "play disruption"; and, indeed, Gandhi continues with a momentary negative reaction to his whole undertaking: "I therefore wonder for a moment whether it might not be proper to stop writing these chapters altogether." After which he recovers, luckily, with a typically Gandhian form of self-sanction: "But so long as there is no prohibition from the voice within, I must continue the writing." There seems to be an awareness, however, of having given in to something akin to free association, though dictated by a higher power: "I write just as the spirit moves me at the time of writing. I do not claim to know definitely that all conscious thought and action on my part is directed by the spirit." Again, he recovers, however, and sanctions his own doings: "But on an examination of the greatest steps that I have taken in my life, as also of those that may be regarded as the least, I think it will not be improper to say that all of them were directed by the spirit." Now he can dismiss his "hostile" readers: "I am not writing the autobiography to please critics. Writing it itself is one of the experiments with truth." And he can distribute the blame for writing at all: "Indeed, I started writing [the autobiography] in compliance with their [his co-workers'] wishes. If, therefore, I am wrong in writing the autobiography, they must share the blame." This concluding remark is, I think, typical of the Gandhian half-humor so easily lost in translation; and humor means recovery.

[9] Gandhi, *An Autobiography*, Part 4, Chapter 11.

To say more about this sudden disruption, I would have to know (according to my own specifications) exactly in what period of his life Gandhi wrote this particular installment of the autobiography. Was there a real snooper and critic in his life at the time? Or was the imaginary one an externalization of a second inner voice, one temporarily at odds with the one that inspired his every effort? Much speaks for the latter assumption, for the disruption follows a chapter called "A Sacred Recollection and Penance" in which Gandhi describes an especially cruel outbreak against his wife under circumstances (there were many in his life) both sublime and ridiculous. Once, in South Africa, while cleaning her house which had become a hostel, she had refused to empty a Christian Untouchable's chamber pot (*that* combination was too *much*), and Gandhi had literally shown her the gate. After such extreme and extremely petty moments something could cry out in him: What if all his professions of universal love, all his sacrifices of those closest to him by family ties for the sake of those furthest away (the masses, the poor, the Untouchables) were a "pretense"? So here, the reader and reviewer become an externalization of the writer's self-doubt, and I felt so directly appealed to that I began to think of how I might have explained these matters to him in the light of our clinical knowledge. Not without the sudden awareness of being older than he had been when he wrote that passage, I addressed him in an ensuing chapter explaining that, as a student of another lover of truth, a contemporary of his on the other side of the world, I had a more charitable term than "pretense" for the psychological aspects of his dilemma: namely, "ambivalence." I confronted him with another instance of petty and righteous cruelty and attempted to formulate a pervasive ambivalence: that his marriage at the age of thirteen to a girl of the same age and fatherhood in his teens had prevented him from making a conscious decision at an informed age for or against married life; that this "fate" had been foisted on him in the traditional manner by his father, whom he never forgave. Thus, a lifelong ambivalence toward his wife and children, not to speak of sexuality in general, had perpetuated a predicament in his life as well as in that of many of his followers: Are *Satyagraha* and chastity inseparable? That such conflicts in the lives of saintly men are more than a matter of mental hygiene, I need not emphasize here. Gandhi, I think, would have listened to me, but probably would have asked me teasingly why I had taken his outburst so personally. And, indeed, my impulsive need to answer him "in person" before I could go on with my book revealed again that all manner of counter-transference can accompany our attempts to analyze others, great or ordinary.

And what, we must ask (and he might have asked), legitimizes such undertaking in clinical work? It is, of course, the mandate to help— *paired with self-analysis.* And even as we demand that he who makes a profession of "psychoanalyzing" others must have learned a certain capacity for self-analysis, so must we presuppose that the psycho-historian will have developed or acquired a certain self-analytical capacity which would give to his dealings with others, great or small, both the charity of identification and a reasonably good conscience. Ours, too, are "experiments with truth."

I can offer, for such an ambitious aim, only another schema which lists the minimum requirements for what a reviewer of a record and of an event should be reasonably clear about:

B. Function of the Review

	I Moment	II Sequence
1. INDIVIDUAL	in the stage and the conditions of the reviewer's life	in the reviewer's life history
2. COMMUNITY	in the state of the reviewer's communities	in the history of the reviewer's communities

Under communities I here subsume a whole series of collective processes from which the reviewer derives identity and sanction and within which his act of reviewing has a function: there, above all, he must know himself as living in the historical process. Each community, of course, may call for a separate chart: the reviewer's nation or race, his caste or class, his religion or ideological party—and, of course, his professional field.

V

Did Freud live up to our methodological standards? His introduction to what we now know to have been the first psycho-historical essay— namely, the book on Wilson allegedly coauthored by him and William Bullitt[10]—does give an admirable approximation of what I have in mind. But not in the bulk of the book: for here he unwisely relied on Bullitt to review the record for him and to provide him with the data necessary for an application of the laws found in case histories to the life history of a public figure. In my review of this book,[11] I felt it necessary to explain the strange collaboration in this way: As a young man and before he became a doctor, so Freud himself tells us, he had wanted to be a statesman. His deep identification with Moses can be clearly read in his work.

[10] Sigmund Freud and William C. Bullitt, *Thomas Woodrow Wilson: Twenty-Eighth President of the United States—A Psychological Study* (Boston, 1967).

[11] Erik H. Erikson, *The New York Review of Books*, Vol. 7, No. 2 (1967); also *The International Journal of Psychoanalysis*, Vol. 47, No. 3 (1967).

Did Bullitt awaken in the old and ailing man (who, in fact, was dying in exile when he signed the final manuscript) the fading hope that his life work, psychoanalysis, might yet be destined to become applicable to statesmanship? The task at hand, however, was obviously overshadowed by Freud's passionate feelings in regard to the joint subject, President Wilson. About this, Freud is explicit in his introduction, the only part of the book clearly written by him, all other handwritten contributions having been "lost" by Bullitt in one way or another. Freud declares that the figure of the American President, "as it rose above the horizons of Europeans, was from the beginning unsympathetic" to him and that this feeling increased "the more severely we suffered from the consequences of his intrusion into our destiny." Wilson's Fourteen Points had promised that a semblance of Christian charity, combined with political shrewdness, might yet survive the first mechanized slaughter in history. Could it be that the destruction or the dehumanization of mankind by the unrestricted use of superweaponry might be checked by the creation of a world-democracy? What followed Versailles played into a pervasive trend in Freud's whole being: a Moses-like indignation at all false Christian (or other) prophecy. A proud man brought up in Judaism, I concluded, even if surrounded by the folklore and display of Catholicism, persists in the historical conviction that the Messiah has yet not appeared and persists with more grimness the more he has been inclined temporarily to give credence to the Christian hope for salvation. Such over-all prejudice, however, even where clearly expressed, is methodologically meaningful only insofar as the slant thus given to the whole work is thereby clarified *and* insofar as it is vigorously counteracted by an adherence to the other criteria for evidence and inference—and for literary form. On the other hand, where a sovereign acknowledgment like Freud's introduction enters an alliance with a vindictive and tendentious case study clearly written by a chronically disappointed public servant such as Bullitt, then the whole work itself becomes a case study of a fascinating, but in its final form abortive, psycho-historical essay. The Wilson book can serve to illustrate, then, if somewhat by way of a caricature, the decisive influence on a bit of history which results from basic differences in *Weltanschauung* among actor, recorder, and reviewer—that is, a world view, a sense of existential space-time which (as a venerable physicist acknowledged in my seminar in Ahmedabad) is "in a man's bones," no matter what else he has learned.

Freud's example leads me back to the days when I first heard of Gandhi and of Ahmedabad and maybe even of the mill owner—all of which remained latent until, at the time of my visit, it "came back to me" almost sensually in the occasional splendor and the pervasive squalor of India. In my youth I belonged to the class of wandering artists who—as some alienated and neurotic youths can and must in all ages—blithely keep some vision alive in the realities of political and economic chaos, even though, by a minute slip in the scales of fate, they may find themselves among the uniformed to whom killing and being killed becomes a sacred duty, or they may perish ingloriously in some mass furor.

As Wilson's image had set in the cruel night of post-Versailles, it was Gandhi's which then "rose above the horizon"—on the other side of the world. As described to us by Romain Rolland, he seemed to have that pervasive presence, always dear to youth, which comes from the total commitment (for that very reason) to the actuality of love and reason in every fleeting moment. The Event had been contemporaneous with Wilson's Fourteen Points; and if these Points were (and with variations still are) "Western democracy's answer to Bolshevism," so was Gandhi's *Satyagraha* (begun so locally) the East's answer to Wilson *and* to Lenin.

As for myself, I was to spend a lifetime finding an orientation in, and making a living from, the field created by Sigmund Freud. But when I decided in advanced years to study the Event—and all I can say is that at a certain time I became aware of having made that decision—I do not think that I set out merely to "apply" to Gandhi what I had learned from Freud. Great contemporaries, in all their grandiose one-sidedness, converge as much as they diverge; and it is not enough to characterize one with the methods of the other. As Freud once fancied he might become a political leader, so Gandhi thought of going into medicine. All his life Gandhi ran a kind of health institute, and Freud founded an international organization with the ideological and economic power of a movement. But both men came to revolutionize man's awareness of his wayward instinctuality and to meet it with a combination of militant intelligence—and nonviolence. Gandhi pointed a way to the "conquest of violence" in its external and manifest aspects and, in the meantime, chose to pluck out the sexuality that offended him. Freud, in studying man's repressed sexuality, also revealed the internalized violence of self-condemnation, but thought externalized violent strife to be inevitable. And both men, being good post-Darwinians, blamed man's instinctuality on his animal ancestry—Gandhi calling man a sexual "brute" and Freud comparing his viciousness (to his own kind!) to that of wolves. Since then ethology has fully described the intrinsic discipline of animal behavior and most impressively (in this context) the pacific rituals by which some social animals—yes, even wolves—"instinctively" prevent senseless murder.[12]

When I came to Ahmedabad, it had become clear to me (for I had just come from the disarmament conference of the American Academy) that man as a species cannot afford any more to cultivate illusions either about

[12] "Psychoanalysis and Ongoing History: Problems of Identity, Hatred, and Non-Violence," *Journal of the American Psychiatric Association* (1965).

his own "nature" or about that of other species, or about those "pseudo-species" he calls enemies—not while inventing and manufacturing arsenals capable of global destruction and relying for inner and outer peace solely on the superbrakes built into the superweaponry. And Gandhi seems to have been the only man who has visualized *and* demonstrated an over-all alternative.

Less nobly, I should admit that I must have been looking for a historical figure to write about. What could be more fitting than (as my students put it) letting "Young Man Luther" be followed by "Middle-Aged Mahatma"? And here I had witnesses: the survivors of a generation of then young men and women who had joined or met Gandhi in 1918, and whose life (as the saying goes) had not been the same since, as if one knew what it might have been. They included, besides the mill owner and his sister, individuals now retired or still in the forefront of national activity in industry, in the Cabinet, or in Parliament. These I set out to meet and to interview on my subsequent visits to India.

If all this sounds self-indulgently personal, it is spelled out here only far enough to remind the psycho-historian that his choice of subject often originates in early ideals or identifications and that it may be important for him to accept as well as he can some deeper bias than can be argued out on the level of verifiable fact or faultless methodology. I believe, in fact, that any man projects or comes to project on the men and the times he studies some unlived portions and often the unrealized selves of his own life, not to speak of what William James calls "the murdered self." The psycho-historian may owe it to history, as well as to himself, to be more conscious of what seems to be a *re-transference* on former selves probably inescapable in any remembering, recording, or reviewing and to learn to live and to work in the light of such consciousness. This, incidentally, also calls for new forms of collaboration such as the father of psychoanalysis may have had in mind when he met the brilliant American diplomat.

To confound things a little further, there are also *cross-transferences* from one reviewer of the same subject to another. For example, in a book on Gandhi's main rivals for national leadership, *Tilak and Gokhale* (both of whom died before his ascendance), S. A. Wolpert[13] calls Gandhi a disciple of Gokhale, and, worse, calls Gokhale Gandhi's "guru." Now, Gandhi, while comparing Tilak with the forbidding ocean and Gokhale (his elder by three years only) with the maternal Ganges and while sometimes calling Gokhale his "political guru," certainly kept *the* guru-ship in his life free for his own inner voice: an important step in Indian self-conception. But why should Wolpert want to call *his* Gokhale *my* Gandhi's guru with such monotonous frequency—and why should this

---

[13] S. A. Wolpert, *Tilak and Gokhale* (Los Angeles, 1962).

annoy me? The italics indicate the answer which (as I would judge from my perusal of the literature on Luther) points to a pervasive aspect of a reviewer's "genealogical" identification with his subject as seen through his method, which may make history more entertaining, but rarely more enlightening unless seasoned with insight.

VI

In India, intellectual as well as political travelers could always count on being lodged with friends of means or with friends of friends, and the mill owner related the sayings of many interested house guests—among them, Gandhi. He had offered me a terrace as a study, saying quietly, "Tagore has worked here." But to be a guest in a man's house is one thing; to be a reviewer of his place in history is another. When I returned to Ahmedabad to interview the mill owner regarding the mill strike, he became strangely distant and asked me to meet him at his office in the mill. This, he made clear, was business: What did I want?

I should say in general that the clinician turned historian must adapt himself to and utilize a new array of "resistances" before he can be sure to be encountering those he is accustomed to. There is, first of all, the often incredible or implausible loss or absence of data in the post-mortem of a charismatic figure which can be variably attributed to simple carelessness or lack of awareness or of candor on the part of witnesses. Deeper difficulties, however, range from an almost cognitively a-historical orientation—ascribed by some to Indians in general—to a highly idiosyncratic reluctance to "give up" the past. Here the myth-affirming and myth-destroying propensities of a post-charismatic period must be seen as the very stuff of which history is made. Where myth-making predominates, every item of the great man's life becomes or is reported like a parable; those who cannot commit themselves to this trend must disavow it with destructive fervor. I, for one, have almost never met anybody of whatever level of erudition or information, in India or elsewhere, who was not willing and eager to convey to me the whole measure of the Mahatma as based on one sublime or scandalous bit of hearsay. Then there are those whose lives have become part of a leader's and who have had to incorporate him in their self-image. Here it becomes especially clear that, unless a man wants to divest himself of his past in order to cure, purify, or sell himself—and there are always professions which receive and sanction such divestment—he must consider it an invested possession to be shared only according to custom and religion, personal style and stage of life. The interviewee, not being a client, does not break a contract with either himself or the interviewer in not telling the whole truth as he knows or feels it. He has, in fact, every right to be preoccupied with the intactness of his historical role rather than with fragmented details as patients and psychotherapists are—often to a fault. After all, this man had been Gandhi's counterplayer in the Event, and he had (as Gandhi knew and took for granted) used all the means at his disposal to break the strike. About this he was, in fact, rather frank, while he seemed "shy" about those episodes which had proven him to be a gallant opponent and faithful supporter. What kind of "resistance" was *that?*

Let me be diagrammatic: The old man's insistence on anonymity turned out to be a lifelong one. In old newspapers I found more than one reference to his charitable deeds which in feudal manner he had always considered his own choice and his own affair. "This is business, not charity," a union official quoted him as saying when he handed him a contribution; and it will be remembered that he did not identify himself when, as a young industrialist, he left money at the *Ashram* gate. Here was a lifelong trend, then, possibly aggravated by some sense of *Moksha,* which supervenes both good deeds and misdeeds. It is not so easy to judge, then, what a man (and a foreigner) does not want to remember or does not want to say or cannot remember or cannot say.

By the same token, the old man's businesslike attitude was later clarified in its most defensive aspects as resulting from an experience with an inquisitive visitor, while in general it seemed to reflect a sense of propriety as though he wanted to delineate what in this matter was "my business" and what his. I have already indicated that this same attitude pervaded even Gandhi's sainthood. When Gandhi said to his friends, who wanted to starve themselves with him, "Fasting is my business," he added, "You do yours." But, then, both he and the mill owner belonged to a cultural and national group referred to in India (admiringly as well as mockingly) as *banias*—that is, traders. And while the whole strike and its outcome are often considered a *bania* deal by Gandhi's many critics (Marxists, or Maharashtrians, or Bengalis), there is little doubt that Gandhi chose to unfold his whole *Satyagraha* technique first in a locality and with people who spoke his language and shared his brand of mercantile shrewdness. And behind such life-styles there is always India and that larger framework of cosmic propriety, which is called *dharma*—that is, a man's preordained place in the cyclic order of things and their eventual transcendence. *Dharma* can excuse much wickedness and laziness, as can Fate or God's Will. But it will help determine, from childhood on, what a man considers proper and what out of line; above all, it provides the framework within which the individual can knowingly take hold of the law of *Karma,* the ethical accounting in his round of lives.

I felt, then, literally "put in my place" by the old man's "resistance." In fact, when he asked me after our first interview what, if anything, I had learned, I could only say truthfully that I had gotten an idea of what

Gandhi had been up against with him and he with Gandhi. Only afterwards did I realize how right I was and that the cause of my initial an-
noyance had been due to a certain parallel between Gandhi's and my
relationship to the mill owner. Had I not gladly accepted the wealthy
man's hospitality when I was a newcomer to India so that I could venture
out into the dangers and horrors of that land from an initial position of
friendship and sanitary safety? And had not Gandhi gladly accepted his
financial support when he came back from South Africa, in many ways
a newcomer to India after twenty-five years of absence? And had not both
of us, Gandhi and I, developed a certain ambivalence to our benefactor?
Here, a Marxist could find an opening for legitimate questions; and while
he is at it, he might well consider the relationship of the social scientist
to the foundations which support him. The common factor which interests us here, however, is the unconscious transference on any host—that
is, the attribution of a father or older-brother role to anyone in whose
home one seeks safety or in whose influence one seeks security. I should
add that in my case this theme seems to be anchored in the infantile
experience—and, strictly speaking, this alone makes a real transference
out of a mere thematic transfer—of having found a loving stepfather in
an adoptive country. Every worker must decide for himself, of course,
how much or how little he should make of such a connection, and how
little or how much of it he should impose on his readers. But first, we
must become aware of it.

Now an equally brief word on the other side of the coin—namely, the
often sudden and unsolicited revelation of such highly personal material
as dreams, memories, and fantasies in the course of interviews. In my
case, these were offered by a number of informants in the more informal
settings of social get-togethers. Accepting them with gratitude, I was
always determined to make use of them only as an auxiliary source of
insights, not to be attributed to individuals. I do not know, of course,
whether revelations of this kind are common in such work or appeared
in mine because my interviewees knew me to be a psychoanalyst. If this
most personal data eventually proved to have some striking themes in
common, I cannot say whether these themes are typically Indian or typical
for men who had followed Gandhi. Here are the themes: a *deep hurt*
which the informant had inflicted on one of his parents or guardians and
could never forget, and an intense wish *to take care of abandoned crea-
tures,* people or animals, who have strayed too far from home. I had
secured from each interviewee the story of how he first met Gandhi only
to learn with increasing clinical admiration how determinedly and yet
cautiously Gandhi had induced his alienated young followers to cut an
already frayed bond with their elders. Tentatively, then, I saw these
revelations as an indirect admission of the obvious fact that followers can
develop a more or less conscious sense of having vastly outdistanced their

original life plan by serving a man who had the power to impose his superior *dharma* on his contemporaries, making a modernized use of the traditional need for a second, a spiritual, father. A resulting powerful ambivalence toward him is often overcompensated by the submissive antics of followership. And followership divides too: Gandhi's disciples had to accept what was his own family's plight—namely, that he belonged to all and to no one, like the mother in a joint family. Gandhi's was a unique maternalism, happily wedded in his case with a high degree of paternal voluntarism, but not always easily shared or tolerated by others.

Followers, too, deserve a diagram. Whatever motivation or conflict they may have in common as they join a leader and are joined together by him has to be studied in the full complementarity of:

C.

	I Moment	II Sequence
1. INDIVIDUAL	the stage of life when they met the leader	lifelong themes transferred to the leader
2. COMMUNITY	their generation's search for leadership	traditional and evolving patterns of followership

As to the last point, Gandhi was a master not only in the selection and acquisition of co-workers, but also in assigning them to or using them in different tasks and ways of life—from the position of elected sons and daughters in his ascetic settlement to that of revolutionary organizers all over India and of aspirants for highest political power, including the prime ministership, for which he "needed a boy from Harrow."

The monumental compilation of Gandhi's works[14] undertaken by the government of India (and now under the charge of Professor Swaminathan) permits us to follow Gandhi's acts, thoughts, and affects literally from day to day in speeches and letters, notes and even dreams (as reported in letters), and to recognize his own conflicts over being invested with that charismatic cloak, the Mahatmaship. That publication will permit us for once to see a leader in a life-crisis fighting on two fronts at once: the individual past that marks every man as a defined link in the generational chain, and historical actuality. One thing is clear: On the verge of becoming the father of his nation, he did not (as he has been accused of having done) forget his sons, although the manner in which he did remember them was not without tragic overtones and consequences.

[14] *Collected Works of Mahatma Gandhi* (Ahmedabad).

VII

The psychoanalyst, it seems, makes a family affair out of any historical event. Does anybody, we may ask, ever escape his internalized folk and learn to deal with the cast of his adult life on its own terms? The answer is yes and no. Certainly, where radical innovation depends on very special motivations and is paired with strong affect, there its impetus can be shown to draw on lifelong aspirations and involvements. It is true that the psychoanalytic method rarely contributes much to the explanation of the excellence of a man's performance—which may be just as well, for it permits the factor of grace to escape classification and prescription—but it may indicate what freed him for his own excellence or what may have inhibited or spoiled it. It so happens that the Ahmedabad Event *was* something of a family affair not only in that Gandhi's counter-players were a brother and a sister, but also because Gandhi here tried to do what is proverbially the most difficult thing for a leader—to be a prophet in his own country. The proverb, too, may gain a new meaning if we can locate the difficulty in the prophet's conflicts as well as in his "country's" diffidence. The very intimacy of my story may seem inapplicable to large events; yet the way Gandhi used his local successes to establish himself firmly as his whole nation's leader—a year later he would command nationwide civil disobedience against the British government— would seem to go to the core of his style as a leader. A man's leadership is prominently characterized by his choice of the proper place, the exact moment, and the specific issue that help him to make his point momentously. Here I would like to quote from a political scientist's work which has aroused interest and on which I have been asked to comment because it uses some "classical" psychoanalytic assumptions rather determinedly.

Victor Wolfenstein, in discussing Gandhi's famous Salt-*Satyagraha* of 1930, asks bluntly: "But why did Gandhi choose the salt tax from among his list of grievances as the first object of *Satyagraha?*"[15] This refers to the occasion when Gandhi, after his long period of political silence, chose (of all possible actions) to lead an at first small but gradually swelling line of marchers on a "sacred pilgrimage" from Ahmedabad to the Arabian Sea in order to break the law against the tax-free use of salt. Wolfenstein's answer is threefold: First, Gandhi "believed that of all British oppressions the salt tax was the most offensive because it struck the poorest people hardest. . . . By undertaking to serve or lead the lowliest self-esteem is raised." This refers to the assumption that Gandhi and other revolutionary leaders overcome a sense of guilt by acting not for themselves, but for the exploited. Wolfenstein's second point is that "the tax on salt constituted an oral deprivation, a restriction on eating." And it is true, Gandhi was preoccupied all his life with dietary prohibitions and dietary

[15] Victor Wolfenstein, *The Revolutionary Personality* (Princeton, 1967).

choices. But then, Wolfenstein introduces psychoanalytic symbolism in a way which must be quoted more fully:

Another line of interpretation, which is consonant with the view I have been developing of Gandhi's personality, is suggested by Ernest Jones' contention that one of the two basic symbolic significances of salt is human semen. If it had this unconscious meaning for Gandhi, then we may understand his depriving himself of condiments, including salt, as a form of sexual abstinence, involving a regression to an issue of the oral phase. In the context of the Salt March, Gandhi's taking of salt from the British can thus be seen as reclaiming for the Indian people the manhood and potency which was properly theirs.

The choice of issues worthy of a *Satyagraha* campaign must interest us in past as well as in ongoing history, and Gandhi's choice of the salt tax has always impressed me as a model of practical and symbolic action. It pointed to a foreign power's interdiction of a vast population's right to lift from the long shorelines surrounding their tropical subcontinent a cheap and nature-given substance necessary for maintaining work-capacity as well as for making bland food palatable and digestible. Here, Gandhi's shrewdness seemed to join his capacity to focus on the infinite meaning in finite things—a trait which is often associated with the attribution of sainthood. Wolfenstein's suggestion—that the power of this appeal is attributable to an unconscious sexual meaning of salt—while seeming somewhat ludicrous as an isolated statement, appears to have a certain probability if viewed in cultural context. Anybody acquainted with the ancient Indian preoccupation with semen as a substance which pervades the whole body and which, therefore, is released only at the expense of vitality, acuity, and spiritual power will have to admit that if there is an equation between salt and semen in the primitive mind, the Indian people more than any other could be assumed to make the most of it. I suggest, however, that we take a brief look at what E. Jones really said and what the place of his conclusions is in the history of psychoanalytic symbolism.

Jones' classical paper, "The Symbolic Significance of Salt in Folklore and Superstition," was written in 1928.[16] It really starts with the question of the meaning of superstitions that the spilling of salt at a table may bring ill luck and discord to those assembled for a meal. Jones brings together an overwhelming amount of data from folklore and folkcustom which indicate that salt is used in some magic connection with or as an equavalent of semen. A peasant bridegroom may put salt in his left pocket to insure potency; tribesmen and workmen may abstain from both salt and sex during important undertakings; Christian sects may be accused of "salting" the Eucharistic bread with semen—and so on. Jones' conclu-

---

[16] Ernest Jones, *Essays in Applied Psychoanalysis* (London, 1951), Vol. 2.

sion is that to spill salt "means" to lose or spill semen as Onan did: suggesting, then, the sexual model of an antisocial act.

But before we ask how salt may come to mean semen, it is only fair to state that through the ages it has had a powerful significance as itself. When other preservatives were not known, the capacity of salt not only to give pungent taste to the blandest diet, but also to keep perishable food fresh, to cleanse and cure wounds, and even to help embalm dead bodies gave it magic as well as practical value: The very word "salary" apparently comes from the fact that this clean, indestructible, and easily transportable substance could be used instead of money. That it comes from the great Sea, the mythical giver of life, makes salt also a "natural" symbol of procreation as well as of longevity and immortality, wit and wisdom, and thus of such incorruptability as one fervently hopes will preserve the uncertain phenomena of friendship, loyalty, and hospitality. The use of salt on its own terms, then, for the ceremonial affirmation of mutual bonds would do nicely to explain the superstitution concerning the unceremonious spilling.

Jones' conclusion is really rather cautious: "The significance naturally appertaining to such an important and remarkable article of diet as salt has thus been strengthened by an accession of psychical significance derived from deeper sources. The conclusion reached, therefore, is that salt is a typical symbol for semen. There is every reason to think that the primitive mind equates the idea of salt not only with that of semen, but also with the essential constituent of urine. The idea of salt in folklore and superstition characteristically represents the male, active, fertilizing principle."

In psychoanalysis, "deeper" always seems to mean both "sexual" and "repressed," an emphasis which made sense within Freud's libido theory —that is, his search for an "energy of dignity" in human life that would explain the fantastic vagaries of man's instinctuality and yet be comparable to the indestructible and commutable energy isolated and measured in natural science. In civilization and especially in his day, he would find pervasive evidence of the systematic repression in children of any knowledge of the uses and purposes of the sexual organs and this most particularly in any parental context—a repression which no doubt used the pathways of universal symbolization in order to disguise sexual and, above all, incestual thoughts and yet find expression for them. Among these, early psychoanalysis emphasized paternal and phallic symbolism more than maternal; yet, if sexual symbolism did play a role in helping Gandhi, as he put it, "to arouse the religious imagination of an angry people," then the Indian masses, with all their stubborn worship of mother-goddesses, surely would have been swayed as much by the idea of free access to the fecundity of the maternal sea as by the claim to male potency.

At any rate, the one-way symbolization suggested in pyschoanalysis, by which the nonsexual always symbolizes the sexual, is grounded in the assumption that the erotic is more central to infantile and primitive experience than are the cognitive and the nutritional. But one wonders: Where survival is at stake, where sexuality is not so obsessive as it becomes in the midst of affluence, where sexual repression is not so marked as it became in the civilized and rational mind—could it not be that the symbolic equation of salt and semen is reciprocal? Could not the ceremonial linking of the two have the purpose of conferring on life-creating semen, a substance so easily squandered, the life-sustaining indestructibility of salt? This is, at the end, a question of determining the place of sexuality in man's whole ecology. But in the immediate context of the chronic semi-starvation that has undermined the vitality of the Indian masses and considering the periodic threat of widespread death by famine, it would seem appropriate to assume, first of all, that salt means salt. In fact, the further development of psychoanalysis will have to help us understand the symbolic representation not only of repressed sexuality, but also of the everpresent and yet so blatantly denied fact of death in us and around us.[17] If reason will not suffice, then new forms of irrational violence will force us to consider the consequences of man's seeming ability to ignore not only the certainty of his own death, but also the superweaponry poised all around him to destroy the world he knows—literally at a moment's notice.

Sexual symbolism may help, I would agree, to understand superstitions and symptoms such as, say, the often self-destructive foodfads Gandhi indulged in: At one time, he excluded natural salt from his diet, while at another his friends had reason to tease him over his addiction to Epsom salt. In such matters, however, he was only the all-to-willing victim of a tremendous preoccupation with diet rampant during his student days in vegetarian circles in England as well as in the tradition of his native country, although he adorned this with his own concerns over the impact of diet on sexual desire. In deciding on the Salt March, however, he was obviously in command of his political and economic as well as his psychological wits. And in any context except that of irrationality clearly attributable to sexual repression, one should take any interpretation that explains a human act by recourse to sexual symbolism with a grain of salt.

VIII

A historical moment, we have been trying to suggest, is determined by the complementarity of what witnesses, for all manner of motivation, have considered momentous enough to remember and to record and what

---

[17] Robert Lifton, *Death in Life: Survivors of Hiroshima* (New York, 1967).

later reviewers have considered momentous enough to review and re-
record in such a way that the factuality of the event is confirmed or
corrected and actuality is perceived and transmitted to posterity. For
recorders and reviewers alike, however, events assume a momentous
character when they seem both unprecedented and yet also mysteriously
familiar—that is, if *analogous events* come to mind that combine to suggest a direction to historical recurrences, be it divine intention someday
to be revealed, or an inexorable fate to which man may at least learn to
adapt, or regularities which it may be man's task to regulate more engi-
neeringly, or a repetitive delusion from which thoughtful man must
"wake up." Psychoanalysis is inclined to recognize in all events not only
an analogy to, but also a regression to the ontogenetic and phylogenetic
past. This has proven fruitful in the clinical task of treating patients who
suffered from "repressed reminiscences"; but out of its habitual and
dogmatic application has come what I have called the *originological
fallacy* which, in contrast to the teleological one, deals with the present
as almost preempted by its own origins—a stance not conducive to the
demonstration of developmental or historical probability.

The diagrammatic formula for a *historical analogy* would be that another event is considered equivalent to the one at hand because it happened.

D.

	I Moment	II Sequence
1. INDIVIDUAL	to a comparable individual at the corresponding stage of his development	to comparable individuals throughout their lives
2. COMMUNITY	in a corresponding stage of a comparable community	at comparable moments throughout history

Let me use as a first set of examples a thematic similarity between
Gandhi's autobiography and that of the most influential Chinese writer
of roughly the same period, Lu Hsün (1881-1937).

The memory from Gandhi's youth most often quoted to anchor his
spiritual and political style in his oedipal relation to his father is that
of his father's death. This passage if often referred to as a "childhood
memory," although Mohandas at the time was sixteen years old and was
about to become a father himself. One night his father, whom the youth

had nursed with religious passion, was fast sinking; but since a trusted uncle had just arrived, the son left the nursing care to him and went to his marital bedroom in order to satisfy his "carnal desire," and this despite his wife's being pregnant. After a while, however, somebody came to fetch him: The father had died in the uncle's arms—"a blot," Gandhi writes, "which I have never been able to efface or to forget." A few weeks later his wife aborted. This experience represents in Gandhi's life what, following Kierkegaard, I have come to call "the curse" in the lives of comparable innovators with a similarly precocious and relentless conscience. As such, it is no doubt what in clinical work we call a "cover memory"—that is, a roughly factual event that has come to symbolize in condensed form a complex of ideas, affects, and memories transmitted to adulthood, and to the next generation, as an "account to be settled."

This curse, it has been automatically concluded, must be heir to the Oedipus conflict. In Gandhi's case, the "feminine" service to the father would have served to deny the boyish wish of replacing the (aging) father in the possession of the (young) mother and the youthful intention to outdo him as a leader in later life. Thus, the pattern would be set for a style of leadership which can defeat a superior adversary only nonviolently and with the express intent of saving him as well as those whom he oppressed. Some of this interpretation corresponds to what Gandhi would have unhesitatingly acknowledged as his conscious intention.

Here is my second example: The writer Lu Hsün, often quoted with veneration by Mao, is the founding father of modern China's revolutionary literature. His famous short story "Diary of a Madman" (1918), the first literary work written in vernacular Chinese, is a masterpiece not only (we are told) in the power of its style, but (as we can see) as a very modern combination of a precise psychiatric description of paranoia (Lu Hsün had studied medicine in Japan) and a nightmarish allegory of the fiercer aspects of traditional and revolutionary China. Later in an essay entitled "Father's Illness," Lu Hsün again mixes a historical theme—namely, the discrepancy of Western and Confucian concepts concerning a man's last moments—with the ambivalent emotions of a son. He had spent much of his adolescent years searching for herbs that might cure his father. But now death was near.

Sometimes an idea would flash like lightning into my mind: Better to end the gasping faster. . . . And immediately I knew that the idea was improper; it was like committing a crime. But at the same time I thought this idea rather proper, for I loved my father. Even now, I still think so.[18]

This is the Western doctor speaking; but at the time a Mrs. Yen, a kind of midwife for the departing soul, had suggested a number of magic

[18] Translated by Leo L. Lee for my seminar at Harvard from *Lu Hsün ch'üan-chi* (Complete Works of Lu Hsün; Peking, 1956), Vol. 2, pp. 261-62.

transactions and had urged the son to scream into his father's ear, so he would not stop breathing.

"Father! Father!"

His face, which had quieted down, suddenly became tense. He opened his eyes slightly as if he felt something bitter and painful.

"Yell! Yell! Quick!"

"Father!"

"What? . . . Don't shout . . . don't . . ." he said in a low tone. Then he gasped frantically for breath. After a while, he returned to normal and calmed down.

"Father!" I kept calling him until he stopped breathing. Now I can still hear my own voice at that time. Whenever I hear it, I feel that this is the gravest wrong I have done to my father.

Lu Hsün was fifteen at the time (to Gandhi's sixteen). He, like Gandhi, had come from a line of high officials, whose fortunes were on the decline during the son's adolescence. At any rate, his story clearly suggests that in the lives of both men a desperate clinging to the dying father and a mistake made at the very last moment represented a curse overshadowing both past and future.

It is not enough, however, to reduce such a curse to the "Oedipus Complex" as reconstructed in thousands of case histories as the primal complex of them all. The oedipal crisis, too, must be evaluated as part of man's over-all development. It appears to be a constellation of dark preoccupations in a species which must live through a period of infantile dependence and steplike learning unequaled in the animal world, which develops a sensitive self-awareness in the years of immaturity, and which becomes aware of sexuality and procreation at a stage of childhood beset with irrational guilt. For the boy, to better the father (even if it is his father's most fervent wish that he do so) unconsciously means to replace him, to survive him means to kill him, to usurp his domain means to appropriate the mother, the "house," the "throne." No wonder that mankind's Maker is often experienced in the infantile image of every man's maker. But the oedipal crisis as commonly formulated is only the infantile or neurotic version of a *generational conflict* which derives from the fact that man experiences life and death—and past and future—in terms of the turnover of generations.

It is, in fact, rather probable that a highly uncommon man experiences filial conflicts with such inescapable intensity because he senses in himself already early in childhood some kind of originality that seems to point beyond the competition with the personal father. His is also an early conscience development which makes him feel (and appear) old while still young and maybe older in single-mindedness than his conformist parents, who, in turn, may treat him somehow as their potential redeemer. Thus he grows up almost with an obligation (beset with guilt) to surpass and to originate at all cost. In adolescence this may prolong his identity confusion because he must find the one way in which he (and he alone!) can re-enact the past and create a new future in the right medium at the right moment on a sufficiently large scale. His prolonged identity crisis, in turn, may invoke a premature generativity crisis that makes him accept as his concern a whole communal body, or mankind itself, and embrace as his dependents those weak in power, poor in possessions, and seemingly simple in heart. Such a deflection in life-plan, however, can crowd out his chances for the enjoyment of intimacy, sexual and otherwise, wherefore the "great" are often mateless, friendless, and childless in the midst of veneration and by their example further confound the human dilemma of counterpointing the responsibility of procreation and individual existence.

But not all highly uncommon men are chosen; and the psychohistorical question is not only how much men come to experience the inescapability of an existential curse, but how it comes about that they have the pertinacity and the giftedness to re-enact it in a medium communicable to their fellow men and meaningful in their stage of history. The emphasis here is on the word *re-enactment,* which in such cases goes far beyond the dictates of a mere "repetition-compulsion," such as characterizes the unfreedom of symptoms and irrational acts. For the mark of a creative re-enactment of a curse is that the joint experience of it all becomes a liberating event for each member of an awe-stricken audience. Some dim awareness of this must be the reason why the wielders of power in different periods of history appreciate and support the efforts of creative men to re-enact the universal conflicts of mankind in the garb of the historical day, as the great dramatists have done and as the great autobiographers do. A political leader like Mao, then, may recognize a writer like Hsün not for any ideological oratory, but for his precise and ruthless presentation of the inner conflicts that must accompany the emergence of a revolutionary mind in a society as bound to filial piety as China. In a man like Gandhi the autobiographer and the leader are united in one person, but remain distinct in the differentiation of re-enactments in writing and in action. In all re-enactment, however, it is the transformation of an infantile curse into an adult deed that makes the man.

Common men, of course, gladly accept as saviors *pro tem* uncommon men who seem so eager to take upon themselves an accounting thus spared to others, and who by finding words for the nameless make it possible for the majority of men to live in the concreteness and safety of realities tuned to procreation, production, and periodic destruction.

All the greater, therefore, can be the chaos that "great" men leave behind and often experience in themselves in the years following their ascendance. For the new momentum, which they gave to their time, may now roll over them, or their power to provide further momentum may wane from fatigue and age. Uncommon men, too, ultimately can become common (and worse) by the extent to which their solution of a universal curse remains tied to its ontogenetic version. The author of "Diary of a Madman" at the end of a career as revolutionary writer himself died in paranoid isolation as, in hindsight, one would expect of a man who, all his life, could hear his own voice yelling into his dying father's ear. And Gandhi, who could not forgive himself for having sought the warmth of his marital bed while his father was dying, in old age indulged in behavior that cost him many friends. In Lear-like fashion, he would wander through the tempest of communal riots, making local peace where nobody else could and yet knowing that he was losing the power to keep India united. It was then that the widower wanted his "daughters" close (he had never had a daughter of his own) and asked some of his women followers to warm his shivering body at night. This "weakness" the septuagenarian explained as a test of his strength of abstinence, opening himself wide to cheap gossip. This story, too, will have to be retold in terms of life cycle and history.

What was once united by the power of charisma cannot fall apart without exploding into destructive furor in the leader or in the masses or in both. Here life history ends, and history begins in its sociological and political aspects. How a leader survives himself and how an idea survives a man, how the community absorbs him and his idea, and how the sense of wider identity created by his presence survives the limitations of his person and of the historical moment—these are matters that the psycho-historian cannot approach without the help of the sociologist of tradition-building and institution-forming. He, in turn, may want to consider the "metabolism" of generations and the influence of a leader's or an elite's image on the life stages of the led: Kennedy's rise and sudden death certainly would provide a modern model for such a study.

To return once more to my original interest in Gandhi: I have indicated what I have learned since about his personal idiosyncrasies as well as about his power of compromise. If some say that his ascendance was unfortunate for an India in desperate need of modernization, I cannot see who else in his time could have brought the vast, backward mass of Indians closer to the tasks of this century. As for his lasting influence, I will endeavor to describe in a book his strategy (as enfolded in the Event) of challenging man's latent capacity for militant and disciplined nonviolence: In this, he will survive. In the meantime, I, for one, see no reason to decide whether he was a saint or a politician—a differentiation meaningless in the Hindu tradition of combining works and renunciation—for his life is characterized by an ability to derive existential strength, as well as political power, from the very evasion of all job specifications. In interviewing his old friends, however, I found ample affirmation of his agile and humorous presence, probably the most inclusive sign of his (or anybody's) simultaneous mastery of inner and outer events. And it is in his humor that Gandhi has been compared to Saint Francis. Luther understood such things even if he could not live them; and at least his sermons formulate unforgettably the centrality in space, the immediacy in time, and the wholeness in feeling that lead to such singular "events" as survive in parables—a form of enactment most memorable through the ages, although, or maybe just because, most effortless and least "goal-directed." Now a man has to be dead for quite a while before one can know what parables might survive him: In Gandhi's case, one can only say that the "stuff" for parables is there. Let me, in conclusion, compare two well-known scenes from the lives of Gandhi and Saint Francis.

Teasing was a gift and a habit with Gandhi throughout his life, and elsewhere I have pointed out the affinity of teasing to nonviolence.[19] It was after the great Salt March (he had been arrested again, and while he was in jail, his *Satyagrahis* had been brutally attacked by the police) that Gandhi was invited to talks with the Viceroy. Churchill scoffed at the "seditious fakir, striding half-naked up the steps of the Viceroy's palace, to negotiate with the representative of the King-Emperor." But the Viceroy, Lord Irwin, himself described the meeting as "the most dramatic personal encounter between a Viceroy and an Indian leader." When Gandhi was handed a cup of tea, he asked to be given a cup of hot water instead, into which he poured a bit of salt (tax-free) out of a small paper bag hidden in his shawl and remarked smilingly: "To remind us of the famous Boston Tea Party."

If we choose to insist on the symbolic meaning of salt and would see in this gesture a disguised act of masculine defiance—so be it. But such meaning would be totally absorbed in the over-all artfulness with which personal quirk (Gandhi would not touch tea) is used for the abstention from and yet ceremonial participation in the important act of sharing tea at the palace, and yet also for the re-enactment of a historical defiance, pointedly reminding his host of the time when the British taxed another invigorating substance and lost some colonies which, in independence, did rather well.

Whatever combination of overt and hidden meanings were enacted here in unison, the analogy that comes to mind is a scene from St. Francis' life, when he was asked for dinner to his bishop's palace. A place on the bishop's right was reserved for the ethereal rebel, and the guests were seated along well-decked tables. But Brother Francesco was late. Finally,

[19] Erikson, "Gandhi's Autobiography: The Leader as a Child."

he appeared with a small sack, out of which he took little pieces of dry dark bread and with his usual dancing gestures put one beside each guest's plate. To the bishop, who protested that there was plenty of food in the house, he explained that for *this* bread he had *begged* and that, therefore, it was consecrated food. Could there be a more delicate and yet finite lesson in Christianity?

The two scenes bespeak an obvious similarity in tone, and artfulness; but in order to make them true analogies, comparison is not enough. Other lifelong similarities in the two men could be enumerated and their respective tasks in their respective empires compared. Gandhi was no troubadour saint, but a tough activist as well as an enactor of poetic moments; and he was a strategist as well as a prayerful man. All this only points to the psycho-historian's job of specifying in all their complementarity the inner dynamics as well as the social conditions which make history seem to repeat, to renew, or to surpass itself.[20]

[20] This paper was presented in outline to the American Academy's Group for the Study of Psycho-Historical Processes at Wellfleet, Massachusetts, in 1966.

Selected Bibliography

Many of the articles reprinted carry an extensive bibliography in their footnotes; see especially the articles by Rieff, Langer, and Pye. What follows are merely some additional suggestions.

Freud's own writings are to be found in *Gesammelte Werke*, 18 vols. (London: Anglobooks, 1940-1952); in English, in *The Standard Edition of the Complete Psychological Works of Sigmund Freud*, in progress, 24 vols., ed. James Strachey and others (New York: The Macmillan Company, 1953-). See also the *Collected Papers*, 5 vols., ed. Joan Riviere and James Strachey (London: Anglobooks, 1924-1950). A useful collection is *The Basic Writings of Sigmund Freud*, ed. A. A. Brill (New York: Modern Library, Inc., 1938). The works most relevant to philosophy of history are *Totem and Taboo, Group Psychology and the Analysis of the Ego, The Future of an Illusion, Civilization and Its Discontents,* and *Moses and Monotheism*. Also of great interest is the paper on Leonardo da Vinci, as well as numerous papers, such as "Thoughts for the Times on War and Death," "A Neurosis of Demoniacal Possession in the Seventeenth Century," etc.

Of enormous importance in tracing the development of Freud's thoughts are *The Origins of Psychoanalysis: Letters, Drafts and Notes to Wilhelm Fliess, 1887-1902,* ed. Marie Bonaparte, Anna Freud, and Ernst Kris (New York: Anchor Books, 1957); and Ernest Jones, *The Life and Work of Sigmund Freud,* 3 vols. (New York: Basic Books, 1953-1957).

Especially pertinent to the philosophy of history are such books as Herbert Marcuse, *Eros and Civilization: A Philosophical Inquiry into Freud* (Boston: Beacon Press, 1955); Norman O. Brown, *Life Against Death: The Psychoanalytic Meaning of History* (Middletown, Conn.: Wesleyan University Press, 1959); Lionel Trilling, *Freud and the Crisis of our Culture* (Boston: The Beacon Press, 1955); Géza Róheim. *The Origin and Function of Culture,* Nervous and Mental Disease Monographs, No. 69 (New York, 1943); and Erich Fromm, *Escape from Freedom* (New York: Farrar, Straus and Cudahy, Inc., 1941). See, too, Philip Rieff's chapter, "The Authority of the Past," in *Freud: The Mind of the Moralist* (New York: The Viking Press, Inc., 1959), as well as his articles, "The Authority of the Past—Sickness and Society in Freud's Thought," *Social Research* (Winter, 1954), and "History, Psychoanalyis and the Social Sciences," *Ethics* (January, 1953).

On the application of psychoanalysis to history, see Erik Erikson, "Ego Development and Historical Change," *The Psychoanalytic Study of the*

Child, 2, 359-396 (New York: International Universities Press, Inc., 1946), and "The Nature of Clinical Evidence," in *Evidence and Inference,* The First Hayden Colloquium (Cambridge: The Technology Press of M.I.T., 1958), as background for his *Young Man Luther.* Of unusual interest is Herbert Moller, "The Meaning of Courtly Love," *Journal of American Folklore,* vol. 73, no. 287 (1960). (See also his "The Social Causation of the Courtly Love Complex," *Comparative Studies in Society and History,* vol. 1, no. 2 [January, 1959], for the social context of his analysis.) Fawn M. Brodie, *Thaddeus Stevens: Scourge of the South* (New York: W. W. Norton & Co., Inc., 1959), is a fascinating book, which, like the Georges' book on Wilson, is psychoanalytically informed but does not express this information in formal, technical terms. Ludwig Reiners, *The Lamps Went Out in Europe,* translated from the German by Richard and Clara Winston (New York: Pantheon Books, Inc., 1955), deals with World War I primarily in terms of personalities; it is filled with psychological aperçus, all expressed in a rather understated fashion. (On the general subject of war, see the following: Alix Strachey, *The Unconscious Motives of War,* especially Part II (New York: International Universities Press, Inc., 1957); T. H. Pear, ed. *Psychological Factors of Peace and War* (New York: Philosophical Library, Inc., 1951); Harold D. Lasswell, *World Politics and Personal Insecurity* (Glencoe, Ill.: Free Press of Glencoe, Inc., 1950 [originally published in 1934]); Edward Glover, *War, Sadism, and Pacifism* (London: George Allen & Unwin, Ltd., 1933); R. E. Money-Kyrle, *Psychoanalysis and Politics* (New York: W. W. Norton & Co., Inc., 1951); and Maurice L. Farber, "Psychoanalytic Hypotheses in the Study of War," *Journal of Social Issues,* xi (1955). [I owe these references to Bernard Brodie, to whom I am also indebted for other suggestions.] See, too, Frederick Wyatt and William B. Wilcox, "Sir Henry Clinton: A Psychological Exploration in History," *William and Mary Quarterly,* xvi, 3rd series (January, 1959); Ludwig Jekels, "The Turning Point in the Life of Napoleon I," *Selected Papers* (New York: International Universities Press, Inc., 1953); and Meyer Schapiro, "Leonardo and Freud: An Art Historical Study," *Journal of the History of Ideas* (April, 1956).

Of general interest is *Psychoanalysis and the Social Sciences,* ed. Géza Róheim, Werner Muensterberger, and Sidney Axelrad, vols. I-IV (New York: International Universities Press, Inc., 1947-1958) (changed in 1960 to *The Psychoanalytic Study of Society*); the article by Hans Meyerhoff emphasizing the historical nature of the psychoanalytic method, "On Psychoanalysis and History," *Psychoanalysis and the Psychoanalytic Review,* vol. 49, no. 2 (Summer, 1962); and Walter A. Weisskopf, *The Psychology of Economics* (Chicago: University of Chicago Press, 1955), which applies psychological analysis to the great economic theories and makes an interesting complement to the work of Erikson, Brown, and others treating of the "capitalist" personality.

Bibliographical Notes for the Revised Edition

To the Selected Bibliography of the original edition, I shall add some brief observations on some of the most interesting work in the field since 1963. (I make no claim to even partial completeness; that would be a small volume in itself.) One of the most intriguing and, I believe, important developments has been the so-called Wellfleet Meetings, held from 1965 to 1968 (with the support of the American Academy of Arts and Sciences), where a number of people—usually around ten or twelve —from various disciplines, met at the end of summer for a week of concerted effort and discussion. Erik H. Erikson was the recognized *primus inter pares,* but all who participated took away from those meetings a heightened notion of what psycho-history was about, which informed all their own later work. Other, similar meetings and formation of groups for psycho-history attest to the vitality of the new discipline.

Further evidence is to be found in published work. In the area of what I called Freud's Philosophy of History (Part I), Philip Rieff, *The Triumph of the Therapeutic* (New York: Harper & Row, 1966) is highly noteworthy. Paul A. Robinson, *The Freudian Left* (New York: Harper & Row, 1969), treats of Wilhelm Reich, Géza Róheim, and Herbert Marcuse. The title of Paul Roazen's interesting book, *Freud: Political and Social Thought* (New York: Alfred A. Knopf, 1968) indicates its contents. Chapter XI, "Freud," of my own book, *The Riddle of History: The Great Speculators from Vico to Freud* (New York: Harper & Row, 1966), seeks to treat of Freud as the last of the great classical philosophers of history.

A new sub-area, what one might call the methodological consideration of problems in psycho-history, has emerged, seeming to stand between what I have called Freud's Philosophy of History and The Application of Psychoanalysis to History. Erikson's *Insight and Responsibility* (New

York: W. W. Norton & Co., 1964) and *Identity: Youth and Crisis* (New York: W. W. Norton & Co., 1968) appear to fit partially under this category, although, as with all of Erikson's writings, theory and practice are skillfully combined. More specific as methodological contributions are Cushing Strout, "Ego Psychology and the Historian," *History and Theory* vol. 7, no. 3 (1968); Hans-Ulrich Wehler "Zum Verhältnis von Geschichtswissenschaft und Psychoanalyse," *Historische Zeitschrift*, Heft 208/3 (June, 1969), which has an extensive bibliography included in the footnotes; Bruce Mazlish, "Inside the Whales," *Times Literary Supplement* (July 28, 1966), "Clio on the Couch: Prolegomena to Psycho-History," *Encounter* (September, 1968), "Group Psychology and Problems of Contemporary History," *Journal of Contemporary History* vol. 3, no. 2 (April, 1968), and "Autobiography and Psychoanalysis," *Encounter* (October, 1970); and Fred I. Greenstein, *Personality and Politics* (Chicago: Markham Publishing Company, 1969), which deals with problems of evidence, inference, and conceptualization, although mainly with political science in mind.

In the Application of Psychoanalysis to History (Part II), especially along the lines of life-histories or psychoanalytically-oriented biographical studies, there is in addition to Erikson's *Gandhi's Truth*, already mentioned, Susanne Rudolph, "The New Courage: An Essay on Gandhi's Psychology," *World Politics* (October, 1963); the entire issue, "Philosophers and Kings: Studies in Leadership," *Daedalus* (Summer, 1968), which includes studies on Nkrumah, Ataturk, De Gaulle, Bismarck, Newton, James Mill, and William James, among others; Frank E. Manuel, *A Portrait of Isaac Newton* (Cambridge, Mass.: Harvard University Press, 1968); Bruce Mazlish, "The Mills: Father and Son," *Horizon* (Summer, 1970); Arnold Künzli, *Karl Marx: Eine Psycho-graphie* (Wien: Europa Verlag, 1966), an 800-page book, written from what appears to be primarily a Jungian perspective, and almost totally neglected in the critical literature (except for Herbert Moller's review-essay in *History and Theory*, vol. VIII, no. 3, [1969]); E. Victor Wolfenstein, *The Revolutionary Personality: Lenin, Trotsky, Gandhi* (Princeton: Princeton University Press, 1967); Robert Jay Lifton, *Revolutionary Immortality: Mao Tse-tung and the Chinese Cultural Revolution* (New York: Random House, 1968); and Arthur Mitzman, *The Iron Cage: An Historical Interpretation of Max Weber* (New York: Alfred A. Knopf, 1970), which is actually a psychoanalytic interpretation.

More in the line of group portraits, or analyses, are Robert Jay Lifton, *Death in Life: Survivors of Hiroshima* (New York: Random House, 1967) —Lifton's *History and Human Survival* (New York: Random House, 1970), is a generalized collection—and Kenneth Keniston, *Young Radicals* (New York: Harcourt, Brace & World, 1968). Other important studies of group phenomena are Norman Cohn, *Warrant For Genocide* (New

York: Harper & Row, 1966), with 'ts concluding chapter, "A Case Study in Collective Psychopathology," being of special methodological interest; John Demos, "Underlying Themes in the Witchcraft of Seventeenth-Century New England," *The American Historical Review* (June, 1970), with an interesting combination of demographic and psychoanalytic approaches; and Lucian W. Pye, *The Spirit of Chinese Politics* (Cambridge, Mass.: The M.I.T. Press, 1968). David Hunt, *Parents and Children in History: The Psychology of Family Life in Early Modern France* (New York: Basic Books, 1970) is an interesting test of both Philippe Ariès' pioneering work on the family in his *Centuries of Childhood* (Paris; Librairie Plon, 1960; translated by Robert Baldick, New York: Alfred A. Knopf, 1962) and of Erikson's theories of psycho-history. Fred Weinstein and Gerald M. Platt, *The Wish to Be Free: Society, Psyche and Value Change* (Berkeley and Los Angeles: University of California Press, 1969) is an exciting collaboration between an historian and a sociologist, both using the psychoanalytic approach to history.

A SELECTED LIST OF *Universal Library* TITLES